INFORMATION SHOULD NEVER BE RANDOM

A guide to business and technical writing

LAURIE ANDERSON

Kendall Hunt
publishing company

www.kendallhunt.com
Send all inquiries to:
4050 Westmark Drive
Dubuque, IA 52004-1840

ISBN 978-1-7924-8488-9

Published in the United States of America

This book is dedicated to its readers to help them strengthen their appreciation of words and to learn to use their words deliberately.

Acknowledgements

While my writing was done alone, a myriad of other people have provided encouragement, insights, lessons learned, and examples. My thanks go to

Ethan Yamashita, a student at the University of Washington Bothell, who wrote the samples for this book as part of his technical writing minor education.

My students who helped shape my thoughts about communication's effectiveness.

University of Washington Bothell Computing and Software Systems faculty who taught CSS 301 Technical Writing for Computing Professionals before me or with me, specifically Nancy Kool, Dawn-Marie Oliver, Marie Deschene, Delmar Davis, Morteza Chini, Bob Mayer, and Mary Kirk.

Other UWB CSS faculty who informed my teaching and communications effectiveness, specifically William Erdly, Carol Zander, Mark Kochanski, Erika Parsons, David Socha, Rob Nash, and Robert Dimpsey.

The wonderful faculty, staff, and administrators at University of Washington and the University of Washington Bothell, and more specifically those in its School of Science, Technology, Engineering, and Mathematics (STEM).

My family and friends who didn't hear from me while I was writing and teaching.

Contents

Introduction: Don't Make Your Reader Figure You Out

This chapter introduces the author's background and its impact on the book's structure.

1.1 Learning from Me

In college, I always received good grades on my papers and interpreted that to mean I must be a good writer – that if I wrote something or said something and it made sense to me, then it made sense to the reader. As I worked in the computer industry after graduation, I took that belief into the writing I did there. Unfortunately, it seemed that I didn't write as well as my grades had led me to believe. On the job when someone didn't understand what I wrote, they simply didn't come back to me. They asked someone else for the information they needed.

Of course from the reader's perspective that made sense; they'd tried to get the information from me and were unsuccessful, so they got it from someone else. However, from my perspective, as the author, I didn't know that I hadn't communicated my ideas clearly. I was removed from the communications path, and usually overlooked the next time a question came up. Unfortunately, I discovered the problem with my communication skills in an incredibly awkward moment when the person whom I tried to help indicated that someone else had provided the information they needed – in a meeting I attended.

That revelation changed how I approached my writing. I read a lot of documents and talked to other authors. I talked to my readers and asked questions, learning what they needed and how my work was or wasn't up to the task. As my writing began to perform the tasks needed – successfully – I also learned the benefit of clear communications: I could get what I wanted on the job, whether it was working on a choice assignment, moving to a new position, or traveling to conferences, and so on. If someone didn't understand me or what was going on in my head, I rarely got what I asked for. Not to say I always got what I asked for when I communicated it well, but I had a better chance.

Throughout my career, I worked hard to communicate successfully: reading books; talking to the readers, colleagues, managers, executives; and talking to other writers, to create a system of writing in a business and technical setting that works. A couple decades ago, I moved to a university setting to teach. As students returned to report how they successfully applied my teaching at their internships, I incorporated that feedback into my classes.

This book breaks down that writing process for you so you can capitalize on it and get ahead on the job faster.

1.2 Assumptions about This Book's Audience

As you will read in this book, an important beginning step to any writing task is understanding who your audience is and what assumptions can be made about their prior knowledge. This will ensure that you're not repeating in your document information they already know – the more readers encounter information they already know in a document, the less likely they are to look for and find what they need to know.

For this book, I'm taking a lowest common denominator approach and assuming that readers have taken a couple of English composition courses where you learned how to reflect on what you'd read and communicate those reflections in writing where you were expected to create well-formed paragraphs with tailored topic sentences.

For readers who may have taken additional technical writing courses where they practiced writing forms, such as instructions, resumes, and letters, you may find this writing a refreshing new perspective on content you're familiar with.

For all the readers, this book is structured with small sections with well-defined headings, so you can decide whether you need to read that section to learn its material or whether you already know it and thus can skim or skip it. This is a useful approach in business and technical writing, so as you read, you can learn by example.

1.3 This Book's Approach: Information Organization versus Delivery

This book's approach to teaching business and technical writing is different than other approaches you may have been taught or read. This text separates *how information is organized* from *how that information is delivered to your audience*. This separation makes the application of your learning more flexible for any dynamic work setting.

When this book refers to delivery, it means the way the information arrives to the reader, which could be a document; report; letter, memo, or email; or social media channel, such as discord. These delivery mechanisms would be ingrained in the culture of a business organization and would be learned quickly by any new employee paying attention to how that business does business. Therefore, in this book, delivery is covered in Chapter 6 on best practices for formatting; in Chapter 7 on letters, memos, and email; and in part, in Chapter 5.3 on tables.

Meanwhile, the information that's put inside those delivery channels is universal. That is the focus of this book. If you organize the content you're delivering based on how you're thinking about it in your head, then it's more likely to be random, since you're organizing it based on your random thinking, and to get ahead on the job, information should never be random.

1.4 Structure of the Book

To help you learn, each chapter/section first covers the material, then includes an example so you can learn by mimicking it, and offers exercises/review questions at the end of the chapter/section where you apply the concepts covered.

This book is organized as follows:

Chapter 1 introduces the author's background and the book's structure.

Chapter 2 covers the writing process that consists of three stages: prewriting, drafting, revision. Even if you've already got a writing process that you're used to using, you can find useful insights. If you struggle with the writing process, then use the advice of the chapter to incorporate into your writing process.

Chapter 3 covers how to analyze your audience, which means considering the needs of your reader and tailoring your work to them.

Chapter 4 covers the most common patterns of organizing information. Each pattern structure is covered with examples provided to clarify the best practices explained. The last sections introduce additional common methods of organizing information, plus inserting a pattern into a document, and combining patterns in the same document.

Chapter 5 covers the various parts of a document that are common, misunderstood, or optional depending on the situation introductions, conclusions, abstracts, summaries, tables, creating tables, and citing another sources' work.

Chapter 6 outlines a series of best practices of formatting your information so that it's easily accessible to the reader. However you eventually incorporate your material for final delivery, these best practices can help you improve their look.

Chapter 7 covers the delivery mechanisms of the three common letter forms, memos for internal communications, and email. How email acts like letters, but looks like memos, is also covered.

Chapter 8 covers some best practices, which when followed ensure a successful critique encounter that can strengthen each other's writing: your work by seeing another's work, and the author's work by receiving constructive input to improve their work.

Chapter 9 is not a full grammar guide, but is designed to cover the most common difficulties encountered in business and technical writing: sentence structure (transitions, subordination, parallelism, modifiers), verb choice (passive voice, expletives, nominalizations), word usage (acronyms, abbreviations, jargon, slang, clichés, gender bias, common homonyms, and misused words), and punctuation.

NOTE: Not all exercises have answer keys. Look at the faculty guide information at the Kendall Hunt web pages associated with this book for more resources.

Perfect your Writing Process: Information Never Dies

This chapter covers the writing process that consists of three stages, which are prewriting, drafting and revision.

Writing stage	Goal or purpose	Result at completion of stage
1) Prewriting	To generate ideas	An outline
2) Drafting	To generate words	A writing draft
3) Revision	To polish the words	A polished work ready for the reader

Once you read what happens at each stage of the writing process in this chapter, you'll probably find that you've not been following this process. But before you discard the idea of following this process, see how it can help you and as you practice using it, see how you can shorten it to fit your strengths and help you identify and address your areas of improvement in writing.

2.1 Reasons to Follow a Technical Writing Process

Using the writing process has the following benefits:

- Create predictable results – By following a process, you can know that each time you use the process, you create the same level of quality. It won't be random or hit-or-miss. It will always be the best work you can create, and it will communicate your ideas to the intended audience.
- Save time – Using this process can save you time, even if it may not seem like it at first. For example, if you fix the sentence structure and punctuation of paragraphs you later remove, you've wasted that time. If you draft work, then find out it all needs to be rewritten to organize it better, then you've wasted any time spent trying to make the ineffective draft work.
- Be efficient – You can focus on one part of the writing process at a time. When you're focused, you can work more efficiently and faster, which saves you time. When you try to do more than one thing at once (e.g., organize and draft, draft and edit), then none of the tasks get done well.
- Write independently – In business, you need to be confident in your own writing abilities. You can't always ask someone to read your work before you post it. While there may be larger documents that are written together with colleagues and in those cases, that's when you coordinate with them to read and edit the final result. However, with your emails and other documents you create, you need to be able to work alone, efficiently, accurately, clearly, and concisely. Using a writing process means you can write independently and still create great results.
- Scan efficiently – By using a writing process that you follow consistently allows you to understand better your own documents, and read and understand other similar documents.
- Recognize the lifespan of information – Every piece of writing needs care. Information will endure forever, even if it's poorly written, negatively

persisting in readers' minds. Meanwhile, a document that is well written, clear, and concise will be easier to remember, comprehend, and maintain.

Before you read how this process works, consider any problems you've had with your writing? Those problems could signal how using this writing process could help you produce the best results.

For example:

- *Has your audience not understood (been confused by) what you provided them?* If so, then using the audience analysis process can ensure that you've examined what needs to be done to reach your audience.
- *Do you have trouble with all your ideas flowing in order, instead creating a jumble that never makes sense?* If so, then maybe brainstorming to generate an outline would help. Or maybe having a clear outline of the flow of ideas before you start writing can ensure a clear completed writing.
- *Do you have trouble staring at a blank page when you need to get writing done? Waiting for words to arrive?* If so, then you've been shortchanging the prewriting stage, which is designed to conclude with an outline. With an outline, you would know what to write.
- *Do you think that all you need to do, after you've written your work, is read it for sentence structure and punctuation?* If so, then you've been shortchanging your revision stage and doing too many steps at once, thus not doing any of them very well.
- *Have you ever written something and then been afraid to rewrite it to make it better?* If so, then be brave. Using a process, like this one, means that you can have faith the results will reach the reader, which means that the right content was created. Besides, before you start your edits or some comprehensive edits, you can copy your draft to another file, so that you have the original work intact. Then, later, even if those saved words can't be used verbatim when you need them, they can easily inspire the words you do need at that time. It's always easier to edit existing work, then draft original work.

2.2 The Three Stages to Creating Successful Technical Writing

Once you know these processes and can use them efficiently, then you can practice with how you might economize the process based on your writing abilities and strengths.

2.2.1 Stage 1: Prewriting Stage

The goal of the prewriting stage is to generate ideas, resulting in an outline.

The prewriting stage is what you do before you start writing content. If you are in a habit of opening your word processor and starting your typing, then you're missing out on a lot of helpful techniques that can refine your thinking to ensure what you write is exactly what's needed.

a) Set the scope

To define the scope, you need to decide on what content to deliver to the reader. Should you go into great depth or not? Should you include information surrounding the topic to provide a context or keep to the point? These answers defined the depth and breadth of content to cover in your writing.

b) Identify your audience

Your audience or reader is who is going to read your work. That is, what role do they carry as they read your work? Are they an end user, a developer, a technician, a manager, executive, or ___? Your reader's current understanding of the topic combined with their new informational needs shapes what content you provide and how you deliver it.

Part of identifying who your audience is involves determining what the audience needs to get out of reading your work, then to understand how to present that information clearly, including what is the best combination of pace, point of view (POV), and tone to use (read more in Chapter 3). What you want to learn to do is create writing that

- Provides a consistent *tone*
- Varies the *pace* to create an easy reading of the material
- Offers consistent *POV* that is proper for the writing content

c) Determine purpose

The purpose identifies the goal of the writing: Why are you writing this work? Being specific about your purpose helps you clarify the scope, and helps you identify how the information you provide should be organized. Not all information should be delivered in the same way.

The pattern you use defines where content is placed in the writing, and it varies. See Chapter 4 for more details on deciding on the pattern of information organization.

d) Use brainstorming to clarify ideas

The goal of *brainstorming* is to help you get ideas out of your brain and written down, so you can organize them. These ideas could be the goal, the scope, the content to include, audience analysis – anything that helps to refine your writing plan.

Many writers skip their brainstorming, and miss out because they've never really allowed their brain to run wild with ideas. If you try to both generate ideas and organize them at the same time, then your brain naturally begins to filter information to fit the *organization* task, which defeats the first task of trying to get all the ideas out to review them. So never consider it a waste of time to generate an idea that is not used later on. At the same time, don't feel that every idea you came up with must be used.

There are loads of brainstorming techniques, this chapter covers the most commonly used tools to help you organize information you're researching. It's best to know at least a few brainstorming tools because they are optimized based on how much information you have about the topic, so depending on where you are in a project, different tools are needed.

Brainstorming can be performed individually or within a group.

Remember there are a lot of tools available that can help create brainstorming results. However, the goal of brainstorming is to get the ideas out. This is best done old school with paper and pencil. If you find later that you decide to use your brainstorming to explain your idea to someone else, then use the tool to polish the look. To use a tool to generate it means that you're splitting your brain time and likely to edit your ideas before they get out of your brain for review.

2.2.1.1 Listing

Sometimes also called brainstorming, listing is the most commonly used brainstorming tool. This tool is best when you need to get the ideas rolling around in your head written down so you don't forget them or so that you can add to them over time.

> Useful when you know the most about a topic and what you're wanting to list. See Figure 2.1.
>
> Not useful when you try to both come up with the ideas *and* order them into a list at the same time, which will not produce the best results. Your brain will filter new ideas to optimize putting those ideas you currently remember in order.

Figure 2.1: Sample list, which once generated, could be ordered as needed

Fitness benefits

- Longer life
- Stronger mental acuity
- Restful sleep
- Positive endorphins
- Less fats accumulate
- Heart becomes stronger
- More blood flow to the brain
- Energy and mental stimulation goes up

2.2.1.2 Branching

Branching helps you determine the various components of your topic. This technique is most helpful if your topic has a sequence or maybe a time component to it.

> Useful when you know you already have a sense of the sequence for your topic, but not all the details.
>
> Not useful when you don't know much about your topic or how the ideas interrelate.

Using this technique, imagine your main topic is the trunk of a tree. Then each of the various ideas and subideas represent branches and subbranches of the tree. See Figure 2.2.

Figure 2.2: Sample of branching

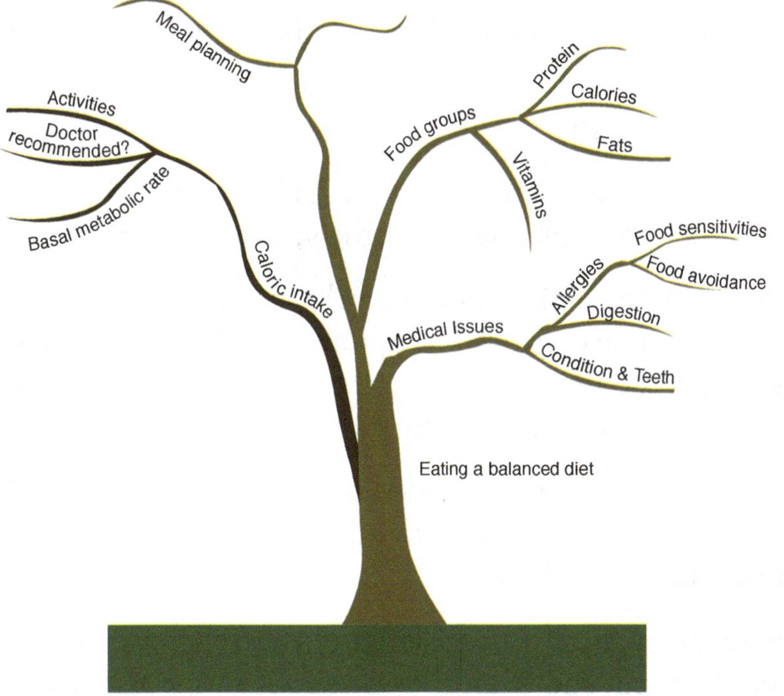

2.2.1.3 Mind Mapping

A mind map allows you to look at your topic from multiple perspectives. This is a great technique to use when you want to have someone else add to your ideas. It is also a great idea to use when conducting research, as you can combine the keywords from your mind map into your search tool to find relevant information.

> Useful when you don't have a good idea of what to do or where to go, because the mind map excels at taking random information and helping you see relationships and connections.
>
> Not useful when you already know what you're planning to do. Another tool can help you organize those ideas faster than a mind map.

To construct a mind map, put your main topic at the center of your page – not the bottom or top – you want to be able to build ideas in all directions from your main topic. Then allow your brainstorming ideas to radiate from the main topic. Allow yourself to draw relationships between the various ideas. See Figure 2.3.

2.2.1.4 Flowcharting

Flowcharting is a process of using established symbols with specific meaning with your ideas placed inside the symbol to convey a concept.

> Useful in programming and other design activities when there is a sequence or time component to the topic. Most useful when the result of the brainstorming will be viewed or critiqued by another person for completeness.
>
> Not useful when there's no need to use the special symbols or those symbols are not useful to other people that may add to the brainstorming ideas.

To create a flowchart, start by familiarizing yourself with the various symbols typically used, and what they mean. See Figure 2.4. Take a moment (even consider using another brainstorming tool, like branching first) to discern the steps/sequence to the topic. Then draw the flowchart, using the proper container shape to hold the concept. See Figure 2.5.

Figure 2.3: Sample of a mind map

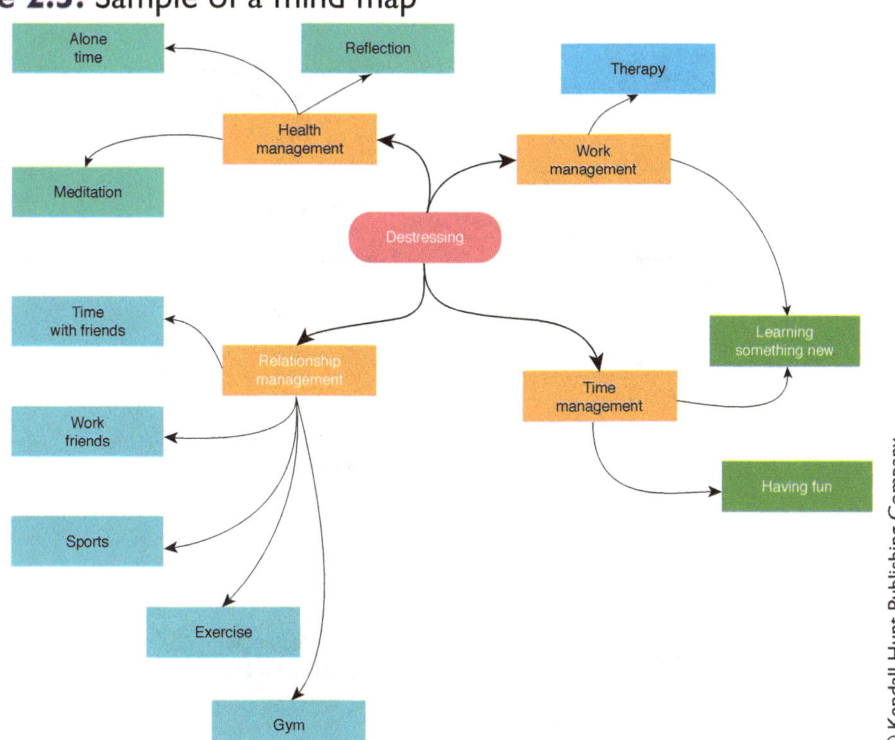

2.2.1.5 Storyboarding

The storyboard technique is used when you need to organize a story, for example, to determine the content for a PowerPoint presentation. The brainstorming tool looks like a comic strip. You can fold a piece of paper into eighths and use each block to brainstorm a panel of the story.

As with any story, there are a lot of ways to tell the story, but probably only one best way to deliver the end point or take away of your story. For that reason, it's best to start brainstorming your story at the last panel. Then decide how best to tell your story to get to that ending. In that way, you can focus on including the information needed to deliver the ending of the story. See Figure 2.6.

Figure 2.4: Flowchart symbols

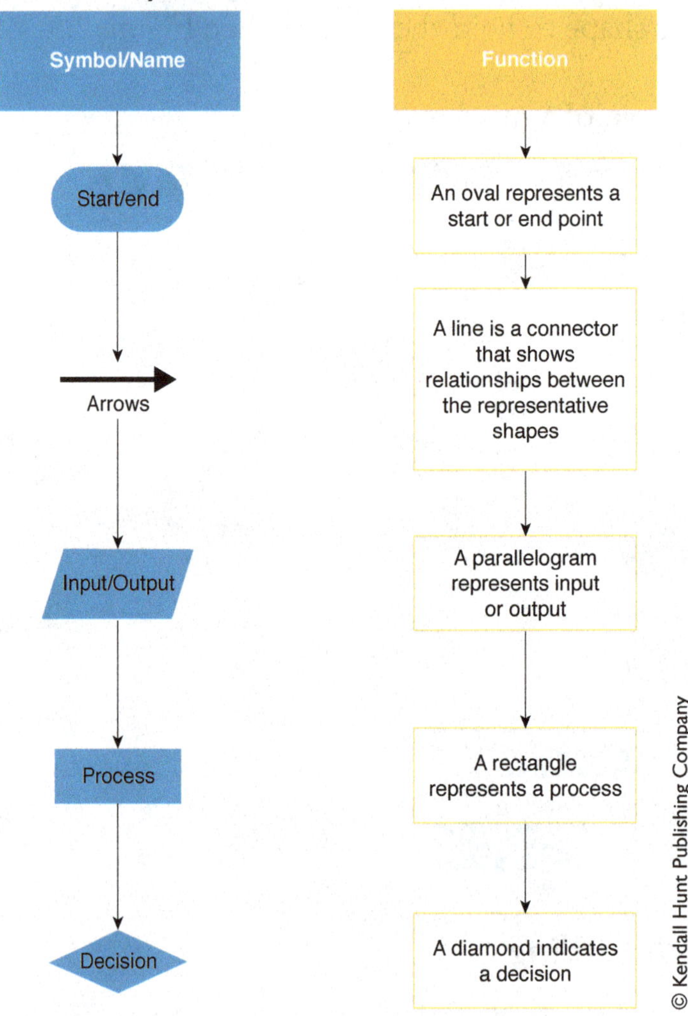

Useful when the result of your work is a story. You can use each panel in the storyboard as a single slide in your presentation or as a series of slides. That way a storyboard is flexible for short or long presentations.

Not useful when there is not a story sequence to your result.

Figure 2.5: Sample of a flowchart

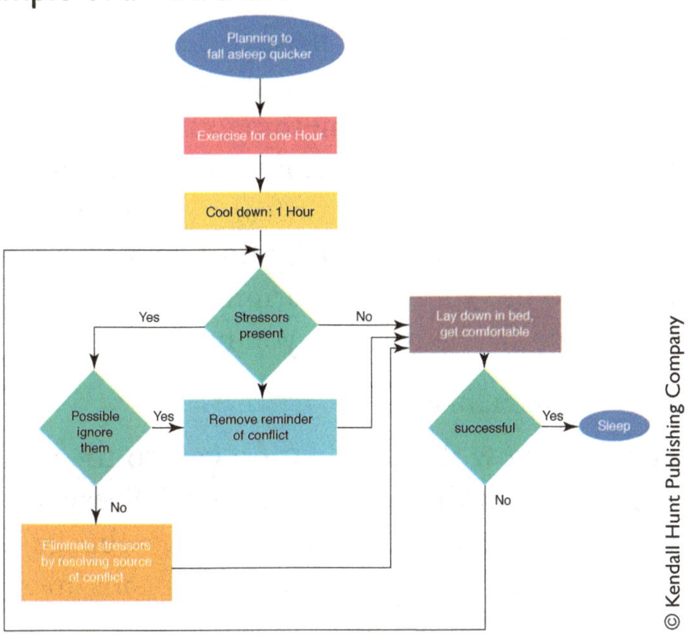

Figure 2.6: Sample of a storyboard

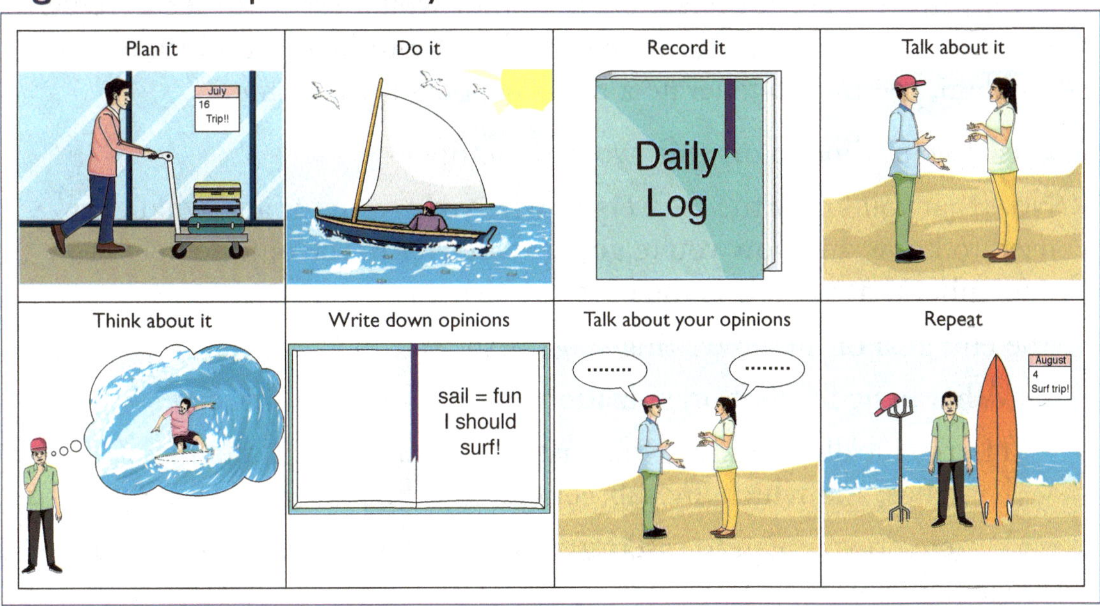

e) Research any needed information

Along with the brainstorming, you need to see what research is required. While the word *research* might bring to mind hours spent surfing the web fruitlessly, it can also mean something as simple as drawing together what you already know about a topic. For instance, you might jot down all the aspects you want to include (or fear you'll forget) based on your *purpose*, so that each idea can eventually find the right home in your writing. You can also use your brainstorming result to help combine search terms to pinpoint the research you need.

f) Plan your delivery mechanism

The *delivery* refers to how the information gets to the reader. Delivery is completely dependent on the situation. Some delivery mechanisms are more common than others (e.g., texting, email, webpage, blog post, news article, magazine, book). Some delivery mechanisms are specialized apps (e.g., Facebook, Twitter, Instagram).

To decide on the delivery method, you need to know where the reader expects to find the information you're providing for them. If you're already in an email conversation, then they would expect to see a "reply." If you were part of a committee tasked with producing a solution to a problem, you might generate a report or possibly a memo.

g) Create an outline to organize your thoughts

Now that you know the answers to who your reader is and what they need to know and how you're going to deliver it, the outline helps you remember that plan. It is the order of ideas.

The end goal of the prewriting stage is the outline.

- What basic form of organization would fit best in this case?
- Hierarchically speaking, what aspects should constitute major headings, and which are subsections or subheadings thereof?
- Where do you plan to insert graphics, information boxes, or other elements of design?

The *pattern* refers to *how the information is organized in the writing*, or what information is placed where. Each pattern requires that each nugget of information be placed in its correct location. For example, in the case of persuasive writing, the thesis or claim that you want to convince the reader to adopt is always placed at the end of the introduction section.

The unique approach to learning business and technical writing from this book is learning the patterns so that for any situation you know where to put the information you have. See Chapter 4, where the most common patterns' organizational structure are covered.

2.2.2 Stage 2: Drafting

The goal of the drafting stage is to generate words, resulting in a rough draft.

At this stage, you turn your outline into words. The main feat of drafting is to turn off your inner critic long enough to let yourself generate the content. Since editing always goes faster than creating original content, simply tell your critic, "thank you for sharing," and move on without heeding it. Don't worry! You'll fix it during the next stage.

As you write, don't feel that you need to write from the beginning to the end. With a good outline, you know what needs to be said, so you can start anywhere you feel most comfortable. You might begin writing in the middle part of the document, then go back to the other parts. For example, I always recommend writing the introduction last because the introduction sets the stage for the rest of the work. If you haven't written the rest of the work, it can be very difficult to write, and frequently requires a complete rewrite once you have written the rest of the work if you drafted it first. So save the time, and write the introduction last.

2.2.3 Stage 3: Revision

The goal of the revision stage is to polish your draft, resulting in work worth reading by your intended audience. Another goal of the revision process is to improve the structure and form of your work to make it low maintenance for further updating, because documents live forever in a business world.

Everyone that has some educational training in writing has been taught to revise their work. Some may think that revision means fixing run-on sentences and punctuation, but to do it well, revision means more than editing.

Now you might think that revision sounds scary, especially if you're afraid of getting rid of any words that you struggled to generate. Rather than being afraid of revising your work, make a copy of that draft before you get started. That way, you can always find any original wording, if you're unhappy with the particular direction your revision process has taken. At the same time, you may find that you drafted content that isn't needed because the reader already knows it. So while you need to delete for the current work, keep it elsewhere safe for when you do need it.

Just like the prewriting stage, the revision stage has a number of substeps. These steps are explained here and discussed in more details in later chapters.

a) Requirements

Have you ever replied to an email, clicked "send" and reread the email, and then realized, oops!, you didn't answer all their questions? We've all been there; that's why this first step is so important.

Start your revision by going back to review the original request. It's so easy to think you've covered all that you were asked to cover, and not realize between the time you started creating the work and now in the process of revising, you forgot various elements of the requirements. This is the time to make sure that you've done what was asked and you didn't inadvertently skip something, for example, something didn't make sense at the beginning.

As you view each instruction, review your drafted work and verify the response to the instruction/request exists correctly in your draft work. If you haven't done it, leave an open space in the document with a note of what needs to be fixed, so that you can get back to it. Once you've completed this substep, you can decide to go back to fill in all missed pieces or collect more revisions and then return to complete the drafted work.

I recommend that you add a marker with your note to indicate there's something to go back to finish. Personally I use a double question mark (??), because I know that sequence should not show up in a finished document and if it exists, I need to go back to finish something. If that's not natural for you, find what does work. For example, some people use the comment feature in their word processor.

b) Page layout and design

You'll be spending a lot of time in this document, so why not make it easy to read right away? Many people wait till the last moment before they publish/print their work to fix the formatting. However, save your eyes and do it sooner rather than later, thus making it easier to refine your work. See Chapter 6 for more details on some formatting refinements.

c) Organization and transitions/headings

This substep means looking at both the organization of the writing and its transitions and headings to identify any issues in your work and fix them. How to approach this substep follows, but see Chapter 4 for details on the patterns' organizational structure and see Chapter 9 for details on transitions.

- Organization – as you examine the organization, use these questions:
  - **i.** Did you follow the organizational structure (pattern) required for the purpose you identified in the prewriting stage? Examine each section per the requirements of the pattern and fix any problems with the structure.
  - **ii.** Be sure that you've included headings for all major sections that clearly explain what content is in that section so your reader can quickly skim your work.
  - **iii.** Is the title/subject line (if present) a clear indication of the pattern you chose and content covered?

- Transitions tell the reader that you're shifting to a new idea (from the current noun context). Transitions are needed in three places:
  - **i.** At the beginning of major sections

    Unlike English composition that has no headings, in business and technical writing, well-constructed headings play the role of a transition for each section heading. Well-constructed headings need to be phrases that include verbs (with the exception of *Introduction* and *Conclusion*). That way, the reader can read a heading and get enough information to presume what that section contains, thus acting as a nice transition.

    Where section headings are not sufficient to provide the reader with an indication of the content, the first paragraph heading might start This section covers . . . or In this section, . . . then describe the contents (See Chapter 4.6.4 Step 7 for more on using "this section covers.").
  - **ii.** At the beginning of paragraphs that shift in content (from the current noun) – When you're changing the noun context in a new paragraph, it's best to put the transition at the beginning of that paragraph to signal that shift to the reader.
  - **iii.** Between sentences that shift in content (from the current noun) but are still providing content based on the topic sentence.

d) Paragraphs

Once you know that the organizational structure works, it's time to address the paragraph level of your document. Well-constructed paragraphs have a couple considerations:

1) Topic sentence and rest of the paragraph – A paragraph is focused on one idea or a group of very closely related ideas. That goal is identified in the topic sentence that tells the reader what the paragraph is about. When you use an "and" in a topic sentence, you're creating a larger task for that paragraph. You want do that deliberately and sparingly, so your paragraphs do not get too large.

2) Rest of the paragraph – The rest of the paragraph builds on the central topic. It's easy when drafting work for a paragraph to digress, so this stage is designed to refocus each paragraph and then be sure that all paragraphs build knowledge for the reader.
3) Length of the paragraph – Paragraphs ought to be just the right size for the reader. Long paragraphs slow down the pace of reading, taking longer to read. If the reader got interrupted while reading a long paragraph, they would most likely have to restart rereading the paragraph to absorb the content. If they got interrupted again and had to start over again, . . . well, you get the idea.

Analyzing your paragraphs is done using two methods. As you work through these methods, you need to fix any problems that arise from the first, before you move to the second method:

1) Perform *glossing** – Glossing is where you get a sense of the flow of information that you've created within each section of your document. This is performed by reading each paragraph within a document section, then writing in three to five words what that paragraph is about. If you're reading online, you could record these words in your word processor's comment feature. If you're reading on paper, then write in the margin to the side of the paragraph.

   When you've completed the glossing for each paragraph in a section, examine the results.

   - If you can't summarize a paragraph to three to five words, then your paragraph is too big.

     To fix, use the Enter or return at strategic places to cut the paragraph into smaller ones.
   - If you use the same words over and over in your glossing, then your writing is redundant. When you say something over and over, the reader will be annoyed that they have to keep reading the same information for whatever extra piece of information you added

*The term glossing comes from Becky Rosenberg Ph.D. previous director of the Writing Center at the University of Washington Bothell.

with the subsequent retellings, or they will skip reading your work and may miss important details.

To fix, reduce redundancies by moving sentences/information around until it's provided only once in the right location for the pattern.

- If you read the glossing words for the series of paragraphs in a section and they seem incongruent, then you may have told the story in the wrong order.

  To fix, re-order your paragraphs until the ideas tell the story for the reader. This fix may require fixing topic sentences and moving other sentences around.

Glossing is not about cutting information out of the work (unless you're being redundant). The goal of glossing is to break paragraphs down to size and to order the paragraphs' information properly. It's about making sure the paragraph's topic sentence matches what is in the paragraph and that it is one bite-sized chunk of information the reader can understand before moving on to the next paragraph and its bite-sized chunk of information.

2) Examine the *sentence-level organization*** within each paragraph – Sentence-level analysis makes sure that each paragraph provides readers with a logical progression of ideas *within* a paragraph – that is, that all subsequent sentences follow from the topic sentence.

   To perform sentence-level analysis, the first step is to number all the sentences in a paragraph based on the role it plays in support of the topic sentence.

   i. Assign a **L1** to the most general, topic sentence.

   ii. Assign a **L2** to a sentence that directly supports a topic L1 sentence. L2 is less general: it modifies, extends, illustrates, and

** The concept of sentence-level numbering comes from Francis Christensen's "Generative Rhetoric of the Paragraph."

qualifies (restricts) and so on, only a L1 sentence. It develops a L1 sentence.

iii. Assign a **L3** to a sentence that directly supports a L2 sentence. L3 is less general/more specific: it modifies, extends, illustrates, and qualifies, and so on, only a L2 sentence.

iv. Assign a **L4** to a sentence that directly supports a L3 sentence. L4 is the least general/most specific: it extends only a L3 sentence.

v. If you find you want to go deeper than **L4** in assigning a number to your sentences, then your paragraph is too complicated, and it's better to start a new paragraph.

vi. With the sentence numbering complete, analyze the structure of the paragraph by looking at the numbers. Does the sequence of **L** numbers create an organized outlined format that makes sense to the reader? For example, does the order resemble an outline? This scheme performs the following:

- Forces paragraphs to be logically organized.
- Ensures you would recognize any jump from an L1 sentence to an L3 or L4 sentence. You can only move from an L1 sentence to an L2 sentence, and know to fix it.
- Helps you recognize that as you move down levels your ideas become more specific, but you can also stay at the same, parallel level OR move up to a higher (more general) level again. This scheme is almost infinitely adaptable and flexible.

Use the practice at the end of this chapter to see this technique in action.

e) Sentences

Now that you know that all the information is organized and in the paragraphs where it should be, the next revision substep is to examine the sentences' structure and polish your word choices. This review is best done in two passes. See Chapter 9 for details on fixing sentence structure and word usage problems.

1) Sentence structure problems
   - Does the POV shift? To fix, search and fix the structure to consistently use the proper POV for the pattern.
   - Are lists parallel? To fix, keep lists in the same English form.
   - Is the sentence a fragment? To fix, ensure that all sentences have a subject and verb.
   - Is the sentence a run-on sentence? When the sentence goes on and on and on and on without proper punctuation, it's called a run-on sentence. To fix, insert proper punctuation.
   - Is the sentence in passive voice? Passive voice is where a sentence is constructed in a way that the subject is not defined or may be unknown. While an occasional passive voice sentence is okay, overuse of passive voice, where the subject isn't identified, can confuse the reader because they do not know who is doing the actions they are reading.

     Do you know if a sentence is passive voice? Add the phrase "by zombies"*** after the verb. Does the sentence make sense? Yes? Then it's passive voice. For example:

     Original sentence: The reading was done.
     Check for passive voice: The reading was done *by zombies*.
     Fix: The students did the reading.
   - Do the subject and verb agree? That is, are the verbs conjugated properly for the accompanying noun? For example, "To be" verb: I am, you are, she is, one is, we are, they are.
   - Are the verbs in the correct tense? To fix, keep the verb tenses consistent with the content, and avoid the use of "will" unless the action *really will* happen in the future.

*** Adding the phrase "by zombies" comes from Grammar Girl Quick Tips on recognizing passive voice: https://www.quickanddirtytips.com/education/grammar/grammar-girls-editing-checklist.

Will

Will ought to be used very selectively in technical writing. When the reader sees that that something will happen, that means that the action takes place in the future, but when in the future: today, tomorrow, next year, fifteen years from now? This imprecision makes use of "will" is a problem because technical writing should never be unclear, and in a business setting, documents live forever.

That is, a document that is created about a project lives while the project is in process, and lingers long afterward, even after the project is completed or obsoleted. Thus, if you use "will" in that document, the reader would never know when that action will happen, which is very confusing. To fix, avoid the future tense, unless you've included a condition statement ("if") or a time frame ("in 2022").

For example:

- *This document will cover x, y, and z* – When will it cover those topics? In this version later in the document? In the next version? Next year? If this document already covers these topics, say, in the next paragraph, then "will" is not required, because it's already happened. To fix, use the present tense: This document covers x, y, and z.
- *If you do this task incorrectly, then you will get an error* – This use of "will" makes sense because it's in an "if" structure that indicates a clear condition. When that task is performed incorrectly, then the reader will get an error.
- *Incoming students will graduate in 2022* – When a date is incorporated, the reader knows when in the future that event will happen. So if the reader sees a date, and that date hasn't passed, then they know it's not happened yet. If it's after that time, then the reader could check up to see if the event has occurred.

To fix sentences after removing will, use other verb forms. Here are some verbs you can consider, depending on what message you want to get across to the reader, "can," "would," "might," and "should."

2) Word choice problems
   - Look for redundancy: For example, overuse of the same word or phrase. It's good to use the same words when you are using jargon. At the same time, overuse of common words may be a sign that the sentence structure is too redundant.
   - Look for expletives: Are there too many "there is/are" or "it is" sentence structures? Some are okay, but too many dull the writing. To fix, remove them by rewriting the sentences.
   - Look for gender bias problems in your writing. These are words that signal only a single gender, when multiple genders are implied, for example, using "he" to refer to multiple genders.
   - Look for pronoun reference problems (e.g., "it," "they," or other pronouns that aren't clear OR using "this" as a subject when the subject isn't clear). For example, "People seeking to get fit often seek out a group of friends who know a lot about fitness. They are also often very organized people." Who are the organized people? Is it the people seeking fitness or the group of fit friends?
   - Look for vague phrases that can mean anything to the reader and thus are unclear. For example, use of "things," "stuff," "technology." To fix, use a precise word/phrase.
   - Look for wordy phrases, where you've used too many words to get your idea across. To fix, reframe to be concise.
   - Look for word choice problems. For example, using the incorrect word, such as homonyms or confusing words, for example, acronyms, abbreviations, or jargon.
   - Look for words/phrases that are likely to change, but you'll forget to change, and so rewriting it now to avoid that word/phrase

would be a better choice. This is about creating low-maintenance documents.

For example, if you wrote There are five tasks to do and then list the tasks, but later you're editing the document and it becomes six or seven tasks, and you forget to change the word five, then your reader would be confused or lose confidence in the accuracy of how many tasks are actually required. Ask yourself whether the exact number is required to be mentioned twice (in the introducing sentence and in the numbered list)?

i. If the number is *not* needed, it's easier to write the introduction as The following tasks are required and make sure they are numbered automatically by the word processor.

ii. If the number is needed and the document likely to be modified by adding more tasks later, then look to change your introduction to the list of tasks to be a heading Five Tasks Required For___, followed by the numbered tasks. Then when you return to the document, you're more likely to see the heading and remember to change the number. Plus if the number is important, you've indicated the importance by placing it in a heading.

- Look for spelling problems.
- Look for where you use a number in the document without following the correct number rule. That is, when do you need to spell out numbers in a sentence? If you don't know the number rules, then you can google search number rules in writing.

f) Punctuation

The last substep in the revision stage is to examine all those small marks – the punctuation – to ensure that they are used properly. See Chapter 9 for details on punctuation.

a) Commas (,) – Used to separate ideas.

b) Colons (:) – Used in time (e.g., 11:00), sentence forecasting, and so on. One common overuse is to put a colon at the end of a heading.

c) Semicolons (;) – There are only two uses for a semicolon. Any other urge to use one is wrong!

1) When you have lists within lists in a sentence, to distinguish between the list elements.
For example, *Before my 2-mile run, I need to stretch, such as doing calf pulls; bring up my fluids, such as drink vitamin water; and remember my special shoes, such as Nike shoes.*

2) To connect two complete sentences.
For example, *I drank an entire liter of water when I got home; the run was very hot today.*

d) Parentheses ( ) – Used to identify additional (extraneous) information, information that is parenthetical to the topic, or that the reader can skip. NOTE: These need to be used properly, as many readers skip reading between parentheses.

e) Slashes (/) – Used to mean "either/or" (e.g., he/she). Using a slash is okay, except for "and/or," which means which? To fix "and/or," rather than say xxx and/or yyy say xxx or yyy, or both.

f) Hyphens (-) – Used to glue words together to create a compound adjective before a noun (e.g., three-dimensional array).

g) Dashes (--) – Used to set off an inner comment. These inner comments tell the reader that what follows is special so they should be used judiciously in business/technical writing. For example, they are used in this section with these bullets to set off the punctuation word from its explanation.

h) Exclamation points (!) – Used to denote surprise or alarm. They are very rare in business and technical writing.

i) Question marks (?) – Used at the end of a sentence to identify the sentence contains a question. These can be easily forgotten, and if you're asking someone a question, you want to make sure they know it.

j) Ellipse (. . .) – Used when you're quoting someone's exact words, but have decided to delete part of the middle of the quote. Where the information was omitted, you use . . . then follow with the rest of the quote. Don't use an ellipse to introduce or end the quote (i.e., at the beginning or ending of the quote). Another use of the ellipse is used to say "you get the idea," which can only be used when you know the reader will get the point.

k) Citations – Used to identify to the reader that information in that sentence was borrowed and links to the references where the information to find the original source is located. To fix, make sure that all of your in-text citations and references/bibliography mechanics are properly formatted according to the citation form asked for (see Chapter 5.4 on citing other's work).

NOTE: If you're using software to generate your citations, you still need to look over the software-generated reference, because all the software out there still has bugs in the code.

This completes all the substeps of the revision stage.

2.3 Writing Process Exercises

1) Do the revision substeps on at least three of your most recent writings. Make a list of your most common mistakes.

2) Take a previous short work of writing that you made.
   a) Apply this technical writing process using the same guidelines. Make a new document with this process. It can contain a different idea from the original.
   b) Do the revision process on the original work.
   c) Compare your notes of the revision. What mistakes did you make? How much of a difference did the technical writing process make?

3) One of the best ways to improve your own writing is to analyze other writing. Read something on the web, an article, social media post, webpage, and so on.
   a) Was the reading *jarring* at any point? Did it stop your reading comprehension or make you lose your way in the content being

delivered? Analyze why that was? Maybe there was a grammar mistake (e.g., the POV shifted making you reflect on the work differently). The more you can learn about these problems, the more you can avoid repeating them in your work.

b) Examine it using the *revision substeps*. How did the author do? Where could they have improved their writing? What can you take away from that example?

c) This series of exercises aids in understanding how the prewriting process works for your process:

   a) Set at timer and write for four minutes. Just write. Set aside.

   b) Set the timer for thirty seconds. Plan what you want to write about. Reset the timer for four minutes, and write using your planning.

   c) Compare these two experiences

2.4 Brainstorming Exercises

These exercises are designed to help you see how each brainstorming technique is optimized based on different initial information and different end result. You may also find that depending on your knowledge level, using more than one technique can help you brainstorm your idea so you flush out your outline more fully.

1) *Listing*: practice with grocery list or to-do list.

2) *Branching*: practice with an activity that needs to get done.

3) *Mind mapping*: practice with a topic that you might use for an assignment.

4) *Flowchart*: practice with what you need to do to complete a current project (at work, home, school).

5) *Storyboard*: practice with a presentation you need to do.

6) *All of them*: practice with your time management.

2.5 Using the Technical Writing Process in Practice

In a business setting, it's important to use these steps as much as possible. At the same time, you can modify them based on your writing strengths and focus where you need the most improvement. You'll find that the more you follow this process, the faster you can use it.

For example:

- Keep a list of common writing issues that show up in your work (e.g., common problems are searching for "will" or be careful that your POV doesn't shift). Keep the list handy so that after you've written something, you can go through the list during your revision steps to ensure your work is polished. And keep your common problem list updated. Your writing will improve as you focus on it, and then you'll find new areas to focus on.
- If you're responding to emails, you can skip through the stages more quickly. Maybe dash off an outline on a post-it to order your thoughts for your response. Then before you hit "reply," reread the original message to be sure that you covered all the points asked for in the message. Look over your common writing issues list, and with a read through and general grammar check and fix, your message ought to be ready to hit "send."
- If you know that you took extra care during the drafting stage to generate well-constructed headings and paragraphs, then it's probably okay to skip the glossing and just focus on the sentence outlining.
- However, if you're writing a larger document over a series of weeks or even months, then use the full process with all the steps to be sure that your work is polished. Remember that the longer you're away from your work, the harder it is to remember where information is located, how you explained

things, and what language (jargon) you used. Thus, you're more likely to become redundant or wordy, or have other issues with your writing.

2.6 Paragraph Analysis Exercises

Review the instructions for paragraph analysis that is performed during the revision stage. Each sentence is numbered based on its role in the paragraph, copy out the numbers into its sequence, and analyze the structure to determine if the paragraph is structured well with good flow. Here's an exercise to practice creating well-structured paragraphs:

1) Work in groups, take a simple L1 sentence and practice coherent development.

2) Each person in the group comes up with an L2 sentence that develops the paragraph.

3) By the end of the exercise, your group should have produced a useful paragraph. And all the groups would have developed a series of useful paragraph templates.

2.6.1 Paragraph Analysis Exercise Examples

L1 Schedule frequent breaks during big tasks.

A) Analysis: {L1, L2, L3, L4, L5} NOTE: In A, it goes to L5, this last sentence is a conclusion sentence that unifies all previous content. In this way, it's okay to go this deep, even though that is usually not recommended.

> *Schedule frequent breaks during big tasks. Long periods of concentration are not as productive as spaced out intervals. During efforts that exceed an hour, focus wanes. That's why breaks can bring back your focus and improve creativity. Taking a step back from your task can help you create new solutions instead of hammering away at old ideas.*

B) Analysis: {L1, L2, L3, L2, L3}

> *Schedule frequent breaks during big tasks. Long periods of concentration are not as productive as spaced out intervals. Holding your concentration requires your brain to stay alert, focused, and on task. However, when you space out your efforts, your brain can alternate between being focused and resting. During the rest, your brain can recharge for the next interval.*

C) Analysis: {L1, L2, L2, L2} NOTE: In C, any of the L2 sentences could have additional L3 or even L4 sentences to grow the information delivery.

> *Schedule frequent breaks during big tasks. One way to take a break is to play a game with real playing cards or doodle on paper. Another way to take a break is with bigger movement actions, such as to get up, walk around, and stretch. Or, you can have your mind take a break by doing a different activity, such as laundry, dishes, or meal preparation.*

D) Analysis: {L1, L2, L3, L3, L4, L3}

> *Schedule frequent breaks during big tasks. Long periods of concentration are not as productive as spaced out intervals. Breaks can help your mind recover mental stamina so that you can consistently focus on your task and not get distracted. Breaks can also improve creativity. Taking a step back from your task can help you create new solutions instead of hammering away at old ideas. Even though you may not be actively thinking about it during your break, your subconscious is still working on the problem in ways that your conscious mind does not think to try.*

Analyze Your Audience: Who They Are and What Do They Need

Simply put, analyzing your audience means considering the needs of your reader and tailoring your work to them. However, it's not that simple, and that's why this chapter is included – to piece apart this process.

What do you think about your audience before you begin writing?

- Do you think that you already know who they are and tailor your output to them?

  This may be true when you are writing to an audience that is just like you. When you create work based on how you'd like it organized and your reader is just like you (e.g., students or workers of the same role/title), then you will most likely be successful getting your ideas across. Variations in preferences in information layout would account for anywhere your audience did not understand what you were doing.

- Do you avoid this step to not take the time?

  You might avoid the analysis if you're rushed to create the work (like emails or email replies) or if you don't know how to do it. Then analyzing your audience becomes a daunting task with no way to get it done, so you would skip it.

- Are you so focused on your own ideas, views, opinion that you can't think about who is going to read it too?

  Perhaps you think that your work is so paramount or general that there is no need to think about a specific audience since everybody will read it.

- Maybe you think that it's not your job to do anything special?

  That instead, it's the job of the reader to figure out what they need to know from what you've provided. This thinking is easy to see because it's reinforced by teachers that do just that – they take their time to figure out what you've written, and even when it doesn't make sense, you'll frequently get a good grade, so you don't know how difficult your writing was to understand.

- Maybe you think that it doesn't matter – that the reader is going to read the whole document anyway?

  Perhaps you're thinking that if the reader reads the work from the beginning to the end of the document, reading all the sections, then they'll find what they are looking for. That's what a teacher may do before assigning a grade, but not what happens on the job. On the job, readers will read only what they need to read to get the information they need to get their job done.

- Are you conditioned to see your work as only ever being read once by a teacher/instructor with the sole intention of grading it? Or for your manager to read it, when they get around to it?

  Although your school work may not to be referenced again, on the job, your business and technical writing lives forever. It may be reviewed again at any time. For example, even seemingly inconsequential emails that resolve a design decision may be stored and accessed again and again for decades.

- Do you think that it's not necessary to analyze the audience?

  Perhaps you naturally mimic an organization style that you've seen before and know would work for the current situation. That's great! Interestingly enough, this is a way of unconsciously thinking about your audience by matching your organization to standard structures.

It's worth knowing where you're coming from with respect to the activities of audience analysis because that will influence your willingness and effort you'll put into it.

This chapter explains what analyzing your audience entails – what it means to consider the person who will read your work at the moment they are reading your work.

3.1 Audience Analysis Is the Author's Job

Audience analysis begins with the realization that, as the author, it's your job to make sure that you do everything you can to create a work that makes the information your reader needs easily accessible to them.

Your reader has a job to do. That job requires that they read your work to get it done, so your work stands between their task and what they need to know to do that task. If your work is not accessible – it's formatted poorly so that information is hard to find or takes a long time to read, or the information is haphazardly arranged so it needs to be scoured multiple times to find the relevant information, or the paragraphs are so large they consume most of a page/screen, or any other myriad of problems – then your reader would be unhappy, annoyed, frustrated, and so on. They may search other (less reliable) sources for the information they need or other scenarios. All these struggles may result in them getting behind in their task.

So you need to set your mindset to realize that your job is to know how to tailor the organization of information, format it for ease of reading, and chose words to deliver the content efficiently and effectively.

3.2 How to Approach the Analysis?

As you consider your audience, you may have a specific person in mind – a teacher, a friend, and so on. However in business and technical writing, your work is usually read by more than one person, which only increases the difficulty of analyzing your audience, because you can't think of the task as tailoring your output to the foibles of a specific person you already know really well to tailoring your work to the foibles of all the various readers. Furthermore, you might not even personally know your audience.

If you want to get to know your audience, you might decide to talk to them, to ask them what they need and how to meet their expectations. Again this approach may be worthwhile, if you have the time to get to know the audience. But this interview process would be complicated by the need to talk to all the various readers of your future work and to collate the various responses so that you're producing only one document to meet all the needs. What can you do?

A more manageable approach is to examine the *role* the reader plays as they read your work. This role would dictate the organization, format, and word choice to deliver the content efficiently and effectively. Then use that knowledge to extrapolate the best way to organize the specific information they need to complete their task. First, you need to know who your audience is.

3.3 Who Is Your Audience?

This section examines the most common audience roles and generalizes their job responsibilities. Use the information here to help you understand the background of your primary audience – the specific people who need to read your work.

If the role you need to write for is not in this list, then you can perform a similar analysis for that role using what you've learned by reading this section. Then you can use the assumptions you make about their role to create your work.

3.3.1 Experts

Technical experts are the people whose job is to create the product/services for a business. They may be software developers, design engineers, user interface designers, and so on. They have a technical degree and have built that knowledge further while on the job to excel in producing whatever technology/expertise the business is known for. These experts are expected to create the products/services, understand the growth of the industry, and suggest new directions or respond to the customer requests. These people are known for their expertise. They are smart, clever, and good at problem solving. They can understand complicated concepts and know the jargon associated with their education and expertise. Furthermore, they are able to learn new ideas quickly because they understand how to educate themselves. And they are willing to dive into long, complicated documents to get the information they need.

3.3.2 Executives and Managers

Executives are at the highest level of the hierarchy of the business. They are responsible for overseeing the business direction, its financial future, its customers/services, and the business' image as perceived externally by their customers and internally by their employees. Likewise, managers are part of the hierarchy of the business below its executives. They interpret and implement the tasks identified by the executives that help the business meet its obligations, grow, and turn a profit. To perform those tasks, they have employees reporting to them that they manage. In addition, they see to the welfare of their employees (their salaries, their career development).

Depending on the size of the organization, the executives and managers usually have knowledge of the technology the business is involved in. They may have a technical degree or a business/finance degree. In the latter case, they would have needed to learn about the business technology to be successful in their job. In other cases, they may be the original experts who later moved into management roles. The longer a manager or executive is in their role, the more they have moved away from the intricacies and nuances of the business' technology and more into the roles of managing the business' overall success. This means that based on your situation, you need to decide how much technical explanation is needed in the work you're producing for this audience.

When considering this audience, realize they are very busy people. Their job scope is broad with many varied tasks. Each task may or may not take long, but it requires a lot of varied information from many different areas across the company. They need to synthesize that information, using their own expertise to help make decisions that direct the company's success. This rapid fire, busy day-to-day means that they can get interrupted frequently, while needing to remember and track a multitude of ongoing activities. This means that your work needs to be easily accessible to this audience, so they can find what they are looking for quickly.

3.3.3 Technicians

Technicians traditionally have specific roles with smaller scope than the experts. They might be IT help desk, quality assurance testers, and so on. They may or may not have a technical degree or may have a specialized degree or certified expertise. They understand how to manage their time and get their job done well and efficiently. Technicians have technical expertise in the fields they work in, but may not have the technical background to understand new technologies beyond those they are educated about, and may not have the time to research other new topics.

3.3.4 Others

This category is used to house the audience you don't know. You may know their role, but not their educational background or their specific role in the company or why they need to read your work. You can certainly assume they are knowledgeable about the role they have in the organization, or they'd not have a job. In these cases, it would be worth doing a little research, either by asking someone who might know or asking the person who requested you create the work.

3.3.5 Audience Analysis Summary

Based on the analysis of the various company roles, some assumptions can be made, as seen in Table 3.1.

Table 3.1: Audience analysis summary

Audience roles	**Assumptions you can make about the audience with respect to their ability to read the material to be covered in your work, using HIGH, MEDIUM, LOW**		
	Existing knowledge level of the material	**Ability to absorb new material**	**Interest level to go beyond the content**
Expert	HIGH Can easily absorb complicated information. They would expect it to be logically ordered.	HIGH Can easily absorb new material beyond their current understanding because of their technical expertise, degree, background.	HIGH Usually interested to know the broader scope or context to the material they are reading.
Executive or manager	MEDIUM to HIGH Depends on how much time they have been able to spend to keep up with technologies while in their management role.	MEDIUM What limits them is focus. They are usually pulled in lots of different directions and easily interrupted. Limited by how much the new material relates to the original request. The more it's related, the easier it is to absorb.	LOW What limits them is time. Their multitasking days limit the time needed to absorb other nonimmediate content. Limited by how much the new material relates to the original request. The more it's related, the easier it is to absorb.
Technician	MEDIUM Assume expertise in the material, but not expert knowledge.	HIGH Assume interest to understand new directions the company may develop.	MEDIUM Assume moderate interest to understand a broader scope to their work.
Others	LOW Unless you know, assume they do not know much about the topic.	LOW Unless you know, assume they do not have the technical expertise to easily absorb new material.	Unknown with LOW Unless you know, assume they could be interested in a broader perspective to the topic.

Now that you have these generalizations about your audience, how does that influence what you do? To answer, let's return to your shifted mindset, that is, your job is to tailor the information organization, format for ease of reading, and chose the best words. These topics are introduced here, then covered in this book in detail and when put together, you'll deliver the content efficiently and effectively.

- Tailor the organization – Your reader has a very specific reason for reading your work. Otherwise they won't be reading it; they will be getting their job done. Their purpose determines how your information needs to be organized, that is, the specific requirements as to where information needs to be located in the document. Read more in Chapter 4, where the various patterns of organization are covered.
- Format for ease of reading – To ease your reader's progress through your work, the formatting of the document needs to be consistent and meet their expectations. Read more in Chapter 5 and Chapter 6, where the various elements of technical writing are discussed and how they affect its accessibility.
- Choose the best words is a focus of this book – Each chapter focuses on how word choice makes a difference, how it delivers the content the reader needs, how it signals changes in direction, and how it refines the message for ease of readability. Later sections in this chapter cover these concepts: *tone*, *pace*, and *point of view* (POV), all of which influence your work's accessibility.

NOTE: This book does not cover how to address audiences from varied cultures around the world. It assumes that you're writing for a business that conducts itself in English in the United States.

3.3.6 Example Audience Analysis

Table 3.2 examines these audience roles using the topic of Excel, as in, they may need to learn more about it in some way. It shows how you can begin to make educated assumptions about the readers that can translate into what you need to do to create a document where the information is accessible to the reader.

Table 3.2: Example audience analysis

Comparison	Expert	Manager	Technician	Others
What do they need to know	New ideas, changes to Excel Future plans for Excel Current news about Excel	Concrete actions taken or to be taken Bare minimum data to execute those actions Existing problems that require actions people who are involved Time constraints on projects	How to perform specific activities Addressing potential problems	Basic overview Main functions Importance of subject
Example topics this audience may need information about	Excel's role in business Excel update log Excel plans for the upcoming year Excel development history	Excel back end team report Excel specifications doc Excel idea proposal	How to use Excel's formulas How to create scatterplots Common Excel formatting issues	Welcome to Excel Deciding between Excel and Sheets
How much they know	High	Medium	Medium	Low
Pace	Slow	Fast	Medium	Medium
Technical writing elements to consider including to deliver the content	Application of concepts Follow-up resources Theoretical and process explanations Data figures Citations	Table of contents Data regarding current task Citations and references to people Process explanations	Glossary Definitions Graphics Examples Details in explanations	Glossary Definitions Graphics Examples Formula guide
Elements to not include	Glossary Definitions	Data not related to the purpose Follow-up resources Glossary Theoretical explanations	Theoretical explanations Follow-up resources Data figures	Process explanations Theoretical explanations Data figures

3.4 Who Is the Secondary Audience?

As information in business is shared, it's likely that someone else may read the work you've created – or pieces/parts of it. These secondary audiences are not the primary target, but lurkers, who look to learn what they need to know. They may read all of the work or merely a part of it based on their interest and time available. The primary and secondary audience are compared in Table 3.3.

Table 3.3: Comparing the primary and secondary audience

Comparison	Primary audience	Secondary audience
How does the author know they are the audience?	Certain documents have traditional audiences: a design doc is for the designer. Whoever asked for a document	You don't know unless you're told You can make assumptions: For example, sections about money could be examined by the company accountant or business analysts
Why the person is reading the doc?	The person who needs to read the document to get their job done. Otherwise, they can't get their job done.	A person who decides to look at the document or read parts of it for their information or because they need that information to help them do their job.
Do you acknowledge this reader?	Yes	No
How is the audience acknowledged?	• In the title by using cue words. Managers learn how to ____ • In the Introduction using a phrase similar to: As a <role>, you ___ • For an email/memo/letter, who it's written TO • For a report, the title page would have two corresponding lines: Produced for ___ Produced by ___	• Not acknowledged inside the document • For an email/memo/letter, the secondary audience is written on the CC line

Comparison	Primary audience	Secondary audience
What parts of the doc need to be read?	The parts that help them get their job done. Not necessarily all of the document. Only what's needed. That's why strong, clear navigational headings are so critical.	Only those parts they're interested in

3.5 Tone Determines Accessibility

Tone is the *impression* that you want the reader to be left with after they have read your work. The reader's impression is an unconscious reaction to the work after they have finished reading it that could be understood in terms of an emotion, the feeling the reader holds about the reading. For example:

- Professional, competent, knowledgeable, informed are all these impressions that tell the reader they can trust what they are reading.
- Sloppy, confusing, hard to follow, difficult, full of errors are impressions that leave the reader confused by the language/word choice, and they might not feel comfortable trusting the authenticity or knowledge level of the author.

Tone is determined by a combination of the following:

1) Pace (paragraph length, sentence length, word lengths) (See Chapter 3.6 for more on pace.)
2) POV in use (1st, 2nd, 3rd) (See Chapter 3.7 for more on POV.)
3) Word choice (e.g., each of the following words evoke a different reaction to the same concept: children, child, offspring, youth, kid, teen, youngster, brat, rug rats) (See Chapter 9.3 for more on word choice.)
4) Voice (passive/active)
   a) Passive – The reader does not know who the subject is. For example, Mistakes were made. (See Chapter 9.2 for more on passive voice.)

b) Active – The subject of the verb is known. For example, The students made various mistakes in their work.

5) Delivery, including the following:
   - Format of the final work – For example, email, letter, memo, website, brochure, and report. (See Chapter 7 for more on delivery.)
   - Page layout and design – Headers, footers, page numbers, and so on. (See Chapter 6 for more on document formatting.)
   - Fonts and colors used
   - Paper (if printed) – Its color, texture, weight

The tone you decide to deliver in your work needs to be *consistent* throughout the document.

Consider when reading comics how their combination of look, font, drawings, and word choice may deliver a lighthearted tone that makes you smile or they may deliver a sad, violent, or heart-wrenching tone, depending on the author's intent. That's tone.

To that end, one paragraph should not sound like "baby talk" and then the next paragraph/sentence sound like a lawyer wrote it. As the author, you control your work to deliver the tone that you want the reader to be left with.

At the same time, it's important to realize that just because you're writing in a business setting, not all writing needs to be formal. So it's important to match your tone with what your audience expects.

- If all writing was formal, then your readers would leave your writing with the impression that it is stilted or overly formal. That reaction might translate to their face-to-face interactions with you in which they feel you're unapproachable or overly formal.

- If all your writing was informal (full of abbreviations and slang), that may create an impression with your audience when dealing with you face-to-face that you don't take your work seriously or even that you may not be reliable.

3.6 Pace Influences Accessibility

Pace is the *speed* with which ideas are presented to the reader.

Pace is determined in combination by the length of the following:

1) Paragraphs – The number of lines in a paragraph.

2) Sentences – The number of words in a sentence.

3) Words – The number of characters in a word.

Pace is primarily determined by the length of the paragraph, but is influenced by sentence length and word length. Lots of long paragraphs, sentences, and words *slow* the pace. Lots of short paragraphs, sentences, and words *speed up* the pace and, at the same time, make it sound choppy. Therefore, pace is not uniform throughout a document. That is, it's not always long nor always short, but instead variable.

In the following paragraph, you'll notice a stilted pace because each of the sentences is short:

> *Rest is good. Sleep helps with learning. A lack of sleep is bad. The mind can't think. It is hard to learn things. Thoughts become dull. These words are proof. I sound tired. It seems simple. I need sleep.*

When you write, you want to vary your pace, but in a way that helps deliver the content. Notice the difference in the following paragraph as the sentence length and word choice vary:

> *I just got more sleep. Now I can think properly and make sentences of varying lengths. My sentences are longer. They have more variation in length, which creates a more dynamic flow of language. Better sleep can make a difference. I not only write better, but I also become a better problem solver and reader of information.*

In all cases, pace must be consistently delivered within each section of the document according to its requirements. For example:

- The introduction can have a faster pace so the reader can arrive at the detail in the body sooner.
- The body of the document may naturally have a slower pace, because as more details are delivered, they need to be explained, thus lengthening those sections and paragraphs, which would naturally slow the reading pace.
- The conclusion can speed up again so that the reader can move on to what they need to do now that they've gotten the information that you provided.

3.7 POV Determines Reader's Relationship to the Work

Point of View (POV) is how you, the author, want the reader to *relate* to the information. POV is defined as 1st, 2nd, and 3rd as seen in Table 3.4.

Table 3.4: Comparing the points of view

Point of view (POV)	Uses these pronouns	Use this POV when
1st	Refers to YOURSELF Singular -> *I, me, my, mine* Plural -> *we, our, us, ours*	Singular: Establishes that the writing is about you, the author. Plural: Establishes that the writing is about a group that includes you, the author, and the reader. This is about a shared experience or a shared role. Use of 1st POV creates an informal tone (but, if needed, this can be overcome by other factors, such as more formal word choice and/or strong, firm document page layout).
2nd	Refers to the READER Singular -> *you, your, yours* Plural -> *you, your, yours*	Establishes that the author is writing to the reader directly. Whenever someone reads *you* in a sentence, they put themselves into that sentence. If you're not writing directly to the reader, then don't use "you." Use of 2nd POV creates a medium-formal tone (but, if needed, this can be overcome by other factors, such as more formal word choice and/or strong, firm document page layout).

►

Point of view (POV)	Uses these pronouns	Use this POV when
3rd	Refers to OTHER PEOPLE Singular -> *he, she, it, one, his, hers, its, ones, they, their, theirs* Plural -> *they, their, theirs*	Establishes a discussion where all parties are referred by name or role (e.g., parent, student, manager). The author does not directly refer to the reader nor does the author refer to himself or herself. Use of 3rd POV creates a formal tone (but, if needed, this can be toned down by informal word choice and informal document page layout including font).

3.8 Comparing English Composition to Business and Technical Writing

Table 3.5 compares the English Composition writing style and business and technical writing to highlight the differences in expectation and style of these types of writing.

Table 3.5: Comparing English composition to business and technical writing

Comparison criteria	English composition	Business and technical writing
Audience	Your teacher, but really you're writing for yourself	Always someone else or groups of people
Why is it read?	Writer-centric: To grade it	Reader-centric: To get their job done
Content	"Essays," varies	Single or special purpose writing for business. Content is technical, factual, where accurate is paramount.
How is it read?	From the beginning through to the end	Only the parts needed to complete their work

Comparison criteria	**English composition**	**Business and technical writing**
What writing style is common?	Flowery, long, vague, wordy, creative, even teasing	Concise, proper tone, direct
What writing aids are used?	Writing aids infrequent	Graphics and tables frequent and useful
Document format	Double spaced, indented paragraphs, centered titles, same text font throughout, no special formatting (italic, bold, underline, varied fonts, etc.), no headings, except centered title line on first page	Single spaced, white space between paragraphs, headings using contrasting font, use of bullets, tables, graphics make information easy to find
Last sentence in paragraph	Used as a transitioning sentence to forecast the next paragraph	Traditionally omitted, because documents are frequently edited, so these would need to keep being modified
Due dates?	Turn in when done, never examined again, except maybe for posterity	Living documents, never really go away. Continue to be used, sometimes even for decades after their original authorship

Exercises

1) Explain why you would *not* create the same document for multiple primary audiences.
2) If you need to create multiple documents with the same type of content for different primary audiences, what should you do?
3) Look at the chatty phrasing and consider how you would rewrite it to use a more formal tone.
   a) Let's look at _____ first, then _____.
   b) You'll notice that ___.
   c) This'll be like _____.
   d) You could say that ____

4) Consider the information in the following scenarios:
NOTE: Front matter refers to the information that occurs at the top of all these assignments.

What is being conveyed by the author to the reader? Why?

a) MLA writing assignment front matter

> Last Name 1
>
> Student's First Name Last Name
>
> Professor Laurie Anderson
>
> Composition Writing
>
> October 31, 2020
>
> Centered title of the assignment
>
> First paragraph begins, indented with the work double spaced. All text uses the same font, only Times New Roman 12 throughout. No special formatting is provided in the document. . . .

b) Student generated front matter to a typed writing:

> Student's First Name Last Name
>
> Professor Laurie Anderson
>
> Writing Exam
>
> October 31, 2020

c) Student generated front matter to a typed exam:

> Student's First Name Last Name
> Midterm Exam; October 31, 2020
>
> 1)

5) Practice writing to varied audiences: SCENARIO: You need to tell each of the following audiences that you're a week behind on your project because *make up the reason*. Write a paragraph that tells each audience what they would need to know, based on who they are and what their role is.

What is the reason that you're a week behind?

---

a) *Manager* (who cares most about managing the people that report to him or her and their well-being)

b) *Project manager* (who cares most about the schedule, the project, and all the project pieces fitting together). If you're behind by a week, then your lateness could impact other people working on their pieces. That is, consider whether your work is on the *critical path* or not. What will you say if it is/isn't?

c) *Work colleague* (who is a work friend who you get coffee with, attend work functions), as follows:

i. The work colleague is on the same project as you are.

ii. The work colleague works for the same company but not the same project.

d) *Friend* on social media. Identify the app:

---

e) *Family* that is asking you to come over to have dinner with them that weekend.

f) *Someone else* to practice these skills?

6) Make an audience analysis summary table of a current or past project group.

a) How much do they know?

b) How much are they willing to learn?

c) Are they interested in learning more beyond the original content?

d) What did they need to learn?

7) One of the best ways to improve your own writing is to analyze other writing. Read something on the web, an article, social media post, webpage, and so on.

   a) What is the *tone* that you are left with after reading it? Was the reader successful in developing the tone they wanted? What created that tone? Look at word choice, sentence structure, and so on, to see how the tone was delivered. NOTE: If you're reading a review, news, or social media, sarcasm is one of the most difficult tones to deliver.

Write to the Pattern Defined by Purpose and Audience

Once you know who you're writing to by performing an audience analysis, then you need to know what motivates your audience to go looking for the work you've created – to read your work. That purpose will determine how you need to organize the information you're providing, or what pattern of organization to use.

If you didn't follow a specific prescribed pattern, then the way the information will end up organized is the way it made sense in your head (as the author) at the time you were creating it. However, your audience would rarely perceive that as organized, since they aren't in your head thinking the way you do. So to them it would appear random. And whenever you're trying to convey information, it should never be random!

From the audience's perspective, they have been taught patterns throughout school and other reading they have done. They know where to find information because they have learned patterns.

Therefore, from your perspective, as the author, it's best to use an established pattern. It's what the reader expects and what they can easily understand.

If a pattern does not exist, build on the existing patterns for what your situation requires.

4.1 How to Select a Pattern

This chapter focuses on the most common patterns. To decide on a pattern to use, you analyze your purpose for what you're trying to accomplish, as seen in Table 4.1.

Table 4.1: Document purpose and corresponding pattern to use

Purpose	Pattern	Chapter
To help the reader understand how the author learned, grew, changed, based on an experience	Inductive	4.2
To convince the reader to adopt your thesis/claim	Persuasive	4.3
To help the reader make a decision by comparing the subjects clearly and objectively	Compare and contrast	4.4
To explain *how* to do something	Instructions	4.5
To explain *why* things are done the way they are (best practices) and proper background for use	Process	4.6
To solve a problem the reader has	Problem solution	4.7
To explain how particular causes have produced an effect, that is, why something has happened (in the past) OR to predict why something might happen (in the future)	Cause/effect	4.8
To convey the order of importance associated with a list of elements • *Most important* first – List ordered by importance with most important at the top to maximize ease of relevance • *Least important* first – List ordered to build anticipation for the audience until they get to the most important at the end	Most important to least important OR Least important to most important	4.8
To organize a list of individual elements in numeric order, in alphabet order, or combined as alphanumeric order	Indexed	4.8

Purpose	Pattern	Chapter
To take like-identified groups and identify them in a named class is *classification*	Classification	4.8
To take a whole object and partition it (break it up) into its parts and identify those parts is *partition*	Partition	
To show relationships of information in three-dimensional (3D) space	Spatial	4.8
To organize all the varied complicated information when a single document needs more than one pattern	Combining patterns in same document	4.9

NOTE: While this book's focus is primarily on generating a written result, you can use any of these patterns to organize your thinking, work through a problem, and deliver your thinking in a conversation or discussion.

4.1.1 How to Read This Chapter? Definitions of Pattern Characteristics

Each pattern section begins with a table that includes information about that pattern followed by a detailed discussion of the pattern organization. Table 4.2 defines those pattern characteristics.

Table 4.2: Pattern characteristics and what they mean

Characteristics	Defining the characteristics
Purpose	The purpose defines why the audience is reading the work – the reason – what information they need from reading your work.
Audience or reader	What is the role of the audience who needs the information that you're providing. Combine your knowledge of the information you're providing with their role to produce the best word choice the pattern organization, so your work is accessible to the audience.

Characteristics	**Defining the characteristics**
Secondary audience	Someone else may read the work you've created, or pieces/parts of the work. These readers are not the primary target, but lurkers. They may read all of the work or merely a part based on their interest and time.
Scenario indicators	There are special words that cue the author as to what kind of information the audience is looking for. By listening to the requestor, you can deliver exactly what they need to read. To help you identify when to use which pattern, the cue words are offered.
Point of view (POV)	POV (1st, 2nd, 3rd) should not be used randomly in the patterns, because each POV evokes a specific reaction with the reader. To improve accessibility use the correct POV consistently.
Tone	Tone is the reader's impression of the work. For simplicity sake, this book categorizes tone along a continuum from *informal*, *medium formal*, to *formal* to refer to the resulting overall impression of professionalism the reader perceives.
Pace	Pace is the speed that information is presented to the reader. For simplicity sake, this book categorizes pace along a continuum from *slow* to *fast*.
Organization	Each pattern requires that the information is delivered always where the reader expects to find it. This chapter focuses on the organization of each pattern.
Ethical scenarios	In any writing, situations arise that may cause you to examine ethical situations where you may not be exactly truthful in your writing, where you may feel that you can exaggerate or be vague. Each pattern highlights the different situations that can arise and summarizes the possible scenarios.
Examples	Examples are offered where the pattern might appear in business.
Delivery	Examples are offered of how the pattern might be delivered to the reader in business.

Characteristics	Defining the characteristics
Cognitive skill	Writing builds on or stresses your cognitive (thinking) skills. The patterns stress different cognitive/thinking skills. Sometimes if you're having trouble with a pattern, it can be helpful to hone your thinking skills too.
Writing skill	Each of the patterns build on writing skills that you've honed in your other writing experiences. Knowing which ones are stressed by this pattern can help you focus during your revision stage.

4.1.2 Exercises

1) On the job, you will need to determine, based on keywords in the audience request, what pattern of organization to use.

  a) Consider a recent request for information that you were asked for, what pattern was inherent in the words used in request?

  b) Examine the corresponding method of organizing for that pattern. Would the resulting document be a single pattern or a combination of patterns in the same document?

2) On the job, you may be asked to create a document just like this one for your project. This means you would be given or pointed to an existing document that is already organize the way they want you to produce the information for your project. Your job would be to analyze each section of the document, section by section, find out what information lives in that section for that project, and then create the content in a new document for your project using the same table of contents (TOC).

  a) Take a recent document, article, and so on, that you've read and analyze the pattern throughout.

  b) What keywords told you the organization? For example, Word is followed by the rest of the sentence is a structure that signals a definition follows the "word."

  c) Can you learn and find in a sample the language of each of the patterns in this chapter?

4.2 Inductive Pattern

The inductive pattern is used when you want to tell someone about an experience you had, which changed you and where you grew in some way. This pattern goes beyond the mere storytelling of an experience to the focus on a self-reflective discovery.

4.2.1 Inductive Pattern Summary Table

Characteristics ☞	**Writing inductively**
Purpose	To help the reader understand how the author learned, grew, changed, based on an experience
Audience or reader	Someone you know
Secondary audience	If present, someone you know
Scenario indicators	Learn, change, grow, reflect, self-reflection, your experience (read more in Chapter 4.2.2)
Point of view (POV)	1st POV (singular) to refer to the author (most common POV used throughout this pattern) 2nd POV: used to refer to the reader (only seen in the conclusion, if at all) 3rd POV: used to refer to other people in the experience
Tone	Medium formal
Pace	Medium
Organization	Organized as introduction + the experience + conclusion (read more in Chapter 4.2.3)
Ethical scenarios	• Exaggeration of events, or being biased about events or sequence • Deemphasize issues that occurred, or blaming others rather than taking responsibility for your part in an experience (read more in Chapter 4.2.3.3)

Characteristics ☞	**Writing inductively**
Examples	Explaining your learning from experiences. Job interview answer. Half of your yearly performance evaluation. Within another pattern. (see Chapter 4.2.7)
Delivery	Talking/speaking, email, letter, report, memo, a section within a larger document
Cognitive skill	Being self-reflective about learning from a personal experience
Writing skill	Narrative writing
☞ See Table 4.2 for definitions of these characteristics.	

4.2.2 Deciding on When to Use the Inductive Pattern

Deciding when to use a pattern is based on the cues that you get from your audience. Listen carefully to their questions or watch their actions to help you decide when this pattern is the best choice. This pattern can be used in writing, or when speaking, to organize your thoughts to create a thoughtful answer/reply.

Words that cue you to use the pattern:

- learn, change, grow
- reflect, self-reflection
- your experience

4.2.3 Organization of the Inductive Pattern

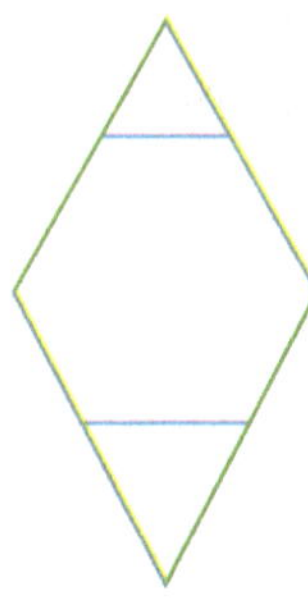

The inductive pattern is organized in three parts: introduction, the experience, and conclusion. Think of this pattern as a diamond cut into three unequal sections.

Top: introduction with the smallest amount of content.

Middle: for the experience, contains the most content.

Bottom: conclusion with less information than the middle, but more than the introduction.

What information goes into each part of the pattern is explained in the following sections:

4.2.3.1 Title

However this work is being delivered, you would need to introduce it in some way. It's always a good idea to introduce this pattern specifically, rather than vaguely or with conclusions already drawn. This helps the reader get prepared for what they are about to learn.

- If you're making this a standalone piece, then this would be a title.
- If this work is delivered as an email, this would be the subject line.
- If this work was part of a larger document, then this would be a heading.
- If you're speaking (like during a job interview), then this would be the first sentence of your reply.

This introduction to your work could parrot the cue words that informed you to use this pattern: for example, Learning from __ or How I changed when __ or, when speaking, To answer your question, __.

4.2.3.2 Introduction

The introduction contains *only* what's needed to get the reader oriented to read the rest of the work, that is, answering the questions: who, what, when, where. You can do this in one sentence. And yes in business and technical writing, it's okay to have a one-sentence paragraph. Since this section is usually just one sentence, you can decide to omit the heading if you choose to be a little less formal.

In the introduction, do *not* offer any summaries or generalizations, or draw any conclusions of your experience, such as the following:

> Summary: All the work was accomplished by __.
>
> Generalization: All students need to take a writing course.
>
> Conclusion: I learned that when I __.

These summaries, generalizations, conclusions stop the audience from being engaged with or staying to listen to your experience or how your experience derived from that conclusion.

When you revise your work, in the introduction, you can find summaries, generalizations, and conclusions, by examining the verb. For example, learned, changed, believed all denote a conclusion or generalization.

> NOTE: English composition encourages conclusions in the introduction, so if you're most familiar with the composition type of writing, then you need to pay special attention to this part of the pattern. See Chapter 4.2.4 for more on how this pattern differs from English composition.

4.2.3.3 The Experience

The experience is written as a narrative that includes your personal reflection.

Organizing the Middle of Your Work

There are two ways to organize the body of the writing where you tell the narrative of the experience and reflect on what happened.

1) **Chronological** – Organize the experience by time, where the headings sequence might be In the beginning or When we started, followed by In the middle or By midway, ending with In the end or When we finished or any other headings of your choice that denote time sequence.

2) **By topic** – Organize the experience by topic/concept, where the headings would be each of the topics that you have used to break up the experience into topics/concepts. For example, if you were going to discuss how a group you were in worked (or didn't work), you might use headings sequence, such as Group formation, Group norming, Group in action, Group difficulties, Group resolution.

NOTE: Never use body as the heading for the middle part of any writing in business or technical writing.

NOTE: Do not organize the body of the work as one large paragraph. A large paragraph makes it difficult to read and comprehend.

Including Your Personal Reflection

Once you know how you're going to organize the narrative of the story, you need to reflect on each of the experiences in each of the organizational areas. Then you need to include language to tell the audience what the experience meant to you or to help them get a sense of how the experience affected you while you were in the midst of it. That is, what your brain was thinking while you were inside the experience, while the action was occurring.

There are two ways that you can interject the reflective perspectives in the experience narrative:

1) In its own paragraph or sentence at the end of the section. This option would focus on creating a reflective concluding statement about that part of the experience.

2) With selected words choice, adjectives, adverbs, and phrases within the narrative discussion. This option gives you the flexibility to incorporate your reflection throughout the narrative.

Be consistent throughout the whole piece with whichever choice you've made to inject the reflective analysis, rather than sometimes standalone and sometimes within the story. Readers find consistency easier to follow.

Avoiding Ethical Writing Scenarios

As with any business/technical writing, it's important to avoid writing untruths. These untruths would vary with each pattern.

For the inductive pattern, avoid the following:

- Exaggerating events, for example, how it unfolded.
- Deemphasizing issues that occurred or blaming others for what occurred. Be sure to take responsibility for your part in the experience.

- Being biased about the events or sequence. It's hard to avoid all bias, but always work to create a narrative that shows your ability to see more than just your perspective of the situation.

4.2.3.4 Conclusion

The conclusion is where you explain to the audience what you learned from the experience in the form of a generalization/conclusion.

This paragraph is in three parts, in this order:

1) **Generalization/conclusion** of what you learned from the experience. This is finally your opportunity to relate the purpose of this work, to help the audience understand how you learned, grew, changed based on an experience.

2) **Applied reflection** or how your learning can be applied. This is written usually in the form of Now, I will__. This is your opportunity to show the audience how you can *apply* this learning in the future in a *broader* context than the one in which you learned it. Application goes beyond just doing the same thing again, but using the learning in a new way.

   For example, if you're using this pattern to write up your reflection of your job experience so that you can make a case to get a raise, this applied reflection is critical. Say you worked on your own to learn a new technology that was used in a project design. No one at your company knew the technology, so you couldn't ask anyone questions, you had to learn it on your own by reading the documentation, watching YouTube videos, asking others in a chat room, and so on.

   When you get to this part of the conclusion, what might you say? Now I can use this tool again. That tells your reader (e.g., manager) that you can do this same job again that you're already doing and getting paid to do. Why would your manager make a case to pay you more to do the same job? What if you said instead, Now I can teach anyone else in the company how to use this technology? Oh, now that sounds worthwhile, if it's needed, and is worth paying you more to do. Or you might say, Now that I know how to self-direct my learning, I can tackle any other new technologies that we need to learn. Again, see how this language shows how the experience can be reapplied to show your growth.

3) **Advice** for your reader. This third part is optional based on who your audience is. If your audience can benefit from your learning, then you could explain how they can benefit similarly from your experiences.

   NOTE: This sentence is the *only* place in this pattern where second point of view (POV) (*you*) would be used.

4.2.4 Don't Confuse the Inductive Pattern with English Composition

While you're using the narrative approach to write this pattern, do not confuse this pattern with English Composition writing. Table 4.3 summarizes how these two styles of writing have a different purpose, different reasons for reading, and so on, which ought to be reflected in your work.

Table 4.3: Comparison of English Composition to inductive pattern

Characteristics	English Composition	Inductive pattern
Audience	Teacher	Someone that you know
Why reading it?	To grade it	To understand how you learned, changed, grew from a specific experience
Document design or format	Double spaced, indented paragraphs, so the teacher can grade it easily and comment	Single spaced, white space between paragraph, headings, so the reader can quickly read it
Writing style	Vague, creative, imprecise, wordy, flowery, even redundant	Clear, precise, specific, direct, to the point, concise, avoids redundancy
Tone	Informal, chatty, even artistic	Not chatty, medium formal tone

Characteristics	English Composition	Inductive pattern
Introduction	Concludes with a thesis or main point of the writing	Only introduces the experience context. No thesis/main point. No conclusions
Conclusion	A summary of the writing	Never a summary. Written in three parts: conclusion, reapplication of learning, (optional) audience takeaway

4.2.5 Prewriting Steps: Creating an Inductive Outline

Various tasks need to be completed during the prewriting stage of the writing process as outlined:

1) Brainstorm the experience itself – How did it unfold? Who was involved? When did you have the experience? This brainstorming helps you construct the introduction.
2) Brainstorm what you ultimately learned from the experience – It's important to know how you're going to conclude this pattern so that the body narrative can lead the audience to that conclusion.
   a) What is overall conclusion you draw from this experience? This would be the first part of the conclusion.
   b) How can this final conclusion be reused in the future? This would be second part of the conclusion – the future application from your learning from this experience.
   c) If your reader is someone like you, how could they learn from your experience? This would be the third (optional) part of the conclusion.
3) Draft the introduction and conclusion paragraphs, now that you know what information they include. This way you can check to ensure the introduction won't have conclusion content and that only the conclusion has that language.
4) Brainstorm the body of the work because now you know what information needs to be included in the body narrative. What parts of

the experience need to be included to support the conclusion? Further, you need to decide the best way to tell the narrative: chronologically or by topic. Be sure to brainstorm your personal reflection of each of the stages so you can include them in your narrative.

5) Draft the body of your work.

6) Include a title/subject that encompasses the experience.

4.2.6 Uses of the Inductive Pattern

You might be wondering when to use such a specifically prescribed pattern. There are many ways in which this pattern can be used.

- Explaining your learning from experiences – When you're visiting with close friends discussing difficult situations and you want to offer solace or insight or recommendations on how an experience you had and what you did could help them understand their situation better or maybe offer a solution of how they can proceed with fewer struggles.
- Job interview answer – During the face-to-face part of the interview, the prospective employer will want to get a sense of who you are as a person and how you've handled yourself in various situations. A common question may be Tell me about a time when you __ where they ask, for example, Tell me about a time when you worked in a group that didn't work out well?
- On the job, as half of your yearly performance evaluation – At periodic interval, businesses perform performance evaluations of their employees to discuss how they are doing great at their job and where they need to improve.

  Frequently, these are done in two parts: you write up your perspective of your performance during the interval and your manager writes up their perspective of your work during the interval. Your side could be written in an abbreviated form of this pattern. For example, for each activity you did, you could abbreviate the introduction/experience/conclusion in its own section or table.

NOTE: This example is where you can change how this pattern is structured and even make the entire pattern one paragraph, depending on what point you want to get across to your manager.

- Within another pattern. Patterns can always be combined within a larger document, so a section could offer an inductive perspective.

However you use this pattern, avoid turning this pattern into one large paragraph. Walls of text seen by large paragraphs slow down the reading pace, making it harder to comprehend. Instead break up the work into paragraphs or even sections with headings and paragraphs. Alternatively, you might consider organizing the experience in a table or some other way to help the reader read the work quickly.

4.2.7 Inductive Samples

What I Learned from Facebook Groups

In the summer of 2020, I created a Facebook group to organize a new book club at my university.

Group Formation

I was concerned about how I would find new members for the club online since there was no Facebook group for our university. Fortunately, my fellow club founders simply direct messaged their Facebook friends and invited them to the group. Our other members came through offline methods such as posters and fliers. I learned that the Facebook group's primary purpose is not for recruitment, but instead serve as a communication center for preexisting members.

Club events

I joined other Facebook groups to understand how others organize their events. Based on my observations, I found out that most groups use polls to establish the theme of the event. They also leave the event organizer's contact information so that other people can either ask questions or ask if they can help. I applied these principles to organize monthly book discussions online. This also required me to practice diligence and transparency by giving the group regular notifications on the crucial event details.

Group Participation

I had more to share with people outside of the regular events. I often posted news on book releases that I thought would pique people's interest. People commented on my posts and also shared unique articles of their own. I felt joy knowing that I was in a group of like-minded individuals, and I was fascinated with each person's unique responses. I realized that these posts helped me better understand and grow friendships with people in the group.

Conclusion

In my time with the book club Facebook group, I learned how to create a community and build strong relationships through hosting events and participating in group posts. I helped to create a strong and healthy community of fellow readers. Now I plan to use my experience to form another community for people interested in coding projects for nonprofit organizations.

Growing Through Starting a Club

Introduction

During my first year of college, I started a club through my campus' club council procedures.

Finding the need for a club

When I first came to college, I experienced difficulty in finding community around my passions. Since it seemed that there were no organized groups on campus that represented my interests, I decided to go forward and create a group that could serve as a community for people like me. We didn't have a model going forward, so I sought help from similar groups across different colleges using my local network of friends and family.

Once I had examples to work on, I decided to seek new members. I was nervous to meet new people, but I knew I was going to need help with creating a club on campus, so I reached out on campus for other potential members. I was relieved to see that there were other people like me who wanted community.

Making the club

Now that I had other people to work with, we established various tasks that needed to be accomplished. It was comforting to know that I did not need to do everything on my own. We needed a certain number of members to qualify as a club. We also needed to receive training from club council before we could be an official club. I pitched in my efforts when I could and did my best to form the club values so that newcomers knew what to expect.

Maintaining the club

Once we were approved by the club council, we planned community-building events in order to build the club and create a reputation. I initiated contact between our leadership and between new members. I also spent my spare time coming up with new ideas for activities. I also devoted time learning new skills that the club could use, such as leadership, presenting, and graphic design. Our club did not have many members, so I worried about our club in the long run, but I was grateful for the people who came, so I spent time with them and made close friendships.

Conclusion

I grew in my ability to understand and communicate with others through interacting with authority figures, community-building, and making new friendships within the club. I plan to use this experience to build camaraderie among my peers in the workplace. My time spent making new friends in new environments can help me establish relationships in the workplace and fit into the social culture quickly.

4.2.8 Exercises

1) Practice your reply to a potential interview, "Tell me about a time when you _____." Fill in the blank with something a prospective employer may want to know about you and then create the outline for a corresponding experience you had.

2) Practice using this pattern with a friend/colleague who is struggling with something in their life. What experience have you had that can offer advice based on how you solve it yourself?

3) Examine the following conclusion paragraph.
   a) What did it do well?
   b) Identify any problems. How would you recommend fixing them?

      Title: Learning JavaScript

      I had a fun time learning JavaScript! It was the easiest coding language that I ever learned. My time learning about JavaScript also taught me to be patient with my mistakes and research the language beyond the class content in order to gain a fuller understanding. Everyone else also had an easy time through the class and they made some incredible programs that I want to attempt in the future. You should change my current position on the team as a software engineer because I have skills in coding and the ability to continue advancing my coding knowledge.

4.3 Persuasive Pattern

This section covers the persuasive pattern. The terms *persuasive* and *position* are both used because, in this type of writing, you work to *persuade* the reader to adopt your *position* that you've taken about a subject.

It is probably the most familiar writing since it's taught in various forms in high school and college English Composition. In this book, the pattern has remnants of the five-paragraph paper, but where the body paragraphs would not get as large.

4.3.1 Persuasive Writing Summary

Characteristics ☞	**Writing position/persuasive**
Purpose	Convince the reader to adopt your thesis/claim
Audience/reader	Someone who is interested in the topic
Secondary audience	Someone who might be interested in the topic, or might want to learn more, or to see what the various claims are about
Scenario indicators	*convince, debate, believe, arguable, stand, pro/con* (read more in Chapter 4.3.2)
Point of view (POV)	3rd POV Do *not* address the reader with "you." When someone reads "you," they put themselves into the sentence. Someone who is considering a thesis would want to consider it remotely. It's more comfortable. Do *not* use "I" or "we" to refer to the authors. With your name on the paper, when the reader reads an opinion that is not cited, it's yours. Saying "I believe" only weakens what follows.
Tone	Formal
Pace	Medium
Organization method	Organized as introduction, body sections, conclusion Your thesis is the main point (your opinion) that you want your reader to adopt. It is placed at the end of the introduction. In the body, a position paper combines opinion (arguments) supported by facts (supports) to persuade the reader to adopt your thesis: • Arguments – Your arguments prove your thesis is true. These arguments are also your opinion or debatable. • Supports – Your arguments are proved to be true by supporting facts. The conclusion is where you explain what the next steps are after you've convinced the reader. (read more in Chapter 4.3.3)

▶

Characteristics ☞	Writing position/persuasive
Ethical scenarios	Logic errors, emotional appeals, exaggeration of the facts to support arguments, inaccurately presenting the opposing views
Examples	Position paper, white paper, debates (see Chapter 4.3.7)
Delivered/formatted	Report, presentation, email, webpage, letter
Cognitive skill	Critical analysis, evaluating others' opinions
Writing skill	Thesis construction, persuasive word choice, organizing arguments and supports
☞ See Table 4.2 for definitions of these characteristics.	

4.3.2 Decision, Deciding to Use the Persuasive Pattern

You would be cued to use the position pattern by someone using any of the following words:

- convince
- debate
- believe
- arguable
- stand
- pro/con

In all cases, you would use this pattern or a revised version of this pattern, when someone is interested in your opinion about a topic and/or where the goal is to persuade the reader adopt your opinion.

4.3.3 Organization of Persuasive Writing

Figure 4.1 shows a position pattern outline, then each element is explained in the sections following.

Figure 4.1: Traditional Persuasive Outline Organized as 3 x 3 + 1

Title

(The title ought to be the position you want the reader to adopt)

Introduction

(Thesis as last sentence)

Argument 1 stated that proves thesis is true

Small paragraph explains the argument and why the argument proves the thesis is true

Support 1 in support of the argument in its own paragraph or a bullet

Support 2 in support of the argument in its own paragraph or a bullet

Support 3 in support of the argument in its own paragraph or a bullet

Argument 2 stated that proves thesis is true

Small paragraph explains the argument and why the argument proves the thesis is true

Support 1 in support of the argument in its own paragraph or a bullet

Support 2 in support of the argument in its own paragraph or a bullet

Support 3 in support of the argument in its own paragraph or a bullet

Argument 3 stated that proves thesis is true

Small paragraph explains the argument and why the argument proves the thesis is true

Support 1 in support of the argument in its own paragraph or a bullet

Support 2 in support of the argument in its own paragraph or a bullet

Support 3 in support of the argument in its own paragraph or a bullet

Conclusion

The topic sentence as the thesis reframed. The rest of the paragraph explains what the reader should do now that they have adopted your thesis.

References

Bibliographic references go here

NOTE: All bolded lines in the outline would be headings in the document to the reader.

The traditional position outline is organized as 3 × 3 + 1: three arguments (minimum) with each argument having three supports (minimum), plus an introductory paragraph after the argument heading.

4.3.3.1 Title

The purpose of the title is to be specific about your position, so the reader knows what idea you want them to adopt. Short, complete sentences that encapsulate your thesis are a great title.

4.3.3.2 Introduction

The introduction of the persuasive writing has two parts: the purpose and the thesis (the last sentence).

Purpose: Used to Introduce Your Central Point

- Length varies, but keep them short. The reader wants to start reading the point of the paper, not an elaborate introduction.
- Tell the reader what they need to know to understand your thesis.

Piece apart your thesis and figure out what needs explaining or defining. This bridges the gap between unfocused speculation within the reader's mind and a working understanding of the author's approach to the topic, thus orienting the reader.

Your Introduction Can Include ....

- The although material (or opposing view)
- Answer: Why your topic needs considering
- Use a
    - Analogy

- Question: A question can only work if the question begs to be answered by the thesis. You cannot ask open-ended or large questions that suggest the work contains research writing not a position writing.
- Specific incident/instance, for example, personal experience. Using a specific, personal experience changes the POV to 1st and should only be used when appropriate for your situation.

NOTE: The topic sentence of the introduction is NOT the thesis statement.

What Not *to Do in the Introduction*

- Do *not* lose the reader by creating a long introduction.
- Do *not* include generalizations in your introduction. If a statement can be made about any number of other subjects, then it's not worth saying. For example, As technology changes __ could mean anything about any industry.
- Do *not* use scaffolding statements that are unnecessary with a well-written introduction. These are statements such as this author believes, I believe __, we will show __, and so on. Likewise don't replace those scaffolding statements with equally awkward statements, such as It is the opinion of the author that __.

  Instead, just state your viewpoint in the proper places according to the pattern. Readers are smart and know that any opinion that is not cited is owned by the author.

  NOTE: Although these scaffolding statements are common in academic journal articles, when seen/heard in business and technical writing, they can lead the audience to assume the reader is unsure or insecure in their beliefs.
- Do *not* begin your arguments or supporting points in the introduction because if your reader doesn't agree, then you've lost your opportunity to persuade them. They'll stop reading.
- Do *not* make the introduction all opinion. The opinion (your thesis) ought to be at the end of the introduction. The material before the thesis

leads to that opinion. If it's all opinion, then the reader is unclear which opinion you're going to prove in the body of the work. That is, which of all the opinions in the introduction is the thesis?

Thesis

The thesis is the point that you want your reader to adopt.

NOTE: The idea is your opinion. Persuasion is designed to convince someone of an opinion, not to convince them of a fact. A research paper is designed to prove a fact.

The thesis is located at the end of the introduction.

- Be specific in your thesis.
- The thesis is debatable or arguable. It is your interpretation of the facts. For example:

  A LinkedIn account is a necessity for anyone who is in or is entering the workplace.

  NOTE: While this thesis has an "or" in it, it is one idea (the necessity of a LinkedIn account for job searching), so it still matches the rule that a thesis needs to be one idea. What is being debated is whether the account is a necessity.
- The thesis is *not* a fact. A fact is not debatable and thus does not require a position paper to convince the reader to adopt it. For example:

  If you forget the password to your Instagram account, then you have to send an email to reset the password.
- Another person's thesis/claim is *not* yours to adopt as your own thesis. For example:

  According to MarketWatch.com, Facebook needs to stop requiring its users to fill in personal information.

- However, you can make someone's claim as your thesis, *if* you rewrite it and then assuming that your arguments go beyond what their claim stated. For example:

  MarketWatch is correct that Facebook needs to stop requiring its users to fill in personal information.

- Do *not* use vague statements.

  Such as the following phrases: y industry benefits from x; y industry has no meaning, and benefits is not arguable.

- Do *not* use the words and, or because then you have created a compound thesis to prove are true. A thesis should be only one idea that you prove to be true.

- Do *not* forecast the arguments as your thesis. That is, do not put your arguments in the introduction.

  You want the reader to read the arguments' supports (in the body sections). If the reader knows your thesis and arguments at the end of the introduction and doesn't agree with them, then they may go away, and you lost your opportunity to persuade the reader. Better to end with the thesis and let the reader read the arguments and supports along the way in the body of the work, giving you a chance to persuade them.

- RECOMMENDATION: Do *not* use than in your thesis because then the arguments turn into a comparison of the two sides, which is hard to be consistent.

- RECOMMENDATION: Do *not* put a not in your thesis. That forces you to prove that something is not true. It's too easy to create logic errors and confuse the reader.

NOTE: The thesis is not the topic sentence of the introduction. The topic sentence introduces the topic. The thesis states the claim you want the reader to adopt and ought to reside at the end of the introduction.

4.3.3.3 Arguments and their Supports

This section explains the body of a position paper that includes all the arguments and supporting facts.

Organization of Body

The organization of the body sections has the following components:

Heading – Each argument has its own heading. Like all headings, if the reader knows what a section contains based on the heading, then they may choose to skip reading it.

The heading needs to be clear enough that a reader can discern from the heading what the argument is about so that they can immediately see how it might prove the thesis is true (see "Because Test" under Section "Tools to Support the Body Construction").

First short paragraph after heading – A short paragraph after the heading explains what the argument is and why it proves the thesis is true.

This means that this small paragraph in part reminds the reader of the thesis. Consider the length of a paper. The farther away the reader gets in reading the body with all the arguments and supports, the more removed in their mind the thesis is. So when they read the next argument heading and then this small paragraph, it explains the argument and why it proves the thesis is true, thus reminding the reader of your persuasive story.

> NOTE: This first short paragraph is not an introductory paragraph to the section. Since this type of writing isn't a research paper, there aren't any introductory paragraphs. If you need introductory information for your reader, then you need to reframe the information and put it in your supports (see Section "Supports").

Arguments – Arguments answer *why* the thesis is true. If the argument does not answer *why*, then the argument does not directly support the thesis and cannot be used. The arguments are your opinion (not a fact) and thus they are debatable. Be sure that each argument is a distinctive reason that proves the thesis is true.

NOTE: Do not carve up the thesis into multiple ideas and then have each argument prove that part of the thesis is true. Remember the thesis is *one* idea. Therefore, the arguments prove that one idea is true in multiple ways.

Supports – The supports prove the argument is true. They are facts interpreted by you to support your argument. Be sure that each support is distinctive. Your supports become weakened if you reuse them for multiple arguments.

In each support paragraph, begin with your fact, then follow it with your analysis that explains why this support proves the argument is true. This analysis can include your opinion.

NOTE: Do not make your opinion your topic sentence of the support paragraph. That opinion at the beginning of the support can easily put off a reader who would then perceive that it's all an opinion piece.

Tools to Support the Body Construction

Two tools can be helpful as you create your persuasive arguments.

Because Test – The best way to know whether your argument proves your thesis is to construct the following compound sentence and see whether it makes logical sense. Read your thesis, add the word *because*, then add your argument as a sentence. If that new sentence is completely logical and clear, then the argument proves the thesis is true. Be careful to avoid logic errors.

Thesis + BECAUSE + Argument = Clear logical statement.

Example: Facebook needs to stop requiring its users to give their personal information + BECAUSE + Personal information allows users to stalk others.

Likewise, the way to know whether your supports prove your argument is true is to take your argument, add the word *because*, and add your support. If that new compound sentence is completely logical and clear, then the support proves the argument is true.

Argument + BECAUSE + Support = Clear logical statement.

Example: Personal information allows users to stalk others + BECAUSE + Gran et al. found that people could be located down to their home address through their full name and birthday.

NOTE: This *because* test is a great tool to use, but do not confuse it with the way to write your thesis or to write your arguments. Let the reader add their own *because* in their mind as they read your work.

Logical Fallacies – Be sure that your thesis and your arguments are not logical fallacies. There's lots of information in the Internet about these pitfalls in logic. Search logical fallacies, using your favorite browser, for more information on logic errors.

Example: Straw man fallacy: I don't believe Jack is correct about global warming because all of his posts are racist and homophobic.

Supports Consist of Evidence or Facts

Remember that supports are of the form: Fact followed by short analysis that explains why the fact proves the argument is true.

Your supports are facts and can consist of any of the following types.

- Statistics or fact (piece of information)
- Quotation – Use of references as your supporting evidence. However, do not begin or end a paragraph with a quote. You must explain the quotes included in your document. Use experts that are authorities on the topic.
- Well-reasoned arguments – When using a well-reasoned argument, you're offering your opinion, but one that anyone would logically agree

with, so it's essentially a *fact*. Use these sparingly in your supports. If all your supports are these opinions, then your work is not very persuasive.

- Comparisons – If you want to combine the persuasive pattern and compare and contrast (i.e., to have a *than* in your thesis), then do it as follows (see Chapter 4.4 specifically how to organize the part-by-part [P/P] comparison.)
  - If your thesis said, X is better than Y. In this case, identify criteria in which X is better than Y. These criteria become your arguments.
  - Each support paragraph needs to be structured with subjects always in the same order, throughout the whole document. For example, if you said, X then Y. Then all paragraphs must discuss X then Y. And a paragraph cannot return to X or Y again or change the order.

Order of Arguments and Supports

The order of your arguments and the supports is important and depends on the context or your story you're using to persuade the reader.

The general rules of ordering your arguments/supports are the following:

- If your arguments/supports build on one another (tell a story), then put them in story order.
- If your arguments/supports are all weighted equally, then order them according to how readers remember what they've read. Readers pay the most attention to beginnings and endings, less so the middle. Readers remember first, the last thing they read/did. Then readers remember the first thing they did/read.
- If your arguments/supports are short in length, then put your best *last*, because readers can stay attentive for a series of short sections, and then remember your best argument.

- If your arguments/supports are long in length, then put your best *first*, because the reader may need multiple sittings to read the paper. With the best first, your reader is more likely to return to your work to finish reading it and then skip any arguments once convinced, finishing with the conclusion.

Transitions with Arguments

The heading for each argument serves the purpose of the transition from one section to the next. No other explicit transitions are needed.

Transitions with Supports

- If your supports build on one another, or tell a story, then you're unlikely to need explicit transitions because the story provides them.
- If all your supports are essentially equal, then you need some sort of transition between supports so that they flow for the reader. In this case, be aware to avoid overuse of "also." Alternatively, you can format your supports as bullets, which provides its own automatic equal weight transition.

4.3.3.4 Conclusion

You should assume that when the reader reads "conclusion," then you've convinced the reader; otherwise, they would have abandoned the reading long before reaching this section. Therefore, do not use the conclusion to summarize your arguments or further attempt to persuade the reader to adopt the thesis. The reader does not want to reread that content.

The purpose of the conclusion is to bring the work to a satisfactory end. It is best constructed in two parts. The topic sentence of the conclusion is a retelling of your thesis. Use the remainder of the conclusion to answer what does this mean? or now what – that is, if the reader is now convinced, they need to know what to do now.

Ways to answer now what include the following. Pick one method, the best one for your topic/content.

- Tie the individual arguments together in a new way – If each argument told its own story, then maybe all the arguments together mean something bigger/greater than the story you've already told.
- Make a recommendation – Tells the reader what you would suggest that the reader specifically do now that they have adopted your thesis.
- Make a prediction – Tells the reader a prediction of what would occur assuming that they adopted your thesis.
- Provide a call to action – Tells the reader what needs to happen in general, not what they need to do specifically. This call to action might identify how others might need to change their actions as a result of this thesis being adopted.
- Follow up on further research – Only use this option if there is more research to actually do. In a detailed persuasive work, you already bring in a lot of research and facts with your supports, so don't suggest that your conclusion do more of the same. That would cause you to lose the persuasiveness of your argument.

What *not* to do in the conclusion:

- Do *not* introduce new information in support of your thesis or arguments.
- Do *not* pick too many "now what" ideas, thereby confusing your audience.
- Be careful about moving to 2nd POV (*you*) as you address the reader what to do now that they have adopted your thesis. You can do this on purpose or you could address the reader by their role they would take on in performing the action.

4.3.4 Prewriting Stage: Creating an Outline

At the end of the prewriting stage, you ought to have an outline that should consist of

1) Your thesis
2) Your three arguments
3) Your supports

4.3.4.1 Mind Map

Use the brainstorming stage to generate a mind map. Your mind map is a critical tool to a successful position paper. It can help you formulate your ideas and perform your research.

Here are ways you can use your mind map, in general, and specifically for this pattern.

- Identify your interest areas
- Find key words to research
- Find out what you don't know or questions to answer
- Find intersecting ideas not previously obvious
- Narrow your topic
- Broaden your topic
- Create your body outline
- Add to your mind map as you research your topic. Each time you find more information, add a bubble to your mind map (include the source of that information so you can cite it properly later)
- Identify your thesis
- Identify your arguments that prove your thesis is true

- Identify the supports that prove each argument is true (do not double up the same support for multiple arguments, as that weakens your arguments and dilutes your supports)

Once you've got your mind map, use it to identify your thesis and arguments that prove your thesis is true. Remember that your mind map can help you throughout the drafting and revising process.

4.3.4.2 Thesis Guidelines

Your thesis should be

- Debatable
- A grammatically complete sentence
- Focused and specific, rather than vague and overly general
- Written in active voice

Good thesis example: Facebook should not require its users to give out their personal information.

4.3.4.3 Arguments Guidelines

Each of your arguments should be

- Formed as a grammatically complete sentence
- Pass the "because" logic test
- Ordered based on the story your paper arguments are telling
- Sufficiently, clearly unique (watch for overlap or duplication of arguments)

Good argument example: Public personal information enables others to stalk people against their will.

Bad argument example: Facebook has a bad relationship with its users.

4.3.4.4 Patchwriting Avoidance

As you research and write your paper, you want to avoid patchwriting. From the web article, "'Patchwriting' is more common than plagiarism, just as dishonest," patchwriting is defined as:

> Patch writing is often a failed attempt at paraphrasing [. . .]. Rather than copying a statement word for word, the writer is rearranging phrases and changing tenses, but is relying too heavily on the vocabulary and syntax of the source material. It's a form of intellectual dishonesty that indicates that the writer is not actually thinking for [him/] herself. (McBride)*

Patchwriting is not the same as plagiarism, but it's not considered original writing either. The problem is when the bulk of your writing is directly from the other source, and there is no originality in the writing, that is plagiarism. Another form of plagiarism is taking content from a source not citing it, claiming it as your own work.

Patchwriting arises when the writer

- Finds an article with a good argument(s), and then "borrows" it/them along with all the facts backing it/them up for their work.
- Searches for ideas and then copies them, or fragments of them, directly from the source into their draft document. From that copy/paste action, it's hard to reframe the work enough for it not to suffer from patchwriting.

How to avoid patchwriting:

- The way to resolve this problem is using your mind map.
- Reshape ideas from the source in your mind map.
- Use the mind map to generate your outline.

---

* McBride, Kelly. "'Patchwriting' is more common than plagiarism, just as dishonest." Poynter.org. September 18, 2012. Web. September 9, 2016. http://www.poynter.org/2012/patchwriting-is-more-common-than-plagiarism-just-as-dishonest/188789/

- Allow your mind map to help to isolate each borrowed idea and then reframe them into your original work.
- Use the time elapsed between reading the original work and the drafting process to create original connections around the facts you borrow.

4.3.4.5 Order of Prewriting/Drafting Tasks

When you're working on creating an outline and begin the drafting stage for a position writing, start with your thesis, arguments, and supports. After you've created that work, consider what ought to be written in the conclusion.

Last, return to the introduction. Only then, do you know what the reader needs to know to understand the paper, that is, only then do you know what to write in your introduction. If you try to draft your work beginning with the introduction and continuing to the conclusion, you end up having to rewrite the introduction and, maybe, the conclusion as well.

4.3.5 Sample Outline

Thesis: Facebook should not require its users to give out their personal information.

> Arg. 1: Divulging personal information makes users vulnerable to online stealing.
>
> Arg. 2: Personal information forces users to risk their personal security to engage online.
>
> Arg. 3: Personal information enables companies to analyze human behavior.

<u>Example of passing the BECAUSE test:</u> These arguments pass the "because" logic test. For example, the following compound sentence makes logical sense:

> Facebook should not require its users to give out their personal information because divulging personal information makes users vulnerable to online stealing.

4.3.6 Uses of Persuasive Pattern

Once you've understood this pattern, there are many ways in which you can modify it to suit your specific situation on the job. For example:

- Use this form during a discussion. You don't have to wait for a writing occasion.
- Use more than three arguments and/or more than three supports.

  NOTE: If you go below a 3 × 3 structure, then your arguments become very weak. Like a stool, your thesis/arguments require at least three legs to stand.

- Incorporate the counter arguments or opposing viewpoints as you explain your position in the body of your work.

  In this bare bones pattern presented in this book, handling the opposing view has been omitted because

  - In most cases in business and technical situations, the other side is well represented by the people that hold those views and thus you don't need to address it in your work.
  - Addressing the opposing view can be misconstrued by those that don't hold that view, which leads to problems with your credibility, thus weakening your ability to persuade a reader to adopt your thesis.
  - You can include the counter argument, in the introduction before the reader sees your thesis by using the "although" clause.

4.3.7 Persuasive Sample

Advocating for a Facebook Tutorial

Introduction

Facebook continues to be a heavily used social media website that changes and evolves with its users. Although it is considered "old" as a technology platform, it is still a relatively new medium for older individuals. They did not need to use social media to connect with family and friends, but the growing difficulty of physical travel makes social media an increasingly enticing solution. Facebook needs to create a walkthrough for its senior users (those over 60 years of age).

Seniors are unequipped to learn how to use social media

Seniors have different needs and challenges to learning social media that Facebook needs to account for, that could be solved by having Facebook provide a senior walkthrough.

- Sixty-two percent of people over 65 years of age are using Facebook in comparison to over 80% of people ages 18 to 49 are using Facebook [1]. This is not only an indicator that seniors are less confident with technology, but it also means that older people are likely to have less friends who can relate and guide them through the process of learning about Facebook.
- Seniors have to deal with false assumptions when using technology such when a study noted that seniors tended to believe pop-up messages were a sign of danger [2]. These can create discouraging misunderstandings throughout the learning process that can deter people from using Facebook.
- A study showed that older people felt the need for external help to understand how to use Facebook [3]. They are uncomfortable with how Facebook currently guides users to learn their functions. Facebook's guide insufficiently teaches the older population how to use its functions.

Facebook's current tutorial relies on past social media experience

The current tutorial only conditionally works for experienced social media users, which is why Facebook needs to create a senior walk-through version.

- Facebook does not address user concerns about people spying on other people's posts or when it is acceptable to post [2]. For most users, this is unnecessary since in social media contexts, posts are meant to be seen by everyone and could be casual in nature, but older individuals expressed fear and did not realize that their posts were a privilege, not a limited resource.

- The way to interact with common navigation tools such as the navigation bar receives no explanation. In an experiment on learning Facebook, the seniors did not know that the navigation bar needed to be clicked on [2]. Facebook is difficult to learn without knowing the basic tools that drive the user experience.
- Elderly people have trouble identifying the purpose of Facebook, considering it a place to search information instead of communicating with friends [2]. Even if they knew how functions on Facebook worked, they are getting less satisfaction from their experience because they do not know the importance of Facebook's role as a social media website.

Inexperienced Facebook users are vulnerable to online manipulation

Facebook has an obligation to protect its users from unwanted influence, which can be incorporated into a senior walk-through.

- Misinformation through private Facebook groups has historically perpetuated extreme political movements without any safeguards [4]. Facebook users who are not experienced with online groups could be swayed into joining dangerous movements on Facebook, unaware that Facebook groups can be used to spread false information.
- Scammers use small and innocuous requests such as friend requests and donation requests to learn more about their identity down to their credit card info [5]. Unless new users are warned, they may think little of scamming attempts, not realizing where the harm comes from.
- Facebook has historically given people's information without much notice, to other tech firms and advertising companies [6]. This allows other companies to subtly target advertisements or services around people's individual interests and personal information, compelling them to make excessive purchases.

Conclusion

Facebook needs to have a tutorial that specially considers the needs of new users above the age of 60 because while they are more than capable of learning social media, they face unique challenges and dangers. To avoid unwelcome discrimination, consider adding a question that asks people about their familiarity with social media plus a question that addresses a general scenario that new senior users may experience. The tutorial can be oriented around this scenario so that there is no judgment and full consent. To identify scenarios to use, research common senior assumptions and survey current users who learned Facebook at an older age.

Bibliography

[1] Aslam, Salman. "Facebook by the Numbers: Stats, Demographics, and Fun Facts." Omnicore. Apr. 2020. Accessed Aug. 2020

[2] Chou, Wen Huei, et al. "User Requirements of Social Media for the Elderly: a Case Study in Taiwan." Behaviour & Information Technology, vol. 32, no. 9, 2013, pp. 920–937.

[3] Xie, Bo, et al. "Understanding and Changing Older Adults' Perceptions and Learning of Social Media." Educational Gerontology, vol. 38, no. 4, 2012, pp. 282–296.

[4] Jankowitz, Nina, and Cindy Otis. "Facebook Groups are Destroying America." Wired. June 2020. Accessed Aug. 2020.

[5] Vishwanath, Arun. "Habitual Facebook Use and Its Impact on Getting Deceived on Social Media." Journal of Computer-Mediated Communication, vol. 20, no. 1, 2015, pp. 83–98.

[6] "Facebook's Data-Sharing Deals Exposed." BBC. Dec. 2018. Accessed Aug. 2020.

4.3.8 Exercises

1) Create three different sample introductions, each one with a different approach. Use this thesis: Facebook needs to stop requiring its users to give their personal information.

2) Create one support for each argument. Make sure it passes the BECAUSE test.

Arg. 1: Personal information makes people vulnerable to online stalking.

Arg. 2: Personal information forces users to risk their personal security to engage online.

Arg. 3: Personal information enables companies to analyze human behavior.

3) Create a mind map on a topic of your choice and trade with a colleague where they can add to your mind map, and you can add to theirs.

4.4 Compare and Contrast Pattern

The compare and contrast (C/C) pattern is used when you help the reader make a decision when there are various choices to compare against. You're probably most familiar with this pattern when shopping online and viewing a product comparison summary table (CST).

4.4.1 Compare and Contrast Pattern Summary Table

Characteristics ☞	**Compare and contrast pattern**
Purpose	The author helps the reader make a decision by comparing the subjects clearly and objectively
Audience/reader	Decision maker, whoever needs to live with the decision that gets made

Characteristics ☞	**Compare and contrast pattern**
Secondary audience	Anyone who may help the reader make the decisions or cares what decision is made
Scenario indicators	Any of these words indicate that the audience needs to make a decision: decide, between, which, choose, pick (read more in Chapter 4.4.2)
Point of view (POV)	2nd POV (Use "you" to refer to the reader)
Tone	Formal (NOTE: Even though 2nd POV is used, the tone can still be formal by using the other factors of tone to compensate)
Pace	Medium
Organization	Organized as introduction, comparison, conclusion (read more in Chapter 4.4.3) The comparison is organized as • A comparison summary table (see Chapter 4.4.3.5.1 – the most common • By paragraphs of text organized either as (see Chapter 4.4.3.5.2) – used when the comparison won't fit easily in a table cell ○ Whole-by-whole (W/W) ○ Part-by-part (P/P) • A combination of table and paragraphs (see Chapter 4.4.3.5.3)
Ethical scenarios	Exaggerate evaluation; fail to be objective in evaluation Even evaluation of criteria: Each subject needs to be evaluated using the same criteria
Examples	Decision paper, position paper, marketing/sales writing, debates (see Chapter 4.4.7)
Delivery	Report, presentation, email, webpage, as part of any other type of document (especially the comparison summary table)

Characteristics ☞	Compare and contrast pattern
Cognitive skill	Critical analysis, author needs to be able to analyze the subjects Even evaluation of criteria: For every subject, the author needs to use the same criteria (and subcriteria) to evaluate each subject
Writing skill	Objective writing (writing without personal bias)
☞ See Table 4.2 for definitions of these characteristics.	

4.4.2 Decision, Deciding to Use the C/C Pattern

You would be cued to use the C/C pattern by someone needing to make a decision choosing from various subjects. The audience would ask for that by using any of the following words:

- decide
- between
- which
- choose
- pick

4.4.3 Organization of C/C Writing

A C/C writing is organized as introduction, comparison, conclusion. This type of writing can be lengthy and requires headings so that the reader can navigate the writing easily.

4.4.3.1 Title/Subject Line

In any C/C writing, you need to let the reader know that the upcoming document helps them with the decision they need to make. Use specific words in the title to let the reader know a C/C writing is coming along. Examples include the following:

- choosing a <identify what the reader is picking by naming the topic, not the subjects>
- comparison of <list the subjects>
- deciding <identify the decision that needs to be made without mentioning the subjects>

4.4.3.2 C/C Introduction

The introduction has four requirements:

1) Acknowledge your audience.

For someone looking for work, __.

2) Acknowledge the decision that needs to be made, without naming the subjects. NOTE: Do not explain the decision in terms of the subjects. That would imply those are the only subjects possible, when in fact, those are the only subjects your work covers.

Correct: For someone looking for work needing to decide how to get your qualifications to the prospective employer, you can examine LinkedIn or your resume to determine if they can get your qualifications to your prospective employer.

Incorrect: For someone looking for work, you need to decide if you're going to use LinkedIn or your resume to get your qualifications to the prospective employer.
(There are other ways to get information to prospective employees and this statement implies these are the only options, thus misinforming the audience.)

3) Introduce the list that is your subjects (the options to choose from).

This comparison examines LinkedIn and resumes.

4) Forecast the criteria (i.e., list them) (not any subcriteria).

This comparison examines LinkedIn and resumes, using the following criteria: purpose, audience, contents, and medium. (See Chapter 4.4.7.)

The *introduction* section must *not* do the following:

- Do not make the decision for the reader.

  Your best choice would be __.

- Do not explain the decision in terms of the subjects.

  You need to pick LinkedIn.

- Do not tell the reader what to do.

  You should __, You need to __, You must __.

- Do not begin the comparisons.

  Linked, the online app, resumes, and an uploaded document are compared.

4.4.3.3 Identifying Comparison Criteria

Before we get started, here's a note of spelling to remember:

> *Criteria* is plural, referring to all the criteria used in the comparison.
>
> *Criterion* is singular, referring to a single factor of comparison.

The criteria that you pick for the comparison can be information that is the same, different, or similar between the various subjects. In all cases, the criteria chosen *must be relevant to the decision that needs to be made* so as to help the reader make their decision.

For example:

- If color is irrelevant, then do not use it as a criterion.
- If price is important, even if the price is the same for all the subjects, it must still be included as a criterion so the reader sees what it would cost (even if it's free).

The criteria ought to be discussed in an order that helps the reader build knowledge or understanding about the comparison (also known as progressive level of disclosure; see Chapter 4.6). For example, make the price last, since the audience can't decide to get something if all they've examined is the price, they need to know what they'd get for that amount.

4.4.3.4 Making Objective versus Subjective Comparisons

In a comparison paper, the reader needs to make a decision about picking a subject based on their own situation and for that reason, you need to provide an objective comparison. See Table 4.4 for a sample of using facts, instead of subjective impressions.

Table 4.4: Comparing facts to impressions

Criteria	Objective (FACTS)	Subjective (Impressions)
Time	2 hours 30 minutes	A lot; half of the morning
Height	6 feet 5 inches	Taller than me
Weight	120 pounds	Just right, heavy, light
Power	240 horsepower 0–60 mph in 5.5 seconds	Outclasses compact vehicles

Here are a few problems that are frequently found in comparisons you'd see on the Internet:

- When the comparison you read is riddled with subjective impressions based on the author's viewpoint (e.g., zz is the best approach), then you, as the reader, have to extract that subjectivity and attempt to figure out how the subjects really compare.
- When comparisons are done in relation to the other subjects (e.g., X is more than Y), then you would need to look up what X and Y are and make the comparison independently. For example, if you read, Subject X costs less. Then you'd need to research both the costs to still determine if you can afford X. Instead, if you read that Subject X is $99 and Subject Y is $110. Then you could do the math of which costs more/less, and also know if you can afford it.
- When the author tells the reader what to do (e.g., pick zz for best results), instead, just avoid this construct in the comparison.

4.4.3.5 Comparison/Contrast Comparison

The comparison sections contain the comparison/contrast. The comparison can be constructed in the following ways:

1) As a CST (see Chapter 4.4.3.5.1)
2) As paragraphs of text organized as either whole-by-whole (W/W) or P/P (see Chapter 4.4.3.5.2) used when the comparison is lengthy and won't fit in a table cell
3) As a combination of both (see Chapter 4.4.3.5.3)

4.4.3.5.1 The Comparison as a CST

The heading for this section would be "Comparison" or some other phrase that cues the reader that this section contains the comparison information.

For a CST, the columns are in the following order with the first column as the criteria (one row per criterion), followed by a column per subject. See Table 4.5.

Table 4.5: Comparison summary table structure

Criteria	Subject A	Subject B	Subject C
Criterion 1	For info re: A and 1	For info re: B and 1	For info re: C and 1
Criterion 2	For info re: A and 2	For info re: B and 2	For info re: C and 2
Source: Provide the full source for the information in the table cells here			

The following sections offer more details on creating this table and formatting it properly.

Selecting Criteria

You want the criteria to be a concept or idea, then the table cell would be how that concept relates.

In other words, when deciding on your criteria, you want to avoid using criteria that would generate "yes" or "no" for the table cell. When that happens, it puts all the pressure on the criteria to make the sense for all readers. For example, if you were comparing laptops, see the two rows in Table 4.6 that show how the question criterion is not an informative row, while the second criterion row is more helpful.

Table 4.6: Example criteria comparison

Criteria	Some laptop	Another laptop
Stylus included?	Yes	No
Stylus	6" resin stylus included with list price	No stylus included. Optional stylus available for additional cost

See Chapter 4.4.1 for the C/C Pattern Summary Table for another example of how to create criteria and table cell content.

NOTE: In any table, as much as possible, the English form of the criteria column (after the heading row) needs to be parallel. (For a discussion of parallelism, see Chapter 9.1.2.)

Establishing a Table with Criteria and Subcriteria

When creating a CST that has criteria that break down into subcriteria, then special formatting requirements are needed to help the reader understand how that information is related. See Table 4.7 for an example.

Table 4.7: Practice table

Column heading	Column heading	Column heading	Column heading
Criterion	Table cell content	Table cell content	Table cell content
Criterion			
Subcriterion	Table cell content	Table cell content	Table cell content
Subcriterion	Table cell content	Table cell content	Table cell content
Subcriterion	Table cell content	Table cell content	Table cell content
Criterion	Table cell content	Table cell content	Table cell content

▶

Column heading	**Column heading**	**Column heading**	**Column heading**
Criterion			
Subcriterion	Table cell content	Table cell content	Table cell content
Subcriterion	Table cell content	Table cell content	Table cell content
Subcriterion	Table cell content	Table cell content	Table cell content
Criterion	Table cell content	Table cell content	Table cell content
Criterion	Table cell content	Table cell content	Table cell content
Source: Full bibliographic source where the information came from			

NOTE: When you have subcriteria, only the criteria are forecasted in the introduction, not the subcriteria. If you tried to forecast both, the sentence would get very convoluted for the reader.

NOTE: If you need to define a criteria term, then the brief definition would go in the table cell where the criteria are identified (in the first column).

Recommendation: Merge the cells for the criteria that break down into subcriteria and format the look of the subcriteria differently (as seen in Table 4.7). You could indent them or tab in a little bit as was done in Table 4.7.

NOTE: See Chapter 5.3 for more information on creating tables.

4.4.3.5.2 The Comparison as Paragraphs of Text

This section explains how to format the comparison when using paragraphs of text instead of a CST. This form is used when the amount of information to explain the comparison exceeds what can reasonably be presented in a table cell.

There are two ways to organize the paragraphs of text (see Figure 4.2 for sample outlines):

- Whole-by-whole (W/W) – or sometimes called subject-by-subject – covers each subject at a time with subsections covering each criterion in the same order, applying it consistently and evenly.

- Part-by-Part (P/P) – or sometimes called point-by-point – covers each criterion at a time and evaluates it consistently and evenly for each subject, always covering the subjects in the same order as subsections.

Figure 4.2: Heading outlines for whole-by-whole and part-by-part compare and contrast showing two subjects (A and B) and three criteria (1, 2, and 3)

[WHOLE-by-WHOLE]	[PART-by-WHOLE]
Introduction (introduce subjects, criteria, and acknowledge decision)	Introduction (introduce subjects, criteria, and acknowledge decision)
Subject A	Criterion 1
Criterion 1	Subject A
Criterion 2	Subject B
Criterion 3	Criterion 2
...	Subject A
	Subject B
Subject B	Criterion 3
Criterion 1	Subject A
Criterion 2	Subject B
Criterion 3	...
...	Conclusion Recommendation (optional)
Conclusion Recommendation (optional)	

Choosing the Comparison Organization Method

How do you decide which organization method to order your comparison? This question is answered in two ways:

1) How does the reader want to digest the comparison?

- Does the reader want to focus on the subjects? Then use W/W.

- Does the reader want to examine the details of the comparison? Then use P/P.

2) What is the result of the comparison?
   - Are the subjects are very similar? Then the best way for the reader to see the differences is with a P/P comparison.
   - Are the subjects are very different? Then the best way for the reader to understand the comparison and make a decision is with a W/W comparison.

Whichever method you choose, pick one method and stick with it. The method you choose must be obvious, by the headings you use as shown in Figure 4.2. That is, the comparison headings would match those words/phrases used in the introduction section exactly.

4.4.3.5.3 The Comparison as a Combination of Both

If you've tried each of the prior methods first, you might have found that either you've got table cells with too much information in them to reasonably present the information or you've found that some of the subsections are too skimpy. In these cases, it may make sense to combine the methods using both tables and sections for those longer comparisons.

When you combine both paragraphs of text and a table, then follow the organization methodology described in Chapter 4.4.3.5.2 on writing with paragraphs of text and insert tables for those small sections that can fit in table cells.

- For W/W, the table you include cannot be a full CST with all the subjects. Instead, you would create the table as only two columns: criteria and the subject being compared.
- For P/P, the table you include is described in Chapter 4.4.3.5.1 using a CST with subsections for the criteria that need paragraphs of text.

4.4.3.5.4 What Not to Do in the Comparison Sections

In the comparison sections, here are some rules of what *not* to do:

- Do not use transitions. They carry emotion and/or impressions. Since C/C is designed to be unbiased, all emotions/impressions need to be removed.
    - For example, however, but, unlike <subject>, only
- Never tell the reader what to do.
    - For example, using verbs like should, must, need to.
    - Reserve this language for the conclusion or recommendation section if you include one.
- Never make the decision for the reader, in the comparison section.
    - Reserve this language for the conclusion, or recommendation section if you include one.
- Do not make conclusions about the subjects, until you get to the conclusion.

Instead, give the facts in the comparison section.

4.4.3.6 The C/C Conclusion

Your *conclusion* section helps the reader make the decision by evaluating each criterion, now that they've read/understood the data about the subjects. It's not a place to evaluate the comparison.

The C/C conclusion is organized in two parts: the topic sentence reiterates the subjects and criteria, followed by an "if" statement as bullets for each criterion (or combined criteria) that helps the reader make the decision. You must have one "if" statement for each criterion, in the same order as the criterion introduction. That way the reader can go through each criterion and see its effect on their choices. These bullets take the following form:

> If <criteria content>, then pick <subject>, (optional <reason>).

You can combine criteria information, if they go together, as follows:

> If <criteria content> and <criteria content>, then pick <subject>, (optional <reason>).

Yes, this is a redundant way of writing, but when using bullets, the reader can see that and easily skim for the information that is relevant to their needs.

NOTE: This is a place where you can tell the reader what to do, because in the conclusion they are looking for that type of resolution, so do not use passive voice in the "if" statements:

> Incorrect: If you'd like xyz, then subject A is a good choice.
>
> Correct: If like xyz, then pick subject A.

4.4.3.7 A C/C Recommendation

A recommendation section is an optional section for C/C usually. As discussed later, you could alternatively use a recommendation and exclude the conclusion, depending on what your audience has asked for.

Like the word denotes, a recommendation is how the reader should decide, that is, what subject is the right choice based on your research and your personal experience with the subjects. This section needs its own heading so that the shift in tone from objective to subjective (personal viewpoint) is clear to the reader.

The recommendation would be a place where you could use 1st (singular) POV to refer to yourself and use personal, biased language as you are providing your own perspective, for example, Based on my personal experience with subject X and subject Y, my recommendation would be . . . .

NOTE: Do not use "if" or "consider" phrasing in a recommendation; those phrasings are reserved for the C/C conclusion.

Also, do not add new comparison content in the recommendation.

4.4.4 Prewriting Stage: Getting Started

Various questions can be completed during the prewriting stage of the writing process to form the outline:

1) Purpose: What decision needs to be made?
2) Audience: Who are the decision makers?
3) Audience analysis: Analyze their knowledge level with respect to the subjects, criteria, and decision that need to be made. What can you assume about the reader's knowledge of the topics? You want to analyze any assumptions you can make about the reader's ability to understand the content so that you know when you need to define terms, what order the criteria should be placed in, and so on.
4) Do you have any secondary audiences? If you have any secondary audiences, what is their role in the decision-making process? A secondary audience might be paying for the subject, even if the primary audience would be using it, or they may be influencing the decision. What do you need to do to reach this audience?
5) What are the subjects?
6) What criteria do the reader need to see evaluated to understand how to make the decision the subject? Select criteria based on the decision that needs to be made.
7) Outline the comparison.

4.4.5 To extend the C/C Pattern

There are various ways to extend the C/C pattern.

4.4.5.1 When the Comparison as Paragraphs of Text Is More Than a Paragraph

If your comparison grows beyond one paragraph, then help your reader keep track of the larger comparison as seen in Figure 4.3.

Figure 4.3: Outline showing headings/subheadings for large comparisons

[WHOLE-by-WHOLE]	[PART-by-PART]
FOR WHOLE-BY-WHOLE Heading Subject A Subheading Criteria 1 Paragraphs of information Subheading Criteria 2 Paragraphs of information Subheading Criteria 3 Paragraphs of information Heading Subject B ...	FOR PART-BY-PART Heading Criteria (1) Subheading Subject A Paragraphs of information Subheading Subject B Paragraphs of information ...

4.4.5.2 To Use Comparison as Paragraphs of Text Requires Criteria Definitions

If you're using the comparison as paragraphs of text, and you need to define your criterion before you explain the facts, then you need to add a definition paragraph before you offer the subject comparison information. Unfortunately, if you need criteria definitions, then you must use the P/P organization method. W/W does not work. Plus, each criterion must be defined. See Figure 4.4.

4.4.6 Uses of C/C Pattern

There are many ways in which you can change this pattern based on your situation on the job:

- You can compare the subjects in a subjective/biased manner, rather than objectively. While biased comparisons are quite common on the Internet in reviews, it forces the reader to extract the author bias. That's

Figure 4.4: Outline for P/P comparison with criteria definitions

Heading Criteria (1) Paragraph: definition of criteria (1) Paragraph Subject A (1) Paragraph Subject B (1) Paragraph Subject C (1) Heading Criteria (2) Paragraph: definition of criteria (2) Paragraph Subject A (2) Paragraph Subject B (2) Paragraph Subject C (2) Heading Criteria (3) Paragraph: definition of criteria (3) Paragraph Subject A (3) Paragraph Subject B (3) Paragraph Subject C (3)

a lot of work to expect the reader to perform. Unfortunately, despite the onerous workload on the reader, this C/C form is quite common. And it can be useful, if your audience are just like you and would make similar evaluations. This is why the ratemyprofessor.com is popular, as the expectation is students rate professors similarly.

- You can alter the contents of the introduction. For example, you may not need to acknowledge the audience. For example, your audience could be established in the TO field of an email without needing to be repeated it in the beginning paragraph.
- You can consider omitting the conclusion section with the "if" statements and only include the recommendation section. This would be common if your reader asked you for a recommendation, and not

to help them make the decision. In this way, they see the facts in the comparison, and see why you made the recommendation you did.

- You can use both the P/P and W/W comparisons. For example, you could start with the P/P to explain the differences between two solutions (where the subjects are the solutions). In the recommendation, pick one of the solutions. Then C/C using W/W, comparing the difference between "before the use of the solution" and "after the use of the solution" as the subjects.
- You can use a CST (a table of columns: criteria and subjects, and rows for each criteria) as a table in another document. For example:
    - To help convince or explain to the reader about an action, by using subjects as *before* and *after*.
    - To inform or clarify specifications information for the reader.

4.4.7 C/C Samples

Comparing LinkedIn to Resumes

Introduction

For someone looking for work, needing to decide how to get your qualifications to the prospective employer, the comparison in Table 1 examines LinkedIn and resumes, using the following criteria: purpose, audience, contents, and medium.

Comparison

Table 1: Comparing LinkedIn and Resume

Subjects	LinkedIn	Resume
Purpose	Publicizes your skillsets and your goals Connects with other professionals online	Displays specific skillset to your target company Connects with recruiters, employers

►

Subjects	**LinkedIn**	**Resume**
Medium	Online Social Media Profile	Printable document
Audience	Recruiters, friends, acquaintances, future connections	Recruiters, employers
Contents	Skills, goals, experiences, connections, as long as needed	Skills, experiences, stylized formatting, up to one page, two pages max

Conclusion

LinkedIn and resumes differ based on their purpose, audience, contents, and medium.

- If you want to publicize your qualification to anyone and you want to learn a social media platform, then use LinkedIn.
- If a prospective employer has asked for your information, then use a resume.
- If you want to have free rein on how you display your skills beyond one page, then use LinkedIn.

Comparison of Facebook and Discord

NOTE: This partial comparison uses P/P with paragraphs of text and includes definitions for the criteria in their own paragraph.

When do you get notified?

Social media websites vary in terms of what events prompt a notification for the user.

Discord notifies users about every message within the channels that they have access to. When there are updates to the status of a friend request, Discord sends a notification. Discord also sends notifications when others react to a message that the user sent.

Facebook notifies people about your birthdays, @ mentions, and events that you are attending. Other notifications on Facebook come from updates to friend requests and comments to the user's post

How can you react to posts?

Social media posts allow people to respond with comments, but for the sake of time, simple reactions consisting of single emotional icons (emoticons) are a crucial tool for users.

Discord can display any emoticon that is in the standard Unicode Emoticon Library. Users can make their own emoticons from their downloaded pictures. Users can display more than one emoticon per post.

Facebook gives people six emoticons to react to the post. One person can react one emoticon per post.

4.4.8 Review Exercises

1) C/C introductory paragraph
    a) What are the four elements that need to be incorporated into the introductory paragraph of C/C writing?
    b) What should you not put in a C/C introductory paragraph?
2) What is the reader's experience of the following word choice constructs in the Comparison section?
    a) You must examine __.
    b) Your only choice would be __.
    c) Subject A has XXX; however, you __.
    d) Subject B has more xxx than subject A.
3) If the comparison section is designed to give facts about the subjects based on the criteria, what word constructs should not exist? Use each example from (2) to turn into a rule.
4) How is the conclusion constructed? What should not be put in a conclusion?
5) How is the recommendation constructed? What should not be put in the recommendation?

4.4.9 Practice Exercises

1) SCENARIO: Answer the following questions based on a comparison of the differences between two classrooms offering the same course at the same time. Audience: A student at your university/college. Decision: A student needs to take the course a student sees on the time schedule that multiple sections of a course are offered, and decides to pick which course to take based on the classroom the class is offered in. Author: you're the author.

- **a)** Audience analysis: What does the audience already know before they read the comparison? In what way do you need to tailor your work to ensure the audience understands the comparison?
- **b)** Decision: What criteria would help the audience choose the best room based on their needs? What considerations about a classroom are important for a student at your university/college? What criteria would ensure objective/factual comparison?
- **c)** Create the CST objectively comparing subjects using the criteria you've identified.

  Table

2) SCENARIO: Answer the following questions based on a comparison of the differences between two instructors teaching the same course. Audience: A student at your university/college. Decision: A student needs to take the course and different instructors are teaching it the same quarter. The student decides to choose which course they enroll in based on the instructor. Author: You're the author.

a) What criteria would you choose and why?

b) Based on that criteria, what facts would allow you to compare the subjects *objectively*.

c) Based on that criteria, what impressions would allow you to compare the subjects *subjectively*.

d) Summarize the reader's experience between the *objective* versus *subjective* comparison.

e) When do you usually see in *objective* comparisons?

f) When do you usually see in *subjective* comparisons?

g) Using the criterion, background, what subcriteria would encompass background? How would you ensure an even comparison of the instructors using their background and any subcriteria you identify?

h) Practice writing, given this scenario:
   - **a)** What would be the email/subject line (title) to the audience?
   - **b)** Write the introduction.
   - **c)** Create the CST.
   - **d)** Write the conclusion.
   - **e)** Write a recommendation.

3) Using what you know about C/C, why is it a problem, in the grocery checkout line, when you are asked "paper or plastic?" (Hint: Think about the introduction paragraph requirements.) What should be the proper question you are asked?

4) Why do you think the C/C pattern is so fixed?

5) What is the reader's experience because of the C/C form?

6) What is the reader's experience if the C/C form was not followed?

7) What is the reader's experience if subjects are *not* compared evenly?

4.5 Instructions Pattern

Instruction writing is similar and different to process writing.

> *Process writing* tells you why things are the way they are, like a textbook, a reference book, a user's guide, or a tutorial.
>
> *Instructions* give you step-by-step or how-to commands to perform a specific task.

4.5.1 Instructions Pattern Summary Table

Characteristics ☞	Instructions
Purpose	Explain *how* to do something
Audience/reader	Uninformed or struggling user
Secondary Audience	None
Scenario indicators	How do I __? (read more in Chapter 4.5.2)
Point of view (POV)	2nd (implied in the telegraphic commands used in instructions)
Tone	Medium
Pace	Fast (short commands, short sentences)
Organization	Stages and steps in chronological order (read more in Chapter 4.5.3)
Ethical scenarios	Miscategorize an error condition. Saying *CAUTION*, when it's really *DANGER* (read more in Chapter 4.5.3.5)
Examples	Online help, instruction manual (see Chapter 4.5.6)
Delivery	Typically online search through an application help feature or website that offers instructions on how to do something
Cognitive skill	Misordering chronological order or sequence of steps (frequently identified by the use of *before* and *after*)
Writing skill	Organizing in stages and steps

▶

Characteristics ☞	**Instructions**
Who creates these documents in a company?	Usually a documentation group/department writes instructional content for products built by a company to ensure accurate/quality writing. Software developers who write code for entering information into forms (which are instructions), for example, any roll over help provided ought to follow proper guidelines

☞ See Table 4.2 for definitions of these characteristics.

4.5.2 Do You Need to Write Instructions?

You would be cued to provide instructions by someone asking how do I __? or how do we __? asking for the method of doing something.

4.5.3 Organization of Instruction Writing

Instructions are organized in stages and steps.

The most common example of instructions are online help. Take a moment to bring up the help of any product you frequently use to see how these instructions are organized. Click on the question mark (?), which is usually the *help* signal. That table of contents are all the stages of instructions provided. Within a stage are the steps.

4.5.3.1 Title and Purpose

Instructions begin with a title line or heading that explains what instructions are being provided. You can even repeat the cue words by saying How to __ as the title/subject line.

Infrequently, this heading is followed by a brief (e.g., one-sentence) paragraph introducing the context of the instructions to follow.

4.5.3.2 Stages and Steps

The heading/purpose is followed by the numbered instructions. The instructions are organized by breaking down the task into individual steps. If there are a lot of steps, then further break down the numbered steps into stages with steps under each stage heading. In this way, you can keep the number of steps in each stage low.

Each stage is its own heading. All numbered steps/tasks are ordered by time. Each step is numbered. Each step begins with a command form of the verb. If you have stages, then reset the step number under each new stage heading.

4.5.3.3 Instruction Writing

This section provides instructions for writing instructions, which can be used by example.

1) Provide introductory information: Definitions, notes, cautions, warnings, dangers, and so on, before the step instructions. These would have their own heading.
2) When your instructions require something to be gathered beforehand, let readers know before they get started. Do not leave readers stranded midstep having to find some tool or piece of information. Consider having a "checklist."
3) Use numbered lists.
4) Place one action per step.
5) Start each action step with a verb.
6) Remove extra information from the steps.

   Provide that additional information in a separate un-numbered line or paragraph at the same indentation as the step information, such as this sentence.

7) Have the pace of your instructions match your audiences' technical capability.

8) Avoid embedding a clause in the middle of the instructions as they force the reader to reconstruct the command.

9) Select your words carefully.

   Users expect more precision and accuracy with instructions. For example, do not use vague words: "a little while" (use "four to five seconds") or "increases" (use "doubles"). When you cannot be specific, use a range.

10) Be careful of constructions with dangling modifiers where the subject isn't clear.

11) End all your stepped instructions with a period, as it's a complete sentence.

12) Organize your instructions so they are not one long list (like this long list). Instead, break up into stages and steps, then group steps under task (stage) headings.

13) Test your instructions.

4.5.3.4 Error Conditions

When writing instructions, especially those that involve electricity and other dangers, then it's important to include cautions, warnings, and dangers, based on these standard definitions:

CAUTION – Possibility of damage to equipment or materials.

WARNING – Possibility of injury to people.

DANGER – Probability of injury or death to people.

4.5.3.5 No "Conclusion"

At the end of the instructions, they end. There's no "conclusion" or "summary" or any other section to wrap up the content.

NOTE: The primary goal of a conclusion is to say "now what?" should the reader do. In the case of instructions, there's no "further steps" of what to do, so there's no conclusion.

4.5.4 Uses of Instructions Pattern

Once you've understood this pattern, there are ways in which you can use it based on your situation. For example:

- Use instructions for online help.
- Consider how understanding instructions can help as you write code where users are entering information into a form. How might you help the reader when they use the cursor to roll over something for more information? Or how might a pop-up help orient the reader? What language forms are best to use?

4.5.5 Prewriting Steps: Creating an Instructions Outline

Various tasks completed during the prewriting stage can help you create efficient instructions.

1) Brainstorm the tasks. It is a complicated task that involves many different sets of activities. For example, installing software may include gathering information needed later during the configuration (especially if the network isn't available to lookup that information), followed by the installation, then configuration, and maybe even customization. Each of these tasks (or stages) would involve subtasks (or steps).

2) Once you know how many stages you need, then organize the steps. Pay particular attention to the use of "before" and "after," which shows that the order of tasks is inaccurate. For example, the instruction Block the tires from rolling before jacking up the car is an example of a compound instruction that is unlikely to end well.

3) Always test your instructions to ensure that you've got all the tasks in the correct order and fully explained.

4.5.6 Instructions Sample

How to Make a YouTube Playlist

These steps cover how to make a new YouTube playlist on your computer.

1) Navigate to your YouTube account.
2) Click on a video.

   This should be a video that you want to add to your new playlist.
3) Click on the "Save" button by the bottom right-hand corner of the video.
4) Click "Create New Playlist" in the pop-up window.
5) Type the name of the new playlist.

   This is valid for any name under 150 characters.
6) Click on the drop-down arrow next to "Privacy."
7) Click "Public," "Unlisted," or "Private."
8) Click "Create Playlist."
9) Click on the next video that you want to add to the playlist.
10) Click on the "Save" button by the bottom right-hand corner of the video.
11) Select the name of the playlist from the pop-up window.
12) Press the "X" on the corner of the window.

    In other words, close the window.

4.5.7 Exercises

1) Examine these steps for making a Facebook post. Rewrite them according to the rules for writing instructions.
   a) The app needs to be open before you can post. Open up Facebook to the default menu.
   b) Tap the "What's on your mind" textbox and type a message.
   c) Add in any images you want, any standard photo type will do, to the post.
   d) Press send.
2) For the following steps on taking a scenic photo, assign a warning level (e.g., CAUTION, WARNING, DANGER)
   a) [Insert warning] Bring precautions against the weather for your camera.
   b) Position yourself at a high vantage point.
   c) [Insert warning] Steady yourself into a comfortable and secure position to avoid falling.
   d) Take the picture.
3) Explain the difference between an instructions and a process writing (Chapter 4.6).
4) Review the instructions for a task in an app you frequently use (e.g., Word or PowerPoint). Analyze how those instructions follow these guidelines, or where/why they deviate from them.
5) Write a set of instructions to accomplish a task on a program that already has instructions. Then, read the official instructions and compare/contrast. Was their word choice more effective? Did they consider mistakes and errors that you did not?
6) Consider the topic: how to make a YouTube video. Make headings for potential instructions for this topic.
7) Watch the YouTube video where the father tests the child's instructions for making a peanut butter and jelly sandwich. (There's a couple of them.) They're funny while showing how difficult exact instructions can be.

4.6 Process Pattern

Process writing and instruction writing are similar and different.

> *Process writing* tells you why things are the way they are, like a textbook, a reference book, a user's guide, or a tutorial.
>
> *Instructions* give you step-by-step or how-to commands to perform a specific task.

4.6.1 Process Pattern Summary Table

Characteristics ☞	**Process**
Purpose	Explain *why* things are the way they are and background for use
Audience/reader	Knows how to do things, does not know the background or context for use or application
Secondary audience	A monitoring agency (e.g., the Federal Aviation Administration [FAA] monitors Boeing's processes and best practices for building airplanes)
Scenario indicators	Any number of words, such as conventions, standards, best practices, standard operating procedures (SOP), process, procedure, user's guide, reference (read more in Chapter 4.6.2)
Point of view (POV)	2nd POV to refer to the reader
Tone	Formal
Pace	Medium
Organization	Progressive level of disclosure (how information is organized) (read more in Chapter 4.6.3)
Ethical scenarios	Overuse of "must." When every rule says "you must", the process becomes overburdened
Examples	US Constitution, an organization's bylaws, User License Agreement (ULA), user's guides, reference manual, "tips for use," best practices, SOP, Request for Comment (RFC), architecture document, employee handbook, tax guide, specification data sheet or specification document, textbook (see Chapter 4.6.6)

Characteristics ☞	**Process**
Delivery	Process can be delivered in many ways, from paper to online, from single-purpose documents to a separate section of a larger document
Cognitive skill	Remembering the assumptions about why things are done a certain way that have now become unconscious thought
Writing skill	Organizing in progressive level of disclosure
Who creates these documents in a company?	Engineers and software developers who are creating the products would write about the processes they followed to generate those products
☞ See Table 4.2 for definitions of these characteristics.	

4.6.2 Deciding to Use the Process Pattern

Process writing is used when the audience knows how to do the task, but doesn't know what conventions or best practices were applied for this particular instance, making process writing a very common pattern. For example, you may be hired because you know certain skills, but you would need to know/learn how those skills are applied at that job. That's process, and it's usually incorporated in some sort of new employee orientation.

You would be cued to use the process pattern by someone using any of the following words, for example:

- conventions
- standards
- best practices
- standard operating procedures or SOP
- process
- procedure
- User's guide
- Reference

Ordinarily, someone doesn't think I'm looking for a process writing. They think unconsciously, I'm looking for something to tell me why things are done the way they are. And consciously think/ask, Are there any best practices for using this ___? Or What are the standard operating procedures for this ___? Or What's the best way to ___?

4.6.3 Organization of Process Writing

The sections of process writing is organized in the order called *progressive level of disclosure*. Progressive level of disclosure means the topics are arranged so the most general concepts are covered first to offer a context or understanding or a big picture of the topic for the reader. Then information is added to build knowledge for the reader. By the time the reader gets to the end, they have a full understanding of the topic.

For example, textbooks and course content are organized to start with certain concepts and then build on them. In a textbook, like this one, each section you read tells you a bit more. As you read along, you build a knowledge base to add to what you already know about the topic. You can understand the ending, because you've read all the parts before. Not only do you understand the topic, but you understand your role. For example, in this book, you understand how to create technical writing patterns.

Process is organized to build knowledge with clear headings, so that it's easy for the audience to confidently to skip any section that they don't need to read because they already know the information, or to return to refresh their memory if they've forgotten. For example,

> **Best tips to become a popular YouTuber**
>
> Creating a theme
>
> Identifying your audience
>
> Making some content

This example covers the general process of becoming a popular YouTuber. These concept headings don't necessarily have a chronological order to it. Consider the last heading. In order to make content, you also need to know your audience. In order to know your audience, you need to know what your channel is about. Each heading provides a progressive order to clarify the next heading.

4.6.3.1 Title

The same words that are used to cue you as to what pattern to use can be used in the title of the document to alert the reader that process writing can be found within (e.g., "Standards" or "Best Practices").

4.6.3.2 Table of Contents

A table of contents (TOC) is not a required element of process writing, but when included it helps the reader skim for the information they are looking for, when they return to the document. The first time through the document, the reader would still most likely read the entire document or skim each section.

Decide to add a TOC depending on the use of the document or the length of a document (i.e., if it's longer, then it's more likely best to add a TOC).

If you don't include a TOC, then include a sentence in the purpose section that includes the list of topics covered in the process document.

4.6.3.3 Purpose Statement

There's no section called "Introduction" in process writing, and this purpose statement may or may not have a heading. When it does not have a heading, the purpose paragraph would begin after the title or subject line, and after the table of contents if present. When it's in a section by itself, it could be called "PURPOSE" or some other idea that gets that point across. How to decide whether you include a heading? If the purpose is more than one paragraph in length, then use a heading for it.

The purpose has two roles: let the reader know why the information is being provided for the reader and orient the reader to the document's contents (if a TOC is not included). If you don't have a TOC, then include a separate sentence at the end of the purpose that explains what major body sections are covered in the document.

NOTE: Never include *both* a TOC and the last orienting sentence, since that duplicates the information, and redundant information annoys readers.

4.6.3.4 Body Sections with Headings and Subheadings

In process writing, all body sections are written with small paragraphs, the details organized using lots of headings and subheadings.

Heading: The heading is a clear indication of what the section is about. The reader ought to be able to read a heading and they know what the section covers – so do not use one-word or one-phrase headings. Be sure that your headings always make it clear what is in that section. Then the reader can decide to skip that section if they already know the content.

The best way to construct a heading is to make sure that headings are phrases with verbs. Use verbs with an –ing form to help the reader understand what the section covers. Do not use the command verb form as that tells the reader what to do and best practices begin by explaining why to do something, followed by the rule.

Why, then rule: Process explains first *why things are (done) the way they are*, including details of what that means and maybe examples, followed by a *rule* or what the reader should do based on that *why* understanding (i.e., how that *why* translates into what the reader should do, that is, the best practice).

Rule as instruction: The rule is written in 2nd POV or telling the reader what they need to do. So while process isn't focused in instructions, instructions naturally exist after the *why* explanation.

The reasoning has to do with human nature. When you tell someone what to do and they don't like the idea or don't want to do it, they will dismiss the command. For example, "Don't park here." Oh, the first thing you want to do is park there, especially when you can't find a place to park. Instead, when why is explained first, followed by the command, then the reader will more easily follow the instructions. For example, "Reserved for Electric Vehicles. Don't park here."

Avoid passive voice: Avoid passive voice when writing the *rule*. For example, to say "it's important to ____" provides a passive voice rule and no explanation of why it's important. Reframe this language. In process, all the best practices are important to follow.

Avoid "if/then": Neither the *why* nor *rule* are <u>not</u> written in terms of an "If . . . , then . . . " statement. An if/then structure implies a choice, and in process, the *rule* is not a choice; it's a best practice. There ought to be only one best way to perform that task. When you find yourself wanting to use "if," then reframe to use "when" instead, as that is a stronger best practice language.

Separate paragraphs: Because the why explanation can be lengthy and you want process to be provided in bite-sized paragraphs, it's best to separate the *why* and *rule* into separate paragraphs. That way the reader can more easily skim the content. When the reader understands the *why*, in many cases the *rule* is obvious, so they may skip it and move on.

Variations: A common variation found in process writing is to omit the rule, because it's obvious to the reader. Another rare variation is to when the *why* followed by *rule* generates overly awkward phrasing, in which case, that can be reversed (*rule*, then *why*).

Paragraph length: You should always have small paragraphs in process writing because they are easiest to skim. This text defines small paragraphs as up to four full lines of Times New Roman 12 text with 1" margins.

4.6.3.5 Example Process Writing

This section contains an example of process writing. You can see the why (first paragraph) is followed by the rule (second paragraph).

> The Purpose of the Technical Writing Dictates the Pattern
>
> Technical writing is written for readers so that they can get some information they need to do their job, which means that the reader can't get their job done until they get the information they require. Furthermore, information broken down into small chunks makes it easiest for the reader to quickly skim or scan for what they are looking for.
>
> Therefore, as the author, you need to organize information in the most efficient pattern based on what the reader is looking for. Furthermore, within each pattern, you need to organize the information with headings and small paragraphs for easy scanning.

4.6.3.6 No "Conclusion"

At the end of process writing, it ends. There's no "conclusion" or "summary" or any other section to wrap up the content. It just ends.

> NOTE: The primary goal of a conclusion in technical writing is to answer "now what?" should the reader do. In the case of process, there are no "further steps" to do, so there's no conclusion.

Writing that has no prescribed ending can be hard for some authors who are used to wrapping up their work between introduction and conclusion bookends, but in process, that is how it is done.

4.6.4 Prewriting Steps to Create Process Writing

Step 1: Purpose

The prewriting tasks begin with identifying the purpose and scope of your process. That understanding ends up being articulated in the purpose statement of the process writing – what is going to be covered and why.

Step 2: Mind map

Organizing the body of the process writing can a harder task depending on when you're doing the writing: right after the best practices were established, or much later after you've forgotten why best practices were established. In each case, it's best to brainstorm the content by creating a mind map. Then group concepts in the mind map into larger ideas, to generate an outline.

Your greater challenge in creating the outline is whether you're writing about content you've forgotten you knew. You know it, but you don't remember all the details of it.

> For example, assuming you know how to drive, do you remember all the driving rules that you read when you took driver's education? Probably not. However, once you're in the car and driving along, you automatically (unconsciously) do what had originally been explained to you, like use a seatbelt, drive on the right-hand side of the road, use turn signals, and look before moving into another lane. Those rules you learned came with why explanations (or rather why things are the way they are), but now that you automatically do them, you act on the rule without thinking about why anymore. The point is that you still drive with that why understanding embedded in your actions.

So if you're creating process writing after you've no longer remembered all the why's, you need to work harder during the brainstorming stage to remember everything, so that you can write them down for the next person who needs to learn them.

In all cases, you need to start with a mind map. Map out all the possible ideas of topics that you need to cover or relate to your topic. These might be the standards or conventions or best practices for this topic, or maybe the SOPs, or even the process. As you brainstorm, identify links between the ideas to help you see connections.

Remember that with all your brainstorming, you still need to add rules to these concepts. The why things are, followed by the rule of what to do. When there's no rule, that's unlikely an avenue to brainstorm about.

> NOTE: Process writing is *not a research paper* (or delivering pure informational content that has no action). So don't brainstorm about history, definitions, or what the topic means in general. These ideas move your thinking into research or just facts. There must be a best practice (action) for it to be process writing.
>
> NOTE: Process writing is *not a persuasive writing* (or trying to persuade someone to do something). So there's no need to convince the reader to *do* the best practice. They are already motivated to do it; they just need to know what the best practice is. So don't brainstorm about *benefits*, *advantages*, or *why do it* questions about the topic. These ideas move your thinking into persuasion/convincing.

Step 3: Order Mind Map into Progressive Level of Disclosure

With your mind map, look at each element and ask yourself, *What is the first piece of information the reader needs to know before all others?* Put a (1) next to that idea. Then ask yourself, *What is the next piece of information the reader needs to know?* Put a (2) next to that idea. Keep following this question, numbering until all elements in the mind map that need to be covered are accounted for. That listing turns into a progressive level of disclosure order of ideas.

Step 4: From Progressive Level of Disclosure to Outline

With this list of progressive level of disclosure topics, you can now create the outline of headings and subheadings. When subheadings relate to one another, they can be placed under a higher-level heading. But remember that each lowest-level subheading has a rule.

Headings are best formed starting with an -ing form of verb (not the command form) with the rest of the heading phrase explaining what the section includes.

Once you've turned all the topics into headings and subheadings, then you've created your outline. Remember, there's no "conclusion" section. Just end.

Step 5: Examine Outline (or TOC) for Potential Problems

The next step is to test your outline to see whether it follows in progressive level of disclosure order. Some tests to ensure your best practices are building properly include the following:

- Look at topics to see whether you're examining them in the right order. For example, when you're looking at the process of an object, it needs to be examined from its biggest form to its smallest form. Not from its small parts up to its biggest form.
- Look at each topic and make sure that each section builds on the previous section. That is, make sure that any section doesn't require knowledge that is explained later in the outline.
- Look at the order of the topics to decide how they are ordered. Process is ordered around *why* things are, which is concept based.

  NOTE: Instructions, process' close neighbor, are organized around time. Work to avoid creating an outline that is ordered around time.
- Look at the order of topics to see whether you find yourself returning to the same topic again in the outline. Process rarely returns to ideas again and again, so reorder topics to cover topics once.
- Look at the topics. When you have lots of ideas that can be grouped together under another topic, use that broader topic as a heading, and use the smaller ideas as a subheadings.
- Look at the subheadings. When you have a subheading, there must be at least two subheadings under a heading. A heading can't have just one subheading; that tells you to collapse the subheading up into the higher level heading.

- Look at the rules. Repeating the same rule over and over suggests an improper organization and makes the *best practice* confusing for the reader. When lots of ideas all have the same rule, collapse all the *why's* into a table or figure that can be easily visible/understandable, and place the *rule* after that.

Step 6: Oops, Forgot that Idea, Now What?

When, after you've completed your outline, you might realize that you forgot to include some content. Sometimes you can find just the right spot to tuck it, but too often, this new point may require you to go back to the mind map and reorder all the concepts again.

Don't be discouraged if that occurs. Your readers will be glad you took the time to fix the progressive level of disclosure.

Step 7: Do You Need Any "This section covers" Paragraphs

If you have a *heading1* (first heading level of a TOC) with subheadings underneath it, then you need to have a paragraph after that *heading1* that tells the reader what topics are covered in that section – hence the phrase this section covers ___ can be used when there is no other way to orient the reader as to the contents of the section.

Use this phrase when the following conditions apply:

- Your organization goes from one heading to another heading with no intervening paragraph.
- You don't know how else to orient the reader to what is covered in this section.

Do not use this phrase when the following conditions apply:

- You have other material to discuss after the *Heading1* that would orient the reader regarding that section.
- It is not a *Heading1* section.

4.6.5 Uses of Process Pattern

Once you've understood this pattern, there are many ways in which you can vary it based on your situation on the job. For example:

- While you're designing the project on the job, write a corresponding process/decision document. This way, when new people come on board with the project, they can read the decision documents and understand why your designs are done the way they are. This document is much easier than you having to remember later what standards you agreed to or why you decided to go with a particular decision. And the new employees to the project can get up to speed much faster without taking your time away to keep explaining again and again.
- A common change to the structure defined in this section is to omit the *rule* because it's obvious after reading the *why*, especially if your audience doesn't want to read the duplicated (implied) information. Take a textbook as an example. It's a form of process writing, without all the explicit rules. Also notice that textbooks frequently break the rule of small sections, to the detriment of the student's comprehension.
- When it's applicable, you can merge both the process and instruction patterns into the same document:
    - When you have an instruction focus, start with the process description paragraph, followed by the step-by-step instructions (similar to car owner's manuals).
    - When you have a process focus, don't feel constrained. Organize by process, but include in numbered instructions within the sections as needed (similar to the Dummy books or a tutorial).
- When you cover the problem/solution pattern (see Chapter 4.7), you take aspects of process writing to reuse for that pattern.

4.6.6 Process Sample

Best practices for making a LinkedIn profile

As you are beginning to consider where you fit into the workforce, you could find yourself relying on LinkedIn to spread your name to other companies. This guide covers the best practices for making a good first impression with your LinkedIn profile.

Understanding the purpose of LinkedIn

LinkedIn is a professional social media website that helps employers and recruiters search through people's occupations and skillsets. Since LinkedIn helps people find jobs, claims of skill or past history online are deciding factors in recruitment.

Keep your online conduct professional and do not bend the truth, even for humor.

Establishing your mission

Employers and recruiters are often looking for specific positions to fill. They have a strong idea of the kind of individual the job requires. Skillsets help to some degree, but the personality, beliefs, and the soft skills are much harder to make claims for. They are only able to deduce your behavior through your posts and your profile bio.

Know what soft skills you possess and what makes you unique as a person. Be intentional about stating and demonstrating these traits in your bio and in your posts.

Creating online connections

Your bio and posts paint a portrait for you, but recruiters also look at your LinkedIn "connections." These connections can provide more insight and corroboration about your character. You may also be curious about various topics and industries or you might want to expand your network. People often use connections to find individuals they want to talk to. These people may be more comfortable talking with you when they learn that you have a mutual friend/connection who can vouch for you or set up the conversation.

Develop your connections on the website by adding in current friends and/or intentionally networking with people.

4.6.7 Exercises

1) Explain the difference between a process and an instructions (Chapter 4.5) document.
2) Order these progressive levels of disclosure headings for operating Snapchat
   a) Making conversations with friends
   b) Making public posts
   c) Finding friends online
   d) Establishing your profile
3) Identify which of these headings would be suited for process and which for instructions. Explain why.
   a) Creating an Instagram account
   b) Understanding Facebook groups
   c) Finding community on Meetup.com
   d) Making a contacts list
4) Identify a hobby of yours and write a process mind map for learning your hobby.
5) Consider a habit that you have. Write the heading and *why* + *rule* for it.
6) For the general topic, Best Practices for Instagram Posts, write a different purpose statement for the given audiences.
   a) An elderly person who is using Instagram to keep up with family and friends while they are unable to leave the house.
   b) A social media coordinator is using Instagram to promote their company.
   c) A young aspiring Instagram star wants to become famous and doesn't yet have a theme for their Instagram account.

7) Look around the Internet and find an example of a process. Print it and mark down each section where the concepts are applied. Analyze why they deviated from the best practices explained in this section. Do they still work? Could they be improved?

8) Watch the YouTube video where the father tests the child's instructions for making a peanut butter and jelly sandwich. (There's a couple of them.)

   They're funny while showing how difficult it can be to remember all the parts of the action that you take for granted. Like the example of remembering the why's behind the driving instructions, process requires you to reremember why things are done the way they are, so you can explain the why.

4.7 Problem Solution Pattern

The problem solution pattern is used when you need to explain how to solve a problem that the reader has. The reader's goal is to find and implement the solution articulated so their problem goes away. This pattern is different than instructions as it goes beyond the "how to do something" to include elements that help the reader solve a problem – essentially, as the author, you need to assume the reader has tried to fix things, but now need help.

4.7.1 Problem Solution Pattern Summary Table

Characteristics ☞	Writing problem solution
Purpose	To solve a problem the reader has
Audience/reader	The reader who has the problem
Secondary audience	Someone who is affected by the problem, but may not implement the solution themselves
Scenario indicators	Using the word problem or any phrase that indicates that the person has a problem that they want help solving (read more in Chapter 4.7.2)
Point of view (POV)	2nd POV: used to refer to the reader

Characteristics ☞	**Writing problem solution**
Tone	Formal – so that the reader can trust that your solution will solve their problem
Pace	Medium
Organization	Introduction (problem) + solution sections + conclusion (convincing) Where the solution(s) are organized using one of the following options: **a)** One solution **b)** A solution with multiple steps **c)** Multiple solutions Where each solution is organized using one of the following options: **a)** Process (progressive level of disclosure) **b)** Instructions **c)** Or a combination of these two methods (read more in Chapter 4.7.3)
Ethical scenarios	Exaggerated claims in solution, exaggerated claims of problem or its difficulties (like ads), solution not adequate to solve the problem but saying it is
Examples	Proposals (in response to a request for proposal [RFP]), FAQs (Q = problem, A = solution), marketing case studies, magazine articles (see Chapter 4.7.7)
Delivery	Problem solution can be delivered in various forms, from online webpages or emails to documents or books

Characteristics ☞	**Writing problem solution**
Cognitive skill	Thinking logically about the problem and its solution(s). Handling the reader's objections: "Why can't my reader do what I tell them to do?"
Writing skill	Organizing solutions and objection handling, writing the conclusion (persuasive tone)
☞ See Table 4.2 for definitions of these characteristics.	

4.7.2 Deciding When to Use the Problem Solution Pattern

You would be cued to use the problem solution pattern by someone using any of the following words:

- "Problem"
- Or any words that indicates that the person has a problem

4.7.3 Organization of Problem Solution Pattern

The problem solution pattern is organized with an introduction, solution(s) sections, and conclusion.

4.7.3.1 Title

The title of problem solution writing tells the reader that the solution to their problem lies here. Be sure to use words that frame that for the reader. For example:

Incorrect: Technical writing patterns

Correct: Picking which pattern to organize your technical writing document

4.7.3.2 Introduction

The introduction's role is to acknowledge the reader's state and orient them to how the solution section(s) are organized. It has four tasks to complete, so it's common to break it up into multiple paragraphs, so as to avoid having your reader lose interest before they reach your solutions.

The tasks of the introduction section are the following:

1) Acknowledge the audience who has the problem. With this acknowledgment, the reader knows that you know who they are. This acknowledgment may occur in the title or title page of the document instead of this section.

2) Acknowledge their problem to tell the reader that you understand the problem they have.

   In the brief explanation of the problem (a sentence or two), you need to be clear enough so that the reader knows that you know what problem they have. This gives the reader confidence to know that the solutions you're offering will actually solve their problem.

3) Convince the reader that the problem is serious. This task is not to convince the reader that they have a problem. Remember that in problem solution writing, the reader knows they have a problem and is looking for a solution. This part of the introduction convinces them that the problem is serious. That is, they need to solve it now. They shouldn't wait any longer. Use facts and statistics to illustrate the gravity of the problem.

> For example, say that the reader's kitchen sink drips and they need to get it fixed. That's the problem. Why is it serious? It wastes gallons and gallons of clean water each day; water that they are paying for. Over even a short period of time, that wasted water can cost a lot of money (for best effect, you could estimate the amount).

   NOTE: Do not say This <problem> is serious to tell the reader that the problem is serious. That is rarely a good way to convince someone.

4) Forecast the way the solution is organized in the solution sections, to orient the reader as to how the solution section of the document is organized before they get to that section. Yes, for best results, you must use one of the following exact sets of phrases:

   i. A solution

   Telling the reader that there is one solution to solve their problem.

   ii. A solution with multiple steps

   Telling the reader that the solution has several steps that must be followed in a particular order. NOTE: Avoid using the phrase "multistep solution," which can be confusing.

   iii. Multiple solutions

   Telling the reader that more than one solution exists for this problem.

   When you organize your solution using this option, you must tell the reader how to choose the various solutions. E.g., First fit? Use as many as possible? All of the above (which makes that sound more like a solution with multiple steps)? Include this explanation in the introduction or in the conclusion.

4.7.3.3 Solutions Sections

The solutions sections tell the reader specifically what to do to solve their problem. That could be written in terms of instructions or process writing depending on how much prior knowledge the reader has about what they need to do to solve the problem.

The solutions section should only contain the solution – that is, how to solve the problem.

> Avoid talking more about the problem in the solution. The reader knows the problem they have, so focus on how to solve it.
>
> Avoid convincing the reader to solve the problem in the solution. The reader wants to solve their problem, so you don't

need to convince/persuade them to solve it. Some benefits to the solution (which is persuasive) might leak into the solution as you describe how to solve it, but don't focus on benefits in the solution.

Organizing the Solution Sections

In the solution sections, organize the solutions sections matching which of the three options you used in the introduction. These solution sections are explained first, then summarized in a figure.

- <u>A solution</u> – Explain how the solution works, organize the solution and headings in progressive level of disclosure order of information.
- <u>A solution with multiple steps</u> – Each step of the solution has its own heading. The heading is the step (instruction/rule). The paragraph(s) underneath the heading provides additional information to explain how that step works. That information can be organized in progressive level of disclosure or could be organized as numbered instructional substeps. Be sure the step headings are ordered chronologically. You can number these headings to provide further clarity for the reader.

  NOTE: This structure flips the process order of why/rule to instead show rule/why.
- <u>Multiple solutions</u> – Each solution has its own heading. The paragraph(s) underneath the heading provide a discussion of how that solution works. That information can be organized in progressive level of disclosure or could be organized as numbered instructional steps.

  Consider how you've organized your various solutions. Do they build on one another? Is each distinctly different? Are some simple, and then get more complicated? Are they ordered in a sequence? Be sure that you've organized these solutions to make it easiest for the reader to figure out what solution for them to adopt.

NOTE: While process writing is similar for to problem solution, there are several variations that apply. While process is written as *Why+Rule* order, problem solution is written as *Rule +How/Why+If.* (The *if* part of the problem solution pattern is the objection handling discussed later.)

Structure of the Different Solution Sections

A solution	**A solution with multiple steps**	**Multiple solutions**
Headings and structure organized as progressive level of disclosure	**1) Headings** as a rule with numbered steps	**Heading** for each solution written as a rule
Solution details in paragraphs	Solution details in paragraphs	Solution details in paragraphs
Last section titled: "Alternative Solution" for objection handling	OR	OR
	Numbered instructions	Numbered instructions
	If ____ separate paragraph for objection handling for <u>each step</u>	If ____ separate paragraph for objection handling for <u>each solution</u>

Whether you decide to organize your solution sections as instructions or as process depends on your audiences' familiarity with the topic. This table offers a quick refresher of the differences:

Comparison	Instructions	Process
Audience	Uninformed readers need step-by-step instructions to follow	Readers already know how, only need to understand why things are done a certain why and the best practices
Organization	Instructions are organized as stages and steps. Each stage has a heading. Each step is numbered and begins with verbs	Process is organized in progressive level of disclosure order
Example	Provide step-by-step instructions on how to change a password in a specific application, how to navigate, where to click, what to type and where	Explain to the reader what varied strengths of passwords consists, using a combination of letters, capital letters, and special characters and how to come up with a passphrase to use

Objection Handling

What is objection handling?

Have you ever read a suggestion of what to do and while you were reading it, in the back of your mind, you were thinking, that's never going to work or not likely or not in this lifetime or some other objection to the suggestion? Yes! That is the situation where the reader is objecting to what the author wants the reader to do.

But what if when the author told you at that moment that your brain rejected the idea, if you can't do <the rejected idea>, then do <this alternative idea> instead? Would you be more likely to keep following the reading? Yes. That "if" statement is considered objection handling. It is designed to help the reader through the various possible situations that could thwart the ideal solution you're providing.

> NOTE: The reader doesn't think in terms of "objection handling" but rather "alternative solution."
>
> NOTE: This objection handling is the primary difference between instruction or process, and the problem solution pattern.

You must handle these unconscious objections that occur in the readers' minds when they read your solution. Furthermore, objection handling needs to be handled promptly so that the reader doesn't go away and find another solution, but instead adopts the alternative you provided.

For example, in the case of a company offering the solution versus another company providing a similar solution, if the reader goes away and purchases a competitive product instead, objection handling can be the difference between your company getting that revenue or not.

What is objection handling in the problem solution pattern?

Objection handling is handling the problem that has come up in the reader's mind – that is, solving the inward head shake the reader has while reading your solution by offering an alternative to that solution.

Objection handling means that you acknowledge the internal head shake (why the reader can't use that solution or part of that solution) and counter with what they can do instead.

The best way to offer the objection handling is an "if" statement in its own paragraph:

> If <(some part of) the solution doesn't work>, then <give alternative solution.>
>
> NOTE: You cannot be vague and say if this doesn't work. In the "if" statement, you need to be specific about what their brain is rejecting.

It's best to put the alternative solution in its own paragraph. This is so that the solution is separate from the objection handling (or alternative solution). Even if the "if" statement is just one sentence, it ought to be its own paragraph.

Because if becomes a key word in the problem solution pattern, avoid using if in other parts of the solution language, unless it's the objection handling. Try to reframe using when instead.

What does objection handling NOT mean?

Objection handling does not mean that you are trying to convince the reader that they do not have a problem, that they should just buck up and do what you're telling them to do.

What kind of objections might occur to the reader?

Sometimes, as the author, it can be difficult to come up with the objections the reader is encountering as they read your solution. It's your job to think like the reader, get inside their head, to figure out why your solution might not work. The following ideas suggest why a reader is shaking their head while reading the solution you offer:

- The solution requires something that the reader doesn't have.
- The solution doesn't work, encounters an error message.
- The reader can't do some step because his or her system doesn't look like that or work that way
- The reader doesn't understand some aspect of this solution, so the reader doesn't know what to do.
- The solution doesn't seem reasonable to implement.
- The solution doesn't seem feasible – too complicated or more complicated than they need for their problem.
- The solution seems like it will create a bigger problem than already existed, especially if it appears to be too complicated.
- The solution costs more/too much to implement.

Can you have more than one objection?

Yes, if you have multiple reasons in which the reader is shaking their head, then you can offer multiple if statements. However be careful about how many are offered. Too many may make your solution sound like it's not very feasible.

What's the best way to structure objection handling with multiple solutions?

For multiple solutions, the objection handling can be as easy as "If this solution doesn't work for you, then try the next solution" assuming that you have the solutions organized in an order that supports that structure. However, you can't send the reader from the last solution back to the top of the body of solutions. If you can't take advantage of this cascade option, each solution still needs its own objection handling. In that case, consider what part of the solution they might be objecting to and suggest an alternative to that.

4.7.3.4 Conclusion

The goal of the conclusion is to convince the reader to use the solution or one of the solutions you've offered. If the reader hasn't already decided after reading the solutions that they want to use your solution, this is the place to explain why this solution is the best way to solve their problem. (Consider that the reader may have read other competing solutions and you want the reader to pick your solution.)

It's best not to make the conclusion too long, which might make the reader regret considering your idea. One way is to summarize with a powerful statement, question, fact, quotation, or another device to drive home to your reader that this solution is the best answer to their problem.

Topics to avoid in the conclusion:

- Do *not* discuss the problem again. If you return to a discussion of the problem, you remind the reader of their plight and can destroy all the hard work you'd done of explaining how to solve their problem.

- Do *not* summarize the solutions. The reader does not need to read again what was stated in the body.
- Do *not* introduce additional solutions not mentioned in the solution sections.
- Avoid using if language in the conclusion. This is not a C/C conclusion to help the reader decide on a solution. If you've saved for the conclusion your explanation of how to choose from the various multiple solutions, use specific suggestions – pick the first on that works; try each one, then use the one you like; pick as many as you need; and so on – rather than a series of if statements.

4.7.4 Prewriting Stage: Getting Started

Various questions/tasks need to be completed during the prewriting stage of the writing process as outlined:

1) Brainstorm the problem.

2) Brainstorm who has the problem.

3) Brainstorm who will solve the problem. Who has the problem may not be the same person who solves the problem. The problem solution pattern only addresses to the reader who has the power to solve the problem – the person who can actually do the steps outlined in the solution.

4) Brainstorm what you know about the audience (perform an audience analysis) so that you can target your writing to the reader.

5) Brainstorm/research about the problem. What would occur if the problem wasn't solved? While the reader may realize that a problem needs fixing, they may not understand the ramifications of why it's serious and needs fixing right away. This information would go in the introduction.

6) Brainstorm the solution(s). Identify what type of solution it is.

7) Brainstorm the objection handling. Look at each stage, step, and task the reader has to perform and consider why they might not want to or be able to do that task or part of that task. Think of a way around that objection.

8) Create an outline for the writing.

4.7.5 Uses and Variations of Problem Solution Pattern

The problem solution pattern is one of the most common patterns that you will use, since your jobs will be to solve problems. Once you've understood this pattern, there are many ways in which you can change it based on your situation of the job. For example:

- Use it in emails or when talking to someone who has a problem you can solve for them.
- Use the problem solution pattern as a part or section of a larger document.
- If you're solving a series of problems in various ways, then translate the pattern into a table where you have *columns* as (problem), (solution), and (alternative solution), and *rows* that explain a different problem, solution, alternative sequence.
- Use it as a research paper for an audience that's not looking for a solution, but interested in the topic. In this case, your introduction would need to explain what the problem is to the reader, since you couldn't assume your reader already had the problem and was looking for a solution. You might not want to use "you" to address the reader, but instead use 3rd POV to refer to the type of person (e.g., job title) with the problem.
- Use it as an editorial. The problem solution pattern can be used when writing an editorial to a newspaper or blog posting. In this case, you, as the author, would be offering solutions to problems where the readers may not necessarily have the power to implement the solution, but agree/disagree about whether that is the way to solve the problem.

- Depending on what you know about the audience, you might replace the exact phrase "a solution," "a solution with multiple steps," or "multiple solutions" in the introduction with forecasting a list of the solutions. But be forewarned if you do this. When you give a summary of the solutions themselves in the introduction, the reader may not read further, if they believe they know what that solution entails. So the reader would miss all the details that would make it possible for them to implement the solution successfully.

4.7.6 Problem Solution Sample

Solutions to Maintain Privacy Online

Introduction

Social media has its own world, providing a space for interaction, but at the cost of leaving a footprint online. As a social media user, you leave a trail of information in the form of profile information, posts, comments, and your friends' posts about you. In fact, other people can stalk you online whether you know them or not, which creates the risks of physical ambushes, a loss of control over your information, cyberbullying, identify theft, and even swatting.

There are multiple solutions that can be used to mitigate your footprint online with little cost to your ability to interact with others. You can use as many of these solution as you need to use the Internet safely.

Keep your profile sparse

When completing your public profile, only fill in the required fields. Depending on the type of social media, switch on "friends only" access or the equivalent for your profile. The ideal case is that both your profile is minimal and only friends can see your profile.

If you want to attract only a specific audience, then keep the profile public so that the people you want to have looking for you can find you. Then only include the information they need to know about you. When you need a profile picture for an air of professionalism, hide recognizable details of any background, such as public landmarks, signs, and other people, so that your locations cannot be traced to anywhere you live or where frequently travel.

Befriend only people you trust

Keep your inner circle limited to people with whom you trust to know the details of your profile information. Evaluate your friends list on a monthly basis.

If you find that your friends are not being mindful of your privacy, then unfriend and block the people on this list whom you either feel uncomfortable around or worry that they might disclose your private information. The block can keep them from seeing your posts and learning anything new about you online.

Tell your friends to be mindful of your privacy

Just as you want to be careful what you post, you need to ask your friends to be mindful about disclosing your privacy on their social media accounts. Be mindful of the pictures that people take of you and ask them to respect your privacy by not posting pictures of you or blurring your face if they do post it, and not including your name in the post.

If they post pictures of you against your will, then avoid them online and in person.

Limit the content of your posts

Keep hints of personal information out of your posts. Hints might include your home address, contact information, and work/school association. Only share this information online through direct messages.

If you already shared personal information in public posts, delete them or use privacy filters on your account to hide them from the public eye.

If a public post of personal information is necessary, then delete the post after its purpose is fulfilled.

Comment only when necessary

Treat comments like posts. Filter out the personal information. Since comments are often opinions, only comment when you are comfortable with the public knowing it. Such purposes include asking clarifying questions, an observation that prompts action, or an opinion that you are comfortable sharing.

If there are comments that you already posted with information or opinions that you do not want tied to you, delete the comments. Some people may prompt you for a comment in a casual post, in which case you can choose to either respond through a comment or through direct messages.

Conclusion

This set of solutions is applicable for most social media sites because it relies on common social media practices. Each of these solutions can be implemented simultaneously to maximize your privacy. They are also able to fix past mistakes and not just your actions going forward and thus increase your sense of security when socializing online.

4.7.7 Exercises

This series of exercises builds a problem solution draft. SCENARIO: The reader is the author – essentially, you'll write up a solution to an existing problem you know you have, because you've probably already researched potential solutions so you don't need to do any research on solutions to complete the exercise.

PART I: The Problem

Think of a problem you have: one that you've had for a while, maybe one that you've tried to solve before. For example, for students, pick one of the following:

- ❑ Not enough sleep
- ❑ Too much school work
- ❑ Not enough money
- ❑ Need better study habits
- ❑ Need to exercise regularly
- ❑ Need to learn how to cook or eat better

1) **Brainstorm**: Answer these questions about the problem you picked:
   a) What is the problem you picked?
   b) How long have you had the problem?
   c) What has kept you from solving the problem before now?
   d) Why does the problem need to be solved? Why is it serious?
   e) What possible solution/solutions exist for solving the problem?
2) **Introduction: draft**. Write the introduction paragraph for this problem solution situation, including all four of the necessary elements in the problem solution pattern. (You can either use 2nd POV and assume there are other readers with this same problem who you're writing to, or refer to yourself in the 1st POV.)
3) Review your introduction.
   - ❑ Does it provide each of the four required parts? If not, then fix it.
   - ❑ Be sure that it doesn't add any other information it shouldn't, such as solution summary. Find any that offer a solution summary, such as forecasting the solution.
   - ❑ Rewrite without those words.

PART II: The Solution

4) **Brainstorm**: Answer these questions about possible solutions to the problem:
   a) Identify solution type from the three options.
   b) Identify the solution headings, ensuring that the headings are sufficient to explain what the section contains.
   c) Review the solution headings.
      - ❑ Cross out words that exist in the solution headings that refer to the "problem."
      - ❑ Rewrite.

PART III: The Conclusion

5) **Brainstorm**: Answer these questions about conclusion:
   a) What will persuade the audience that the/these solution(s) offered are the best?
   b) What are the benefits of adopting/using the/these solution(s)?
   c) What will be the result of using the/these solution(s)?
   d) If the solution offered multiple solutions, how would the audience decide among them?
6) **Conclusion: draft**. Write the conclusion paragraph for this problem solution incorporating those brainstorming ideas. It ought to be short and to the point.
7) Review the conclusion:
   - ❏ Cross out any words the say "problem" to the reader. Rewrite without those words.
   - ❏ Highlight any words in the conclusion that identify your writing as "persuasive" writing. Be sure these are kept in or emphasized as you revise your conclusion.

PART IV: The Objection Handling

In this case, you need to figure out why you wouldn't follow your own advice, especially since this is a long-standing problem.

8) Copy your solution section headings down here from 4b.
9) For <u>each</u> body section heading in 8, consider why you would <u>not</u> be able to use/adopt/do the solution that you provided. Write the *if* statement that will offer an alternative solution.

PART V: Draft the Pattern

Not take all these pieces you've created and create the draft from title, to introduction, solution, and conclusion. Review and revise.

4.8 Other Common Patterns and Combining Patterns

This section reviews the patterns discussed in this chapter and introduces additional common methods of organizing information. It also covers selecting a pattern, inserting a pattern into a document, and combining patterns in the same document.

This section allows you to review your knowledge on patterns, and then advance it into more complicated document structures that still deliver well-organized content to the reader.

4.8.1 What Are the Most Common Patterns

This section covers the most common patterns in use in business and technical writing. As each pattern is discussed, its use is explained, along with examples of where you're likely to find the pattern "in the wild." Last, words that cue you to use this pattern are identified.

4.8.1.1 Inductive

Inductive
Specific to General
e.g., performance evaluation

Inductive begins with just introducing a specific incident, then explaining more about that specific incident, ending with the conclusion where you explain what that incident means (read more in Chapter 4.2).

Examples of this pattern are answering a job interview question that asks you to explain your learning from an experience you had (e.g., Tell me about a time when you ___), half of your yearly performance evaluation, or within another pattern.

Words that cue you to use the pattern:

- learn, change, grow
- reflect, self-reflection
- your experience

4.8.1.2 Deductive (e.g., Position/Persuasive)

Deductive
General to Specific
e.g., lab reports, position

Deductive begins with a conclusion, then explains how that conclusion is derived, giving specifics, ending with a "now what" or, for English composition writing, a summary of the information.

Examples of this pattern are lab reports, position paper, white papers, or debates. For the position, the thesis (or idea you want the reader to adopt) is the conclusion (read more in persuasive pattern in Chapter 4.3).

You would be cued to use this pattern if you realize the reader wants the bottom line first (generalization/thesis/conclusion) before they hear any of the specifics.

4.8.1.3 Compare and Contrast

C/C
(Ideal for objective comparisons)
e.g., product evaluations

C/C is used to help the reader make a decision by providing choices that are evaluated against a set of criteria (read more in Chapter 4.4).

C/C is organized as an introduction, comparison, ending with the conclusion. The comparison section has three possible ways of organizing the comparison, depending on how much information needs to be delivered:

1) As a CST

2) By paragraphs of text organized either

   a) as W/W or

   b) as P/P

3) As a combination of CST and P/P

Examples of C/C writing include product specifications seen in marketing/sales writing and a decision paper.

You would be cued to use the C/C pattern by someone using any of the following words:

- decide
- between
- which
- choose
- pick

4.8.1.4 Chronological

Chronological

TIME, SEQUENCE
e.g., resume, instructions

When using chronological, information is organized by time or sequence. The Western world focuses on time, and thus, organizing your information by time or sequence makes the most sense. But this is not the default pattern, as time sequence imposes another perspective if all you wanted to do was explain something.

Examples of time-ordered information are as follows:

- Instructions, such as when you click on the ? in an application to ask for help or WikiHow website, where each instruction step is numbered and begins with a number. (Read Chapter 4.5.)
- Resumes have two sections that have time sequence: Education and Work Experience, which are ordered in *reverse chronological order* (most recent first), since that is what is most important to the reader.
- Form (e.g., tax form, online form)
- Roll over instructions in an online form
- Recipe (the instructions part)

You would be cued to use time/sequence by someone using any of the following words:

- How do I __
- What is the order to__

4.8.1.5 Progressive Level of Disclosure (aka Process)

Progressive Level of Disclosure
e.g., process, textbook, tutorial, general summaries

Progressive level of disclosure is the way to order information to build knowledge. This is the way we learn, and it's the way we're taught subjects (we learn to add, then subtract, then multiply and divide; in calculus, we learn limits, then derivatives). One piece of information builds understanding on which the next piece of information is explained (read more in Chapter 4.6).

This pattern can be confused with time or sequence order, but building knowledge is not the same as deciding on the order that something needs to occur (i.e., chronological).

Examples of this pattern are many:

- US Constitution
- An organization's bylaws
- User License Agreement
- User's guides
- Reference manual
- "Tips for use"
- Best practices
- SOP
- Request for Comment (RFC)
- Architecture document
- Employee handbook
- Tax guide
- Specification data sheet or Specification document
- Textbook

If nothing else presents itself as the pattern to use, then the *default organization pattern* is progressive level of disclosure. If the reader is trying to understand something, then this is the pattern to use.

You would be cued to use progressive level of disclosure (specifically the process pattern) by someone using any of the following words:

- conventions
- standards
- best practices
- standard operating procedures or SOP
- process
- procedure
- User's guide
- Reference

4.8.1.6 Problem/Solution

Problem/Solution

e.g., proposals, FAQ

Problem/solution is used to provide a solution to the audience that has a problem they cannot solve. These are quite common and seen in articles, web pages, and business documents of many kinds (read more in Chapter 4.7).

This pattern is organized with an introduction, solution(s), and conclusion. The solution section can be organized in three ways, depending on the form the solution takes:

1) A single solution

2) A solution with multiple steps (where the audience must perform each step of the solution)

3) Multiple solutions (where the audience might be able to pick one or many of the solutions to solve their problem)

Examples of this pattern are proposals (in response to a request for proposal [RFP]), FAQs (where the Question is the problem and the Answer is the solution), and marketing case studies.

You would be cued to use problem/solution by someone using language where they ask for a solution to a problem they have.

4.8.1.7 Cause/Effect

Cause/Effect

(why something happened, future prediction)
e.g., critical analysis

Cause/effect writing is used to explain two types of causal relationships to the reader:

1) Explain how particular causes have produced an effect, that is, why something has happened in the past.

2) Predict why something might happen in the future.

The cause/effect writing is organized with an introduction, analysis, and conclusion.

- The introduction orients the reader and ends with the effect conclusion of the analysis.

- The analysis can be organized in two ways:
  1) Effect/causes: After the effect as the thesis at the end of the introduction, there is a section (heading) for each of the causes.
  2) Cause–effect chain: After the (final) effect as the thesis at the end of the introduction, each section explains the series of causes that lead to another effect, in the cause effect chain. To help the reader, each link along the cause/effect chain is explained in its own section.
- The conclusion answers the "now what" for the reader. What should they do now that they understand this analysis?

Examples of this work would be some type of critical analysis. You would be cued to use the cause/effect pattern by someone using the following words:

- cause
- effect
- why
- how did (e.g., How did this happen?)

NOTE: This can be tricky because how do I ___ would cue you to use instructions. The verb tense tells you if it's instructions or cause/effect.

4.8.1.8 Most Important to Least Important

Most Important to Least Important

e.g., ordered lists

Most important to least important is for *lists* only – that is, where the information you're offering is a series of items that have a specific grouping associated with them. If you have a list of items and you want to convey their importance by order to the reader, then you would use an ordered bulleted list.

From the reader's perspective, they would need to know what each element on the list is; otherwise, the list of "importance" would instead appear random to the reader. For example, if you were providing a list of ten important things to do when applying for a job, the reader would need to know what the individual tasks that would appear on the list involve. Then, in this importance list, what they would be learning is the order of importance to do them in, based on the author's perspective.

You would be cued to use this pattern if someone asked you what was important or asked for a list and implied they wanted it based on importance.

4.8.1.9 Least Important to Most Important

Least Important to Most Important

(CLINCHER order)
e.g., Sales Pitches

Least important to most important is for *lists* only – again, where the information you're offering is a series of items that have a specific grouping associated with them. In this case, you would use this pattern, when you want to build anticipation for the audience as they get to the most important element on the list.

You would be cued to use this pattern if you were creating a sales pitch: Why you should buy this ____? The author builds greater reasoning with each list element, and by ending with the most important reason (assuming the reader gets to the end of the list), then the reader is convinced, and the author can move to the *buy now* stage.

4.8.1.10 Ordering Lists by Other Criteria

While *importance* is a common way to order a list, any list can be ordered by any criteria. To make it clear to the reader what criteria are used, use the sentence before the list or heading to list to explain to the reader how the list is organized.

For example, you might think of instructions as a list (of steps) organized by time. In this case, time is the criterion by which the list was organized.

There're lots of ways to organize lists. You could order a list of items to purchase by time (buy them in this order), maybe because each purchase is dependent on another, or order them by importance (buy till the money runs out).

4.8.1.11 Indexed

Indexed

(Organize in numerical or alphabetical order)
e.g., glossary of terms

Indexed refers to organizing a list of individual elements in numeric order, in alphabet order, or combined as alphanumeric order. Everyone is taught the alphabet and the sequence of numbers, and therefore knows how to find something alphabetically.

Examples include a dictionary, glossary of terms, bibliography or references, and index in the back of a book.

You would be cued to use this pattern when all elements are equal (i.e., so they aren't organized by some other criteria) and the audience wants to find any element easily/quickly.

4.8.1.12 Classification and Partition

Classification and Partition

(C) Place items in categories
(P) Break items into parts
e.g., catalog

Classification and partition are actually two different methods of organizing information that have always been talked about together. This is, in part, because when using either of these methods, there must always be another organization method used along with it. They cannot be used alone. And frequently, these are used together.

Classification is used to take like-identified groups and identify them in a named class. All things can be classified for identification/naming – from the foods you eat (breakfast, lunch, dinner, OR vegetarian, paleo, keto, etc.), to the clothes you wear (jeans, shorts, t-shirts, sandals, etc.), to the classes you take (premajor, degree core required, electives, etc.), and on and on. Classification helps to classify masses of information for someone else to understand what group it's associated with.

Partition takes a whole object, and partitions it (breaks it up) into its parts and identifies those parts. Frequently, the parts are then classified. For example, if you were going to take a machine, like a lawn mower and partition it, you would take all its parts and classify them into the various parts: engine, blade, wheels, handle, and so on. Any object that is composed of parts can be referred to in its partitions.

As you can see once individual elements have been classified or partitioned, they still need to be organized in some way. You could index the list, organize them chronologically, order them spatially, or any other way that improves reader comprehension.

You would be cued to use classification if someone wanted to group elements together to help understand them. Again, once you'd classified them, you'd still need to order the elements within the classes.

You would be cued to use partition if someone wanted to group the parts of a whole into classes to help understand them. Again, once you'd partitioned them, you'd still need to order the elements within the classes.

4.8.1.13 Spatial

Spatial
(for screens, physical objects)
e.g., maps, planets

Spatial is a way to show relationships of information in three-dimensional space to the reader. These relationships are conveyed by incorporating figures or objects, flowcharts, maps, and so on, inside a document in combination with other patterns. In these cases, there would be notations or pullouts to point to certain parts of the visual representation that are then referred to in the document text where more context or information could be provided.

For example, if you were going to show how to assemble some piece of furniture, the instructions would include multiple figures showing spatially how the pieces fit together, along with numbered instruction steps.

For example, you might have a research paper discussing the planets of our solar system beginning with the planet closest to the sun, and going out from there. To include other related data, your paper might offer a table comparing the planets by size, estimated weight, likelihood humans could live there (other criteria to provide information to the reader).

4.8.2 How to Insert a Pattern into a Document

To insert a pattern into a document to orient the reader to what they are going to read, there are three components to consider. They are not all necessary for all patterns. This table sorts out what to include for each pattern.

What to include	How to insert the pattern into a document	Use this option for these patterns
Heading and pattern	• Create a clear heading to orient the reader to what the section is about • Insert the pattern	• Indexed
Introduction or Purpose section and pattern	• Create a clear heading to orient the reader to what the section is about • Add an introductory paragraph or sentence that tells the reader how the section is organized • Insert the pattern	• Chronological (e.g., instructions) • Process (progressive level of disclosure) • Most important to least important • Least important to most important • Spatial • Classification and partition

What to include	How to insert the pattern into a document	Use this option for these patterns
Introduction, pattern, and conclusion	• Create and use clear headings for all sections • Heading *Introduction*, then explain the purpose and orientate the reader to the upcoming sections • Insert the pattern with proper headings • Heading *Conclusion*, then offer a "now what" analysis	• Inductive • Deductive • Compare/contrast • Problem/solution • Cause/effect

4.9 How to Combine Patterns

Most documents use a combination of patterns in the same document because you would need to get various ideas across to the audience in the same document.

When considering how to organize your work, if there's not an exact prescribed pattern that would work best or one that's not been used before, then for each section, consider how the information could be organized the best to convey your content and use that pattern for that section.

If nothing else presents itself as the pattern to use, then the default organization pattern is progressive level of disclosure. If the reader is trying to understand something, then this is the pattern to use.

4.9.1 Exercises

1) Look at any other reading: article, webpage, book, document, and so on. Look to see how each section as organized or how the document as a whole was organized.

a) Where did they follow these patterns discussed in this chapter?
b) Where did they use their own style?
c) What can you learn from the new variations? Is this a variation worth remembering that you could use yourself in the future?

2) Discuss how many different unique patterns can be used to deliver content given the following topics. Use the equation: **organizational pattern = purpose + delivery (audience).** Turn this equation into a table with columns: (purpose), (audience/delivery), (pattern) to identify all the possible patterns for each topic. The **purpose** may be provided with the topic or you may need to make it up.
   a) Why did you choose your university/college?
   b) Registering for courses at your university/college.
   c) Reducing the time required to register for classes or to change your schedule at your university/college.
   d) Increasing the ties between your university/college and local business/industry
   e) Preparing someone for a job interview
   f) Reasons you choose your university/college
   g) Three most important changes you'd like to see at your university/college
   h) Student organizations on your university/college campus
   i) Your car's dashboard
   j) Current price of gasoline
   k) Come up with your own topic idea

3) What combination of patterns would deliver the following content? Organize your answer in a table with the following columns: (information that needs organizing), (pattern), (how is the pattern used), (how is the information shown to the reader). Order the rows of the table based on the order the information is provided.

a) How are patterns combined in a typical recipe book (in the order they're used)?
b) How many patterns are combined in a traditional resume (in the order they're used)?
c) How are patterns combined in a manual to assemble a lawn mower (in the order they are used)?
d) How are patterns combined to display a webpage of clubs at your university/college (in the order they are used)?
e) How are patterns combined to explain what you learned on a field trip to your manager/instructor (in the order they are used)?

EXERCISES ANSWER KEY

4.2.8 Inductive Exercises Answer Key

1) Learning JavaScript

Ideally, readers will have noticed that this paragraph does not have a future application other than the optional third point about what the audience should do after reading this document. It also has many redundancies in the beginning and takes the focus off of the author in the Everyone had __.

4.5.7 Instructions Answer Key

Answers for some of the exercises that have specific answers are here.

1) Examine these steps for making a Facebook post. Rewrite them according to the rules.
   a) The app needs to be open before you can post. Open up Facebook to the default menu.
      i. Open up Facebook to the default menu.
      The app needs to be open before you can post.

   b) Tap the "What's on your mind" textbox.
   c) Type a message.
   d) Add in any images you want to the post.
      Any standard photo type will do.
   e) Press send.

2) For the following steps on taking a scenic photo, assign a warning level (e.g., CAUTION, WARNING, DANGER)
   a) [CAUTION] Bring precautions against the weather for your camera.
      i. The camera is the main focus of attention. The consequence of not following this rule is damage to the camera.
   b) Position yourself at a high vantage point.
   c) [DANGER] Steady yourself into a comfortable and secure position to avoid falling.
   d) Take the picture.

3) Explain the difference between an instructions and a process document (Chapter 4.6).

   An instructions document provides a step-by-step guide to accomplish a task. A process document explains why the best current practices are the way they are. Both documents aim to help the reader accomplish a task the best way possible. Unlike a comparison document, the writer gives a clear answer. They also do not have a conclusion because there is no need for a next step to end the document.

4.6.7 Exercises Answer Key

Answers for some of the exercises that have specific answers are here.

1) Explain the differences and similarities between a process and an instructions document.

An instructions document provides a step-by-step guide to accomplish a task. A process document explains why the best current practices are the way they are. Both documents aim to help the reader accomplish a task the best way possible. Unlike a comparison document, the writer gives a clear answer. They also do not have a conclusion because there is no need for a next step to end the document.

2) Order these progressive levels of disclosure headings for operating Snapchat

- **a)** Establishing your profile
- **b)** Finding friends online
- **c)** Making conversations with friends
- **d)** Making public posts

3) Identify which of these headings would be suited for process and which for instructions. Explain why.

- **a)** Creating an Instagram account

  Instructions, because there are specific concrete steps that need to be taken in order to create an account.

- **b)** Understanding Facebook groups

  Process, because there are multiple concepts that need to be expressed instead of a directions with specific order.

- **c)** Finding community on Meetup.com

  Process, because this has more general and abstract practices that could be used to find community.

- **d)** Making a contacts list through Gmail

  Instructions, because there is a specific order that needs to be followed in order for the task to be accomplished. There is no best practice here.

4.9.1 Exercises Answer Key

1a) Why did you choose your university/college?

Purpose	Audience/delivery	Pattern
How do I get educated for the job I want? Show how this university/college can solve this problem	Parents	Problem/ solution
What school provides the best learning/ tuition for the degree value proposition?	Parents	Cause/effect
Persuade audience that university/college is the best school for my needs, making each reason an argument	Parents	Position paper
Order list of reasons by the criteria of importance	Prospective student	Most important to least important
Decide which school is the best for my needs? Compare to other schools that offer similar degree	Prospective student	Compare/ contrast

2a) How patterns are combined in a typical recipe book (in the order they're used)?

Information that needs organizing	Pattern	How used	How the organization is shown to the reader
Book of recipes	Classification	Tells the reader what class of information is in the book. For example, dinner recipes, seasonal recipes, or regional foods.	Book title Distinguishes from all the other recipe books the audience might be considering

Information that needs organizing	Pattern	How used	How the organization is shown to the reader
Each section of the book	Classification	Organized by the classification of the book title, for example: • If the book is about regional foods, the sections might be organized by time: breakfast, lunch, dinner, desserts • If the book is organized by a particular ingredient, then the sections might be organized from easy to hard	Table of contents
All the recipes in each section	Based on a criterion to organize	Recipes in a section are organized to aid browsing, usually combining the classification of the book and the dishes. They might be organized by, for example: • Ease of creation (easy to hard) • Number of ingredients needed (small to large) • Time to create (short amount of time to more time)	Table of contents Could be included in an Index too

Information that needs organizing	**Pattern**	**How used**	**How the organization is shown to the reader**
Each recipe			
Image. What the dish looks like plated	Spatial	(If present) Shows the reader what the dish could look like served on a plate, with garnishes	Picture
Context: when to use, how to use	• Inductive (narrative) • Summary • Abstract	(If present) Offers an orientation to the reader, like when the recipe might be used (time of day, season of the year, event), or maybe a personal story of when the author has used the recipe to best effect	Introduction
All the stuff to put into the dish	Classification	Separately lists the wet ingredients from the dry ingredients in baking to combine in different dishes	List of ingredients
	Chronological	Ordered by when (time) they are added to the dish. This is why a recipe says "Salt and pepper to taste" as the last instruction	
How to make it	Instructions	Tell the reader each step to create the dish	Instructions
List of contents by name	Indexed	An index may be organized by the recipe title, which means the reader needs to know its name, OR there may be an index by main ingredients to search all recipes that contain that ingredient	Index in the back of the book

Perfect Common Parts of Your Writing

This chapter covers the various parts of a document that are common, optional depending on the writing content, and sometimes misunderstood.

5.1 Writing Introductions and Conclusions

Two common parts of writing are the introduction and conclusion. These play a specific role for the reader and are discussed in this section.

5.1.1 Writing Introductions

The purpose of an introduction is to orient the reader to the rest of the document – to set the reader's expectations about what they will read. It is not designed to summarize the document for the reader.

At the same time, introductions do *not* need to entice the reader to read the rest of the work. This perception to entice the reader originated with

English Composition where you were taught to make the introduction enticing. However, in business and technical, the reader must read the work to get their job done, so they don't need to be enticed to read it.

NOTE: Sometimes writers are confused about the difference between an *introduction* and an *abstract*, so abstracts are covered later in this chapter.

5.1.1.1 Tasks of the Introduction

The introduction needs to resolve the following tasks: two are required, one is optional.

1) Cover the purpose of the writing, concisely.

The purpose is why the document was prepared for the reader or why the reader would need to read it. For example,

- For compare and contrast, the purpose statement could be the audience acknowledgment stating the decision.
- For research or analysis, the purpose could be explained in the research question.
- For persuasive, the purpose could be the thesis statement.

2) Prepare readers to comprehend the rest of the work – that is, to help the reader understand how the information that follows is organized. For example,

- For compare and contrast, the orientation is informed by the list of subjects and determining criteria.
- For problem/solution, this orientation is provided in the sentence that forecasts the type of solution or in the list of the solutions discussed in the body of the work.
- Using the direct form of orientation always works, such as This paper covers __ or This document covers__. Readers appreciate directness.
- Using personal directness of a scaffolding orientation statement works, but can sound awkward, such as In this paper, I will discuss __. These personalized scaffolding statements are frequently found in academic writing.

3) Optionally, the introduction can encourage the reader to continue reading – to keep flipping through the document.

The encouragement is in the form of some additional information that lets the reader know that the information they are looking for exists here. This is not the same as enticing a reader to read a document with a literary hook or vague language to lure the reader to keep reading. This optional encouragement is concrete, not vague.

5.1.1.2 Overview of the Introduction Structures for Common Patterns

Pattern	Tasks	What's in the introduction or purpose section
Compare and contrast	Purpose	Somewhere in the introduction say "compare and contrast," since the reader is looking for a comparison. Then the list of subjects prepares them to continue reading.
	Orient reader	Providing the list of criteria orients the reader to how to read the rest of the document.
Process	Purpose	Process has a special section at the front that is the purpose statement, telling the reader why they are reading this process.
	Orient reader	Somewhere in the purpose, forecast the list of topics that are covered to orient the reader to the contents or provide a table of contents.
Position	Purpose	The introduction should only explain what the reader needs to know to understand the thesis. Additional content can distract the reader.
	Orient reader	The thesis explains to the reader what the paper is trying to prove to be true and orients the reader to rest of the writing.

▶

Pattern	Tasks	What's in the introduction or purpose section
Problem solution	Purpose	By explaining the problem to the reader, explains the purpose. By, explaining why the problem is serious can encourage the reader to want to solve the problem now.
	Orient reader	The orientation is provided in the sentence that forecasts the type of solution or in the list of the solutions discussed in the body of the work.

5.1.1.3 Bad Advice or Pitfalls of Writing Introductions

It's common for writers to remember advice once given about writing introductions that no longer applies.

With business and technical writing, the following advice is considered bad advice because the reader knows they need to read what you've written since otherwise they can't get their job done. Therefore performing these tasks can seem contrived and annoy the reader.

- Make the introduction snappy or clever.
- Hook the reader.

At the same time, the following pitfalls should be avoided when writing introductions:

- Writing the introduction as only one long paragraph – An introduction that handles the two tasks and one optional task can be done in just a few sentences. If your introduction needs to be longer, then consider breaking it into multiple paragraphs. Creating one long introductory paragraph turns off your reader from reading it and maybe even the rest of your work.
- Knowing when to stop including content – The introduction *only* introduces the work; it does not summarize the work to follow. Introductions should only include what the reader needs to know to be oriented to read the rest of the document.

NOTE: If you have a long introduction, you might be putting too much content into it or have begun to include writing that should be in the body of the work. Even with long documents (10–20+ pages), an introduction can still be short: one page.

- Being obvious – Saying In this paper, I will discuss __ is redundant. If your name is on the paper or the email came from you, they know it's from you. Plus that saying is six words where This paper covers __ is only three words, providing efficiency in your writing. Or better yet, just begin the discussion and skip all such preparatory phrasings.
- Using the future tense (will) – Very often authors start writing with the introduction and they haven't written the rest of the document yet, so they use phrases, this document will, because in the mind of the author it doesn't exist yet. However, when the audience reads that statement, it also tells them that that content doesn't yet exist, which is rarely the impression the author wants the reader to have.
- Apologizing – Saying I don't have much information about __ or I didn't get to include __ does not give the reader confidence about what they are about to read.

  Instead by providing a clear orientation statement in the introduction that explains what the document covers, then a smart reader would go someplace else, if your document doesn't include what they want to know.
- Using well-worn statements – With the growth of technology __ is a great example of a well-worn statement often used when an author doesn't know how to begin their work. The problem with a well-worn statement is that they are too common, can mean anything, and thus don't provide any useful content to the reader. Avoid them.

5.1.2 Writing Conclusions

The corresponding bookend to an introduction is the conclusion. Not all writing requires a conclusion, but when you're writing one, it has specific requirements. In business and technical writing, and even scientific writing, the conclusion is designed to cover the writer's *conclusions* about the material covered in the document. It is never a summary.

NOTE: Sometimes writers are confused about the difference between a *conclusion* and a *summary*, because in English Composition, a conclusion is merely a summary. Summaries are covered later in this chapter.

5.1.2.1 Tasks of the Conclusion

The conclusion is designed to help orient the reader to what comes next after reading the document. The conclusion has two parts: the topic sentence and the rest of the conclusion.

1) Topic sentence – The topic sentence of a conclusion is the main point of the document, but not a word-for-word repeat. You don't want to be redundant. This sentence ought to be the only summary found in a conclusion section of your writing.

   NOTE: If you want to write a summary, then don't call it a conclusion; call it a summary.

2) Purpose of the conclusion – After the topic sentence, the purpose of the conclusion is to tell the readers what they need to know now that they know all they've read and understood in the document so far. This is where you, essentially, answer the question "now what?" – now what does the reader do with this knowledge you've provided them?

   NOTE: Avoid writing the conclusion as a *reminder* of what has been said or to stress key points of the document contents – these would turn your conclusion into a summary.

5.1.2.2 Overview of the Conclusion Structures for Common Patterns

Pattern	What's in the conclusion
Compare and contrast	Topic sentence reframes the subjects and criteria, followed by bullets that are "if" statements for the criteria that help the audience make the decision
Inductive	Done in three parts: **1)** Conclusion(s) of what you'd learned **2)** Statement of how the author will apply the learning in a new way later in their life **3)** (Optional) Explain how the audience can use the lesson in their own life
Problem solution	Assuming the reader is still unsure whether to pick the solution identified in the body sections, the conclusion section explains why the solution is the best one to solve their problem. In the case of multiple solutions, this is one place where the author can explain how to choose between the various solution options (without using "if" statements, which are reserved for the objection handling or C/C conclusions)
Process	No conclusion exists, since there's no "now what" to process
Position (or persuasive)	The topic sentence reframes the thesis and then answers "now what." Examples might be the following: • Add significance or application • Call for more research • Make a recommendation or a prediction • Identify why this is important to address in <identify a time frame>

5.1.2.3 Bad Advice or Pitfalls of Writing Conclusions

English composition teaches students to write a conclusion as a summary, reminder, or selected key points of what was covered in the document. However in business and technical writing, the reader does not want a summary, that is, they do *not* want to reread what they've already read. That only wastes their precious time. So never summarize in a conclusion in technical writing.

If you're going to create a summary, then name it that in the heading. In business writing, a summary is typically created for busy managers and executives, called an "Executive Summary" and placed at the *front* of the document (see Chapter 5.2).

5.1.3 Exercises

1) Look at your recent writings of introductions and conclusions.
   - **a)** Be sure that headings or transitions exist that make those sections clear for the reader.
   - **b)** Analyze each sentence in the introduction to identify the role it plays of the two tasks and optional task. If the sentence has another role, then it probably belongs elsewhere in the document or maybe is not needed.
   - **c)** Analyze each sentence in the conclusion and identify whether the topic sentence exists and remains as the single starting sentence. Are there any places where the role of the topic sentence is repeated? Does the rest of the conclusion provide a clear "Now what"? If other sentences do not contribute to these two roles, then it could be better suited elsewhere or maybe is redundant.

2) Analyze the Chapter 1 of this book. What parts solve the requirements of the introduction? What makes it a strong introduction?

3) Explain why there is no "conclusion" chapter to this book.

4) Find an introduction and a conclusion for a topic. It could be your own writings or an online source. Write a summary of the paper or source that corresponds to the introduction and conclusion – with assistance from Chapter 5.2. Analyze and write down what the given introduction, conclusion, and summary achieve.

5.2 Writing Abstracts and Summaries

The context of abstracts and summaries in this writing is based on a *business work setting*.

NOTE: When writing a summary/abstract in a *scientific setting* (Biology, Chemistry, Physics, etc.), they are the *same* concept, and you write it, like for a journal article, as a summary, even if it's called an abstract.

5.2.1 Requirements for Writing Abstracts and Summaries in a Business Setting

This table presents an framework of notable differences between abstracts and summaries.

Requirements	**Abstracts**	**Summaries**
Dictionary definition	"Summary" is the first definition. Even so, there are connotative differences in a business setting	To reduce in size, provide the highlights of the original
Purpose	To entice a reader to read the larger document that is attached to or accessible from the abstract. In this context, an abstract is like a movie trailer that entices the audience to see the movie or how the back of a book blurb entices the reader to read a book.	For general summaries, they summarize a larger document so the reader can avoid having to read the larger document from which the summary was derived. For executive summaries, included with the original document, they make it possible to get by with just reading that summary and selected parts of the original document.

▶

Requirements	**Abstracts**	**Summaries**
Audience	May be interested in the topic, and can become more interested to read the full document after reading the abstract.	Busy; do not need details, or do not have time for all the details at this moment. By reading a summary, the reader can get the information they need to get their work done.
Where is it located?	Usually located *separate* from the rest of the document. In a report, it's on the title page. If the goal is to get the reader to download the paper from the company webpage, then the abstract is accompanied by a link (usually for the price of the reader's email address and other private information).	General summaries are usually located *separate* from the original(s) they are summarizing, since the reader isn't intending to read the original documents. Executive summaries are located in the *front* of the original document between the title page and table of contents (TOC), so that the reader can read the summary, turn the page to the TOC, then find whatever other sections they want to read for details.
In-text citations allowed?	No, because it is a separate entity conceptually, so it cannot cite other sources that are resolved in the original document (since it's not available).	For general summaries, they can cite the original, and include a reference section that lists all original sources. For executive summaries, they are considered a separate entity, so they cannot cite other sources. Likewise, an executive summary is *not* like a "prologue" to a book and thus should not refer to later sections of the document.
POV	3rd, even if the rest of the document is in another POV	3rd, even if the rest of the document is in another POV

Requirements	Abstracts	Summaries
Pace	Fast, so that the reader quickly dives into the document	Medium
Tone	Enticing, you want to write it in a way that encourages the reader to read the original document. This can be a little chatty if it entices the reader. Avoid overly chatty language, as that sets more of an informal tone.	For a general summary: Conclusive (formal), you want to write it in a way that is authoritative and complete, so the reader feels okay about not reading the full original document For an executive summary: Formal. Never chatty. Even if the original document has a different tone.
Organization pattern	Large ideas only to entice reader order in progressive level of disclosure order. Can use questions to entice reader (but not too many that would overwhelm or confuse the reader).	For a general summary, use a story telling mode, where it unfolds the information starting with the largest concepts, then information that leads from that information – progressive level of disclosure. For an executive summary, follow the exact order of original document, where each section is summarized into the main points for the reader.
Ethical scenarios	Mentioning/enticing the reader about content not covered	Not mentioning all the main points of the original document Bringing up points not in original doc Personal bias, twist, or exaggeration
Delivery	Use the same page layout as where it is located	Use the same page layout as where it is located

Requirements	Abstracts	Summaries
How to write (read more in Chapter 5.2.3)	**1)** Brainstorm what can entice a reader to go into the document. By analogy, for a movie trailer, if it's a comedy, you would see funny scenes; if it's a Disney animated musical movie, you would see the character sing a few lines of the song. **2)** Organize into progressive level of disclosure	**1)** Brainstorm all the main ideas of the document **2)** For a general summary, organize it into progressive level of disclosure. For an executive summary, follow the exact order of original document putting different major section information into separate paragraphs.
Word limits/ lengths	Could be limited by where it is placed. If the abstract is part of a journal article, then it is placed in a database that can be searched. The database field for the abstract is likely limited. If the abstract is placed on a webpage to draw attention to the corresponding document, then its length is limited by the readers' attention span when they arrive at that page, usually 100 to 150 words, up to around 500 words (if formed into multiple paragraphs).	General summaries ought to be kept as short as needed for the busy reader. Consider around 10% of original works. Executive Summaries should be kept to 1 to 5 pages based on the length of the original document (~20–100 pages).

Requirements	Abstracts	Summaries
Examples in business (See samples at the end of this section)	Found at the beginning of articles, position papers; on websites "paper available for download" where reader gives their email to receive. Seen in research papers, article searches in databases.	General summaries are seen in business when busy managers ask an employee to research a topic and summarize it for them, so they can get up to speed quickly. Executive summaries are found at beginning of long documents, business plans, proposals, product designs, etc.
Cognitive skill	What would inspire a reader to read the original document? Thinking about what to say that would encourage the reader to read more.	Deciding the big details from the small details; what's important? You want to only include the main points, conclusions, and important details, not try to summarize all the small details too.
Writing skill	Writing enticingly and writing concisely	Writing concisely. And organizing all the main points (minus all the minutia). Requires good use of transitions to signal shift.

5.2.2 What to Produce: Abstract or Summary?

By now, it's clear that abstracts and summaries are not really as similar as you might have thought because they have very different purposes and audiences. Unfortunately, most people don't know this, and they use these words interchangeably.

Thus, it becomes your job to discern the context of what the audience, or requester, really wants you to write and then write that. To make this determination, you might consider determining the purpose or goal of what you're being asked to write.

5.2.3 Writing Abstracts and Summaries

Once you know you need to write one of these, you need to identify what information out of all the information in the document needs to go into the abstract or summary. There are two parts to this task: determining what is important and organizing it into a story. Furthermore, there are special considerations when revising your drafted work.

5.2.3.1 Ways to Determine What's Important

To find out what is important to include in your abstract or summary, there are specific places to find that information in a well-ordered document. The following list offers places to examine:

- Look at the title or subject line
- Look at headings, subheadings, or the original outline
- Look at the orientation statements after the major headings
- Look at the introduction that explains the document purpose and orients the reader to the structure of the document
- Look at topic sentences
- Pay attention to key words: terms (but don't define terms in the abstract or summary)
- For a summary, pay attention to transitions that can indicate scope change or interpretation, for example, "results"

5.2.3.2 Analogy to Abstracts/Summaries: Telling a Story

If you're still wondering how to determine what's important when identifying content for an abstract/summary, you can use the analogy of telling a story when thinking about how to organize an abstract or summary.

You are familiar with storytelling; you already know ways of organizing random information into a story form, since most of us tell stories to our friends and family all the time. For example, someone might say to you, "Tell me about your weekend." That's an invitation to tell a story: a summary, if you will. Since that invitation was not request for a full rendition of every weekend activity, you would need to sort through all your experiences and find the most important parts to cover.

Likewise, once you've identified the important parts of an original document that needs to be covered in the abstract/summary, then you can organize the ideas in the form of a story. A story has only one starting point that meets the purpose of the story. Start there. Then add the next part of the story, and so on, until the whole story is told.

Stories can be told differently, which means that your voice, or storytelling mode, shows up in the writing of an abstract or summary. As much as possible, you'd want to match that storytelling tone to the situation, just as you would match your story to who is hearing it, for example, a manager or executive versus your friend.

5.2.3.3 Revision Reminders

Once you've written the abstract or summary, as with any writing, it's important to revise the work. This section identifies special considerations for these small pieces of writing.

- Audience analysis – Assume your audience has interest in the topic. The purpose of these writings is not to generate interest.
- First sentence – Always avoid having the first sentence of your abstract and the first sentence of your introduction be the same. If the reader sees the same sentence in the Introduction after reading the abstract, they may feel that too much is duplicated and to avoid wasting their time, skip important content.
- Verb Tense
  - Use past tense. These are written in the past tense.
  - Avoid future ("will") – Sometimes there's the urge to write the abstracts in the future tense ("will") with the idea that the reader is about to read

that content in their future. However, to the reader, the future tense says that the content doesn't exist yet, but is still to come in the future. That is rarely the impression you want the reader to have.

- Using present tense – You would use present tense if the activity discussed in the abstract is still ongoing at the time the reader is reading the abstract. As you revise your work, determine whether the action is continuing still; if so, then use present tense.

- Sentence subordination – Use subordination to condense information (read more in Chapter 9.1.1).
- Word choice – Use only words with weight. Being concise means that every word counts (read more in Chapter 9.2).
- Background – Do not include history, definitions, or other introductory information. Do not define acronyms, terms, jargon, and so on. If the reader doesn't know a term, then they will look it up.
- Citations – No in-text citations. Do not include quoted material or in-text citations or references to sections of the original document or its figures/tables. These writings should be able to stand alone, with the exception of a General Summary.

5.2.4 Sample

The following abstract and summary samples refer to the content in this section.

Abstract Sample

The section explained how abstracts and summaries can be seen as interchangeable in the scientific community; however, in the business contexts, their purposes differ significantly. Their content is also geared for specific audiences. In order to make an abstract or summary, the author describes how to identify the important ideas out of the material. These should be placed in an abstract or a summary. Once written, the author provides points of revision to edit the abstract or summary.

(78 words)

General Summary Sample

According to this section, abstracts and summaries in the business context have different purposes in order to serve their respective audiences. Abstracts are meant to draw the reader in with general information so that they become interested to read the rest of the document. Summaries are meant to give insight into all of the information in the document that the reader must know so that they can avoid reading the entire document.

Not everyone knows the difference between an abstract and a summary, so the chapter advises the writer to consider which format best serves the requested task and the context of the writer's audience. Once they know what format to write, the writer also needs to identify what information is important to record and to organize the information into a story.

The author gives various locations and indicators such as the introduction, headings, and topic sentences where important information can be found. These indicate what the main ideas of the text are. The author provides the analogy of crafting a story to describe the process of making an abstract or a summary. Like an orderly story with a beginning and an end, the writer needs to place the main ideas in a comprehensible order to make a coherent abstract or summary. In addition, when someone tells a story to their friend, they shift the story to match the context of the friend in the given setting. Similarly, writers of abstracts and summaries also need to consider their purpose and their audience.

After writing up an abstract or a summary, the author reminds the writer to go back and revise it. The writer must ensure that the writing follows the conventions of its format, such as using past tense verbs and taking out any work that requires a citation. The author also gives tips to shorten the text by using sentence subordination, making concise word choices, and leaving out historical or introductory information.

(323 words)

5.2.5 Exercises

1) Practice writing summaries of lectures after your classes. It is a good practice, and you can use the write-up later as you study for exams.
2) Find a previous paper that you wrote. Write an abstract for the paper.
3) Make a summary and an abstract of your day.
4) Identify three places in your life where you require summaries and abstracts.

5.3 Creating a Table

Tables reduce the amount of text that a reader needs to read to to get the information they require, thus making it possible to deliver the content quickly to the reader. However, not all tables are created the same. It depends on how the reader wants to digest the information you're providing.

5.3.1 Choosing the Type of Table to Use

This section explains two ways to construct a table: as a shortened form of paragraph and a comparison summary table (as seen in Chapter 4.3).

5.3.1.1 Table as Shortened Paragraphs

If you're abbreviating paragraphs of text into a table, the reader would read the table as a series of rows. Each row would be like the paragraph of information broken down into separate columns.

For example, when you look at a course syllabus, you might see policies that govern the class/course. That could be written as a series of headings and paragraphs, or it could be done as a table. A benefit of this paragraph-turned-table is that it ensures that the reader gets consistent information for each topic area. For example, in a series of paragraphs on Class Policies, the instructor might forget to mention how the policy was going to be enforced.

This inconsistent delivery of information is challenging for readers, as it opens questions not immediately answerable.

Class Policies

Policy	**Description**	**Enforcement**
Due time	Assignments are due at the time class begins, so that during class time, students can build further knowledge based on the homework.	See late policy
Late policy	Any work turned in after the due time will have 10% of the assignment's worth deducted each day until it's turned in, or three days have elapsed, then it's worth no credit.	Done automatically by the course management system

Likewise, a business could also construct a table of policies that could be included in their employee handbook.

Business Policies

Policy	**Description**	**Enforcement**
Privacy policy	Customer information is only accessible by the customer and is securely protected from cyber attacks.	Checked through monthly penetration testing
Return policy	Any product or service can be fully refunded if the customer completes the online refund form on the company website.	Verified through email confirmation of completion and validity

5.3.1.2 Table as a Comparison Summary

A comparison summary table compares subjects based on an established criteria; they might be referred to a specifications chart/table in some technical contexts.

This special type of table is read by first reading across the heading row across, then reading down the columns. The column headings are, in order, criteria, followed by a column per subject. This is a common table form seen in any product specification chart. See Table 5.1 for the structure and a sample in Table 5.2.

Table 5.1: Comparison summary table structure

Criteria	Subject A	Subject B	Subject C
Criterion 1	Info re: A with 1	Info re: B with 1	Info re: C with 1
Criterion 2	Info re: A with 2	Info re: B with 2	Info re: C with 2
Source: Provide the full source for the information in the table cells here			

Table 5.2: *Comparison of Card Stock*

Subjects	Dimensions (Inches)	Price ($/Sheet)
White Dove	8.5 × 11	0.12
Heavyweight	8.5 × 11	0.10
Blush	4.5 × 6.5	0.06
Jewel	2 × 3	0.04
Recollections	5.5 × 7.5	0.08
Cardstock Paper. Michaels. n.d. Michaels.com. Accessed July 3, 2020.		

Only rarely are comparison summary tables organized with subjects as rows, and that would be if there are only a couple to few criteria that would ever be considered and instead lots of subjects.

The standard for creating a comparison summary table is to have the column order the criteria (or characteristics) followed by the subjects. Yet as you add more subjects, the formatting may break the portrait width of the page.

- For printed documents, then it's okay to switch to a landscape orientation for the table for that section of the document, then return to portrait orientation.
- For web design, you would need to adjust the font size or other characteristics of the table, or maybe even consider whether all the

subjects are needed, or how to organize the information so that it's easily viewed in a webpage.

5.3.2 Formatting a Table

With well-formed column and row headings, the table cell can have small fragments or can even be reduced to a number that would require sentences or paragraphs of text to get the same content across to the reader. As you may have already noticed, this book uses tables frequently to deliver related content quickly.

While it's easy to insert a table in a document, it's best to use these best practices of table formation so that the reader can quickly absorb the table content. Poorly formed tables or tables that are not consistently formed take time to understand, and thus lose their effectiveness.

A properly formatted table is shown in Table 5.3; the rules that went into creating that table follow.

Table 5.3: Demonstrating a well-formed table

Column heading	Column heading	Column heading	Column heading
Row heading	Table cell content	Table cell content	Table cell content
Row heading	Table cell content	Table cell content	Table cell content
Row heading	Table cell content	Table cell content	Table cell content
Source: Full bibliographic source where the information came from			

When designing and formatting any table, follow these rules for best results:

1) Start with a purpose/goal and use the purpose for the table title. Make the table title clear to its purpose, but avoid a table title that is so long that its text wraps to more than one line.

2) Design rows/columns so that as new information is added to the table, it easily grows *down* (by adding rows). Avoid growing tables by adding columns, as the table outgrows the page portrait orientation.

For example, Table 5.4 would break very quickly (i.e., no longer be able to be easily formatted) for a class with a large number of students. Meanwhile, Table 5.5 grows easily for any number of students in the class. Furthermore, by viewing Table 5.5, the instructor might see that there's something wrong with their class design, since students' papers turn-in rate declines as additional assignments come due.

Table 5.4: *Tracking student work*

Assignments	Student A	Student B	Student C
Assignment #1	On time	On time	On time
Assignment #2	Late	Late	Late
Assignment #3	Missing	Missing	Missing

Table 5.5: *Tracking student work*

Students	Assignment #1	Assignment #2	Assignment #3
Student A	On time	Late	Missing
Student B	On time	Late	Missing
Student C	On time	Late	Missing

3) Always label the first table cell as a *column* heading.

If your word processing software is sophisticated, split the cell crosswise and label it as a column heading underneath, and row heading like Table 5.6.

Table 5.6: *Tracking student work*

Assignments / Students	Assignment #1	Assignment #2	Assignment #3
Student A	On time	Late	Missing
Student B	On time	Late	Missing
Student C	On time	Late	Missing

4) Since we read left-to-right, order columns accordingly to build knowledge as someone reads the table, like Table 5.7.

Table 5.7: *Ordering left and right example*

Criteria	**Card Design A**	**Card Design B**	**Card Design C**
Approval Rating (*/7)	6	4	5
Price ($/Card)	0.15	0.09	0.10

5) Create a table title on the line before the table. Start with Table followed by a numeral number that increases for each subsequent table in the document, a colon, and then a title for the table (the table's purpose). See Table 5.8.

NOTE: The table title should not be placed *inside* the table (see Table 5.9) because it is used to identify the table to the reader. If it's placed inside the table, then visually, the table seems to spring up on the reader.

Table 5.8: *Sample table showing title above table*

Criteria	**Subject A**	**Subject B**
Row heading	Table cell content	Table cell content
Row heading	Table cell content	Table cell content

Table 5.9: *Sample table showing title inside the table*

Criteria	**Subject A**	**Subject B**
Row heading	Table cell content	Table cell content
Row heading	Table cell content	Table cell content

Alternatively, you can use a heading to introduce a table, as is done in this text.

6) Pick the table number sequence for each document and use it consistently. You have two alternatives for numbering tables.
   - Number tables sequentially as Table 1, Table 2, Table 3, and so on.
   - Number the tables using scientific notation only if you have section or chapter numbers. Then change the first number to correspond with the section/chapter number and second number for each subsequent table, as is done in this text.
     - ✓ Changing section/chapter numbers: Table 2.1., Table 2.2
     - ✓ Increasing for each new table in a section/chapter: Table 1.1, Table 1.2
7) Have row and column headings (for all rows/columns). This means that the very first column needs to have a heading that identifies what's in that column. Never leave the first column table cell blank.
8) Make column/row headings look different than the table cells, for readability.
9) Use grid lines in your table, so readers can see what lives in each table cell. Your reader should never guess what table cell information goes with what column/row headings.
10) Align the left edge grid of the table with the T in Table like in Table 5.10. In Word, when you create a table, the first column may jut out to the left and if so, it needs to be brought into alignment with the text.

Table 5.10: *Sample table showing improper table alignment with the table title*

Criteria	Subject A	Subject B
Row heading	Table cell content	Table cell content
Row heading	Table cell content	Table cell content

11) Always left-align the first column. See Table 5.11 for a misaligned table.

Table 5.11: *Sample table showing first column misalignment*

Criteria	Subject A	Subject B
Row heading get jagged	Table cell content	Table cell content
Row heading	Table cell content	Table cell content

12) Always align all cells of a column the same way. The eye jerks around if table cells in a column are not all aligned the same, like it does in Table 5.12.

Table 5.12: *Sample table showing problems with column/table cell misalignment*

Criteria	Subject A	Subject B
Row heading	Table cell content	Table cell content
Row heading	Table cell content	Table cell content

13) Use abbreviations the reader would know and sentence fragments to reduce table cell content inside table cells. That is, avoid creating complete sentences within a table – remember the purpose of the table is to reduce the text and delivery content quickly. Avoid ending punctuation. You may notice that this book break these rule in places where complete sentences with the corresponding ending period makes the most sense.

14) Use enough white space to read content easily in the table cell. See Table 5.13, where the table grid ought to be spread out to improve readability of the table.

Table 5.13: *Table showing poor grid spacing*

Criteria	Subject A	Subject B
Row heading	Info about Subject A	Info about Subject B
Row heading	Info about Subject A	Info about Subject B
Row heading	Place on teacher's desk	Info about Subject B

15) Avoid a heavy grid that is distracting to the reader, like Table 5.14.

Table 5.14: *Table showing heavy, distracting table grid*

Criteria	Subject A	Subject B
Row heading	Info about Subject A	Info about Subject B
Row heading	Info about Subject A	Info about Subject B
Row heading	Place on teacher's desk	Info about Subject B

16) If you're going to do math on a column of numbers, then right-align the column, so the numbers line up for easy computation.

17) Omit information that is not relevant to your purpose.

5.3.3 Integrating Tables and Figures into a Document with Titles

You'll notice in this text, tables designed for quick access to information are sometimes introduced with a heading. Alternatively, tables are introduced with a table title line. If you have a table title, then you need to refer to the table within the body of the text, before it appears in the text, followed by the table. This way, a table doesn't suddenly spring up on the reader.

Once you've referenced and shown a table/figure, you can refer to it again. Since it's already been seen, the reader knows where to find it.

NOTE: This rule applies for figures that have been introduced with a figure title.

The following additional rules apply when integrating tables/figures into a document using titles:

1) When referenced in the text, Table and Figure are capitalized and you use a numeral to identify the number as shown in the following examples:

- Table 1 shows where __.   Figure 1 shows where __.
- As shown in Table 1, the __.   As shown in Figure 1, the __.
- __ is reported in Table 1.   __ is reported in Figure 1.
- __ (Table 1) __   __ (Figure 1) __
- (See Table 1.)   (See Figure 1.)

2) Match the text reference with the title. That is, do not use table 1 or figure 1 to refer to Table 1 and Figure 1. You want the text reference to look the same as how it actually appears in the document. Likewise, avoid using the phrase fig 1 to refer to Figure 1.

3) Do not use location words as the text reference, such as the figure below since it's ambiguous, and tables/figures may move or there could be multiple figures "below" so the reference would be unclear. That's why there's a number, so you can use it for the reference. Likewise, avoid using both table/figure number and "below," that's wordy/redundant.

4) Tables and figures should be numbered *separately* (starting both at 1).

On occasion, some authors number both tables and figures sequentially. That's because for the author, it's easier to keep track of one list ("What's the next figure number?") than two lists ("What's the next table number?" and "What's the next figure number?"). However, for the reader, it's confusing to see "Table 1" followed by "Figure 2," followed by "Table 3," and so on.

5) When you reference the table/figure, that's the best place to discuss any information you want the reader to understand about the table/figure. A long discussion of a table/figure would follow the table/figure so that the reader would see the reference, see the table/figure, and then read the lengthy discussion. An example of a table and figure follows as their formatting is slightly different.

Here's a sentence to introduce the Table 5.15 before the table appears in the document. If the table needs to be explained that would appear before the reader sees the table.

Table 5.15: *Sample table*

Criteria	**Subject A**	**Subject B**
Row heading	Table cell content	Table cell content
Row heading	Table cell content	Table cell content

If you need to interpret the table for the reader, then that longer discussion occurs after the table in its own paragraph, so that the reader would see the reference to the table, see the table, and then read the table interpretation.

Figure Example:

Take somewhere in the paragraph to mention Figure 5.1 before the figure appears in the document.

Figure 5.1: *Sample figure*

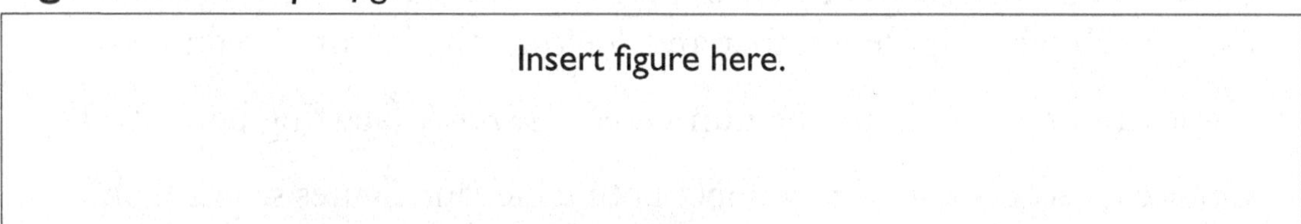

Use this caption space under the figure to interpret the figure for the reader, so that the reader would see the reference to the figure, see the figure, then read the discussion. This discussion is put in a caption that is a left and right indented and the paragraph centered under a figure.

6) Include enough white space on the page before and after the figure/table, so it's not crowded.

7) Provide a separate merged cell at the bottom of the table (like Table 5.16) for any Legends, Notes, or Sources (read more about source citing in Chapter 5.3.4).

Table 5.16: *Table showing merged rows for NOTE, Legend, and one Source*

Column heading	Column heading	Column heading	Column heading
Row heading	Table cell content	Table cell content	Table cell content
Row heading	Table cell content	Table cell content	Table cell content
Row heading	Table cell content	Table cell content	Table cell content
NOTE: Add any notes that relate to the interpretation of the table			
Legend: Add this row for any legend notations			
Source: Last name, First name. "Title." Publisher. Publisher date. Location. Access date.			

5.3.4 Identifying Sources in Tables

If the information in the table is not yours (you sourced it from someplace else), then you need to identify where the information came from. This information would be put in the last (merged) cell of the table so that the reader can find the source of the original information.

If the whole table's information came from a single source, then format the source as seen in Table 5.17.

Table 5.17: All information came from one source

Column heading	Column heading	Column heading	Column heading
Row heading	Table cell content	Table cell content	Table cell content
Row heading	Table cell content	Table cell content	Table cell content
Row heading	Table cell content	Table cell content	Table cell content
Source: Last name, First name. "Title." Publisher. Publisher date. Location. Access date.			

If your table was partly sourced from someplace else and partly from your information, then you need to use the documentary note system of citing where information came from, so the reader knows which information came from where. Place the notation in one of the following places to signal the reader what information was borrowed and from where as follows (see Table 5.18):

1) If you place the notation in the *column* heading, then all the information in that column came from that source.

2) If you place the notation in the *row* heading, then all the information in that row came from that source.

3) If you place the notation in a *table cell*, then only that piece of information came from that source.

Table 5.18: Properly formatted table with multiple sources

Column heading	**Column heading [1]**	**Column heading**	**Column heading**
Row heading [2]	Table cell content	Table cell content	Table cell content
Row heading	Table cell content	Table cell content	Table cell content
Row heading	Table cell content	Table cell content [3]	Table cell content
Sources: [1] Last name, First name. "Title." Publisher. Publisher date. Location. Access date. [2] Last name, First name. "Title." Publisher. Publisher date. Location. Access date. [3] Last name, First name. "Title." Publisher. Publisher date. Location. Access date.			

You might wonder why a full source is needed when showing the source in the table. That's because good tables get borrowed. If your table gets borrowed, once it's in another document, the full source can still help the reader find the original source.

Just like you wouldn't put a citation reference in a document heading, do not put the documentary note system reference in the Table title because if you create a Table of Illustrations, then the citation reference would show up there, and that's strange for the reader.

5.3.5 Using Word to Format a Table

You should assume that all documents are living: they will grow, shrink, can be borrowed from, and so on, throughout their life span. Therefore, it's important to format a table during initial creation using your word processor's table properties, rather than taking time every time you edit your document to rework all the tables in the document so that their formatting makes them easy to read. Rarely is that post-processing time available.

If you are using Microsoft Word, then use this list of tasks to perform on a table after you've constructed it so that it is automatically nicely formatted no matter where the table ends up in the document.

- So the column text won't wrap, adjust columns alignment.
- So headings repeat at top of next page when tables span page boundary, select table headings, Right-Click, select Table Properties, select Row tab, set Heading Row Repeat.
- So rows do not span a page boundary (it's easier to read a table across pages), select (whole) Table, Right-Click, select Table Properties, select Row tab, *disallow* "Row to break across pages."
- So the Table Title stays with table when colocated at a page boundary, select Table Title, Right-Click, select Paragraph, select "Line and Page Breaks" tab, set "keep with next."
- So the Table Title lays just above the table, without any white space, select Table Title, Right-Click, select Paragraph, adjust the "After" space to be "0."
- To create a row for Source, Notes, or Legend, select all cells in last row, Right-Click, select Merge Cells.

NOTE: Each of the Sources, NOTES, or Legend, must be in their own merged table cell so that the reader can easily find the information.

5.3.6 Exercises

1) Since the purpose of the table would be to deliver content quickly, see how each of the patterns can be converted into a table. While the whole pattern may not be able to be included in a table, the body of the pattern would fit nicely:

- **a)** Inductive: Create a table for the Experience section showing rows and columns.
- **b)** Persuasive: Create a table for the Arguments and Supports sections showing rows and columns.
- **c)** Process: Create a table for the Best Practices sections showing rows and columns.
- **d)** Problem Solution: Create a table for the solution sections showing rows and columns.

2) Find an online article with a table and analyze how that table followed the principles from this chapter:

- **a)** Does the context of the table's creation align with its purpose?
- **b)** How is the table structured? As a shortened paragraph table or a comparison summary table or some other variety?
- **c)** Could the table accommodate new information easily?
- **d)** How does the order of the row headers reflect the importance of the information? Would you change the order if you had the ability?
- **e)** How does the article space the table between other information.
- **f)** Was it referenced or did it spring up on the reader? What is your impression of how the table was handled?
- **g)** Was there text to explain the table? Where was it located and was it sufficient?

3) Read an article online that appears to show correlating information and turn it into a table, then analyze your results:

- **a)** Did you use a compressed paragraph table or a comparison summary table structure?

b) What were the column headings and row headings?

c) Was there information missing from the article, so that you had blank/empty table cells? Did you notice that information was missing when you read the article, and if so, did you find that confusing when you read the article?

d) If the article had originally been a table, would you have understood the content better?

5.4 Citing and Integrating Sources

This section focuses on the theory of integrating sources into your documents.

You've integrated sources before in your other writing. Maybe you knew exactly what you were doing. Maybe you tried something but didn't know whether you did it right. The goal of this section is to make sure once you've completed this reading that you can cite your sources and know that you've done it correctly with confidence, because citing sources will never go away, in school or in business.

5.4.1 Definitions

Citation – A citation is a way of giving credit to borrowed information, such as quotations, ideas, figures, words, facts, and even when you restructure borrowed information using your own words.

Paraphrase – A paraphrase means to reframe the original source wording, using your own words. This means coming up with a new sentence structure different from the original (not just replacing key words with synonyms).

Quotation – A quotation is when you use quotation marks (" ") around words that you've borrowed exactly from someone else. If you read words and put them inside your work in exactly the same order, then you need to quote them.

You can quote single words (especially required when you quote a word or phrase that was created or first stated by the author). You do not need to use quotes around commonly used words or technical terms.

If you quote a large number of words in a sequence in your document (e.g., around forty words according to the APA style guide), then you need to use a *block quote* in your document. The block quote needs to be in its own paragraph indented on each of the right and left sides.

5.4.2 How to Cite Sources: A Two-Step Process

There are two steps to citing a source. Both of these two steps are always required, when citing sources.

1) In-text citation

PURPOSE: This step has two purposes.

a) To tell the reader that an idea, fact, number, phrase, figure, table, image, and so on, in your work was borrowed from someone else.

b) To give enough information about that source in the in-text citation so the reader can correlate it with the list of references at the end of the document. The in-text citation information should be minimal (too much is distracting to the reader), yet contain enough information to enable the reader to quickly find the full bibliographic information at the back of the document.

NOTE: The The information in the in-text citation is always the same information that is at *the beginning of the line* in the reference at the back of the document, so that the reader can match up these two elements.

2) Reference at the back of document

PURPOSE: To tell the reader where to find the original source where the idea, fact, number, phrase, and so on, lives.

NOTE: Never use *just* a URL, anywhere.

Because both steps are always required, you should never use just a URL as an in-text citation, because it short-circuits these two steps into one.

Furthermore, a URL is never sufficient for the reference at the end of the document to explain where your source came from because they change and then the reader won't be able to find the original source, and even if it didn't change, it requires the reader to be online to find out where the information came from. Thus, your work is not a standalone document.

However, with the full reference information, the reader has enough information to find the source, if it's moved, and furthermore if the reader is not online presently, they can get a sense of the source of information by the citation information provided.

5.4.3 Why These Steps can be Confusing

Currently on the Internet, webpages combine these two steps into a hyperlink, and short-circuit the information so much, that only a URL is provided to highlighted text. In that one hyperlink, you know both that this information was borrowed and where to find the original source.

But even this new trend of hyperlinks has the flaw that URLs change or online information is taken down. So frequently, you can find that hyperlinks you try to follow in an online article may take you to a page-not found error.

Furthermore, academic document standards haven't caught up with this hyperlink trend. The belief is that your work is a standalone document, and does not require an Internet connection to help the reader understand what sources you used to ground your work.

Depending on where you work, you may find that your business may also ask for more of an academic citation form.

5.4.4 What Do In-Text Citations Look Like

This section shows sample citation formats and explains their differences. Last, this section mentions the rule to avoid wordy in-text citations.

5.4.4.1 Example MLA citations

- "If your audience is knowledgeable, you don't need to give a lot of background knowledge" (Calkins 49).

  This example quotes a person whose last name is Calkins. The words that are used can be found on page 49. All the rest of the information to find the original source is found at the end of the document.

- According to Calkins, "If your audience is knowledgeable, you don't need to give a lot of background knowledge" (49).

  This example moves the explanation of the author into the sentence. This sentence is a way of showcasing the original author's name to the reader.

- Calkins observes that a presentation can move more quickly if the audience is versed in the subject (49).

  This example both showcases the author's name, but rather than quoting the exact words, it paraphrases those words. Paraphrasing shows advanced effort as you must reframe the original text source – result, the new text is usually shorter than the original and keeps your tone of voice.

References

[1] Calkins, Tim. "How to Wash a Chicken". Publishers Group West, 2018.

5.4.4.2 Example of APA citations

- "If your audience is knowledgeable, you don't need to give a lot of background knowledge" (Calkins, 2018, p. 49).

  In the APA format, the date of the original publication is part of the format. APA requires the date in the in-text citation, because the people who use this format care about the age of information at the same time the reader learns the information was borrowed.

- According to Calkins (2018), "If your audience is knowledgeable, you don't need to give a lot of background knowledge" (p. 49).

The date stays with the author's name, separate from the page number.

- Calkins (2018) observes that a presentation can move more quickly if the audience is versed in the subject.

References

[1] Calkins, Tim. 2018. "How to Wash a Chicken". Publishers Group West.

Notice how the reference at the end has the information in a different order than MLA.

5.4.4.3 Example Documentary Note Citations

- "Calkins observes that a presentation can move more quickly if the audience is versed in the subject" [1].

  In the documentary note system, you can see that the only purpose is to identify that information was borrowed in this sentence. To find the full reference, the reader needs to look under that numbered reference.

  Another major difference in the documentary note system is that the notations use square brackets, [ ], not parentheses, ( ), as seen in APA or MLA.

References

[1] Calkins, Tim. "How to Wash a Chicken". Publishers Group West, 2018. Page 49.

NOTE: The reference in the back shares the same notation of use of square brackets. These are not numbered as in 1., 2. But [1], [2] so that they match what the reader saw in the paragraph text.

5.4.4.4 Always Avoid Word Phrasing When Citing

Whenever possible avoid wordy phrases that introduce the source (e.g., According to Calkins writing in "How to Wash a Chicken", published in 2018, he shows that __). These wordy phrases (sixteen words in this example!) make the audience read too much before they even get to the point you want to make. Instead just cite the fact and use one of the in-text citation methods described in this section or specified by your audience.

5.4.5 Why Do You Need to Know Different Citation Methods?

You need to be familiar with and be able to produce various citation methods.

- To do research and find original sources from any of the various methods.
- To find any original source no matter the citation method.
- To know how to produce citations/references in all the various methods. You don't know which one citation method you'll use for the rest of your life.
- Even with the Internet's one-step hyperlink system, the citation methodology won't go away or cease being important. Everyone will always want to have their ideas recognized when you borrow them.
- If you understand the theory, then you can use any method, or make up your own, based on the situation.

5.4.6 What Do In-Text Citations *not* Look Like in Technical Writing

While there may be some places that have decided to use different conventions, the use of superscripts, subscripts, and footnotes are not common.

5.4.6.1 No Superscripts or Subscripts

In business and technical writing, do not use superscripts or subscripts to denote in-text citations. This is because these forms use a smaller text font that are attached to words and raised/lowered from the words they are attached to. As a result, they are very easily lost to view to the reader in the writing. However, citations need to be visible at all times.

5.4.6.2 No Footnotes

Footnotes are not used in technical writing as a citation system.

A footnote is used to deliver extraneous information that is not needed for the primary purpose of the work. Normally, extraneous information in a document would be placed in parentheses. However, if that information grows to be too long to comfortably fit in ( ), then a footnote is used.

5.4.6.3 Use spaces

In-text citations need to have spaces before the opening parenthesis or opening square bracket. For those programmers whose coding style does not use spaces before a (, remember English is not code. Use spaces!

5.4.7 What Do Sources Look Like

Now that you understand in-text citations, this section covers their corresponding source details that are placed at the end of the document.

5.4.7.1 Heading Word for Sources

There are many options of the word to use in the heading to signal the list of sources and they cannot be used interchangeably. This word appears on a line by itself, formatted as a *heading1* (topmost heading in the table of contents), left justified on the page (not centered like in English composition).

Bibliography – Refers to *all* the information that informed your thinking, even if you didn't quote or paraphrase from one of these sources in your work.

References – It is similar to your bibliography, but is a word more commonly used in a business context than an academic context.

NOTE: The heading is "References" (plural), even if there is only one reference.

Works Cited – It refers to just the list of those sources that you cited in your writing. This list would in most cases be significantly shorter than the full Bibliography list.

NOTE: The heading is "Works Cited" (plural), even if there is only one work cited.

5.4.7.2 Each Bibliographic Entry Information

The bibliographic entries that follow its heading word always begin with the *same* name/words that was in the parentheses ( ) or square brackets [ ] used in the in-text citation. This is the most critical point of making citations work for the reader. Thus, the reader can scan down the list bibliographic entries quickly, reading only the first word at the beginning of each line to easily find the original source.

Never use information located later in the reference line in in-text citation (e.g., the publisher), because that would make the reader have to read every word in every reference looking for that word/phrase.

For example, using

> Calkins, Tim. "How to Wash a Chicken". Publishers Group West, 2018. Page 60.

means the in-text citation could only be (Calkins). You would never use ("How to Wash a Chicken") or (Publishers Group West).

5.4.7.3 General Form

The detailed information that you use as a bibliographic entry has the following pieces of information in the following order (assumes MLA format) and each element should be followed by the punctuation mark.

Shown as

Author. "Title of source." Title of container, Other contributors, Version, Number, Publisher, Publication date, Location. Type of medium. Date information accessed by you.

For any piece of information that is not available, then it is omitted.

NOTE: Bibliographic entries are never listed as bullets or numbered.

Examples

Yang, Fang-Ying, et al. "Tracking Learners' Visual Attention during a Multimedia Presentation in a Real Classroom." Computers & Education, vol. 62, no. 13, 2013, p. 208.

Theriault, Michel. "9 Tips For More Powerful Business Presentations." Forbes. Nov 4, 2013. https://www.forbes.com/sites/allbusiness/2013/11/04/9-tips-for-more-powerful-business-presentations/#3fe9ecb53089. Accessed July 2020.

No Author?

If you don't have the author's name, because there wasn't one, do not make one up. Omit that information, and make the first information on the line the title of the work. Put the title in "quotation marks" so that the reader knows this information is not the name of the author, but a title. Use "quotation marks" in the in-text citation as well: ("title").

Example

> "If you smile and make eye contact, you are building rapport, which helps the audience connect with you and your subject" ("Top Tips for Effective Presentations").

References

"Top Tips for Effective Presentations." SkillsYouNeed.com. 2011. https://www.skillsyouneed.com/present/presentation-tips.html. Accessed 9/15/20.

In some cases, you can use the name of a business/corporation as the author. Do not merely substitute a made up name or shortened website name for the author.

Example

> "There's nothing more impactful on people, their work, and their performance, than trust" (FranklinCovey).
>
> References
>
> FranklinCovey Co. 2020. https://www.speedoftrust.com/. Accessed 9/15/20

When not to Use Business Name as Author?

If you are citing many webpages from a site that has no authors and you've chosen to use the business name instead, then the references at the end of the document would be full of entries that each say "Business name. Rest of entry." That means that when you cite one of those webpages, you would have to distinguish between each of the entries that start with the business name.

Thus, when you use the business name as the author, you rarely gain clarity from a bibliography entry perspective, since the in-text citation would need additional information to distinguish the various entries with the same business name. In an author-date notation system, that would be the date. If the date is not present, as is often it isn't, then you need to use the "title" of the webpage.

So why not use the title anyway and skip the business name? Because you'd want to use the business name if knowing that business name in the text is important to inform the reader at the moment. Since if you don't have the author or date, you use the title.

Format Original Sources using Hanging Indents

All sources are formatted using hanging indents, whereas the text of the bibliographic entry wraps to the second lines and beyond, the information is indented from the first line. Again, this formatting makes it easy for the reader to find the information at the beginning of the line.

For example, comparing no hanging indent:

Yang, Fang-Ying, et al. "Tracking Learners' Visual Attention during a Multimedia Presentation in a Real Classroom." Computers & Education, vol. 62, no. 13, 2013, p. 208.

Theriault, Michel. "9 Tips For More Powerful Business Presentations." https://www.forbes.com/sites/allbusiness/2013/11/04/9-tips-for-more-powerful-business-presentations/#3fe9ecb53089.

To create hanging indents. See how much easier it is to find that information at the beginning of the line?

Yang, Fang-Ying, et al. "Tracking Learners' Visual Attention during a Multimedia Presentation in a Real Classroom." Computers & Education, vol. 62, no. 13, 2013, p. 208.

Theriault, Michel. "9 Tips For More Powerful Business Presentations." https://www.forbes.com/sites/allbusiness/2013/11/04/9-tips-for-more-powerful-business-presentations/#3fe9ecb53089.

To create hanging indents in Microsoft Word, select all your references; right click; select paragraph; under "Special," select "Hanging"; then adjust how far the subsequent lines are indented (default ".5" or maybe a smaller number if that works esthetically.

5.4.7.4 Order of Bibliographic Entries

Because information should never be random and because you want the reader to easily find the information you're providing, your sources should be ordered alphanumerically, which means alphabetically, but with numbers sorted before A's. In that way, for example, 3M would be at the beginning of the list, not ordered with the T's (for "three"). This correlates with the documentary note systems, as all entries are numbered in order [1], [2], and so on.

"Communication Compliance in Microsoft 365." Microsoft. Accessed July 6, 2020. https://docs.microsoft.com/en-us/microsoft-365/compliance/communication-compliance?view=o3 65-worldwide

Sullivan, Jay. Simply Said: Communicating Better at Work and Beyond. John Wiley & Sons, Inc. 2016. Page 15.

Or using the documentary note system

[1] "Communication Compliance in Microsoft 365." Microsoft. Accessed July 6, 2020. https://docs.microsoft.com/en-us/microsoft-365/compliance/communication-compliance?view=o3 65-worldwide

[2] Sullivan, Jay. Simply Said: Communicating Better at Work and Beyond. John Wiley & Sons, Inc. 2016. Page 15.

5.4.8 Citing Sources

This section provides clarity on why you would want to cite a source, when you don't need to cite a source, and when you would want to quote a source exactly (rather than paraphrase). In summary, you should cite borrowed information – assuming it's not common knowledge – but you may not always want to quote it.

5.4.8.1 Why Cite?

There are many reasons why you would want to cite information from a source. The following list offers many such good reasons.

- To use as evidence or add support to your idea – While your opinion counts, there may be times, when your viewpoint is better received by having an additional source that backs up what you're saying.
- To provide better credentials to an idea – If you need to offer credentials for an idea you have, so that it has more weight in the eyes of the reader, then cite another reputable person saying the same thing.
- To establish emphasis on a certain idea – When you cite their works, you are pointing out to the reader that this information has special importance, thus creating a sense of emphasis or attention on that borrowed idea. The reader is thinking, you could have supported any of your ideas, but you chose this particular idea of yours to support and you

chose to do it borrowing this particular piece of information; therefore, it must be important.

5.4.8.2 What Not to Cite?

In your work, you do *not* need to cite common knowledge. The concept of common knowledge is based on whether the *reader* knows the common knowledge (not the *author*).

Common knowledge is defined as any fact that is identifiable by *five different, general references sources*, such as the following:

- Dictionary
- Almanac
- Encyclopedia
- Known by the audience

Examples of common knowledge include the following:

- Current and historical events
- Famous people
- Geographic areas
- Common sayings
- Folklore

Because common knowledge is defined by the reader's knowledge level, *your concept of common knowledge, as the author, will change based on who the audience is, even for the same information.* For example, a group of doctors would know about a medical study in their field or a procedure, while a patient who needed the medical procedure would not have that same understanding of common knowledge. Thus, you need to understand your audience well or, instead, just cite your sources.

5.4.9 Quoting Sources

This section explains when to quote from the source.

5.4.9.1 Why Quote?

Quoting refers to borrowing the exact words from the author. In any writing, there are times when it's better to quote exactly from the source.

- Because you were asked to – You may be asked to quote a specific source in your work.
- To highlight the source – When the source of the material is a well-known expert or someone else carrying great authority (e.g., Bill Gates, the President). Sometimes the best way to get a point across is to show that someone well known said it.
- To change the tone – Even in technical writing where the writing is factual, direct, and concise, you have your own way of writing that is different than a colleague's. Quoting exact words from someone with a different tone/style of writing than yours changes the impression in your own work. Used deliberately and with careful attention to the effect, the result can be quite effective.
- To avoid blame – There may be times when you want to say something that is not an accepted idea, even though it's important to say it. However, if you say it, then you'll be known as the one who said it, and you don't want to be tarred with that claim.

  Thus, you could find someone else who said what you want to say, to avoid being blamed as the one who brought this point to light, and instead, you can be the one who pointed it out to others. Examples of heavily loaded words that may fall into this blame avoidance include "epidemic," "pandemic," "catastrophe," and so on, which would vary depending on your situation.

5.4.9.2 When Should You Not Quote?

In any writing, there are times when it's better to paraphrase the writing and skip the quote.

- Use of quotations gives the impression of a writer who has done very little thinking on their own. If your work needs to show your expertise of gathering and collating, or summarizing other people's work, then paraphrase and cite your sources.
  - For courses at a junior level, senior level, or above, it's more important what you've done with other people's ideas, not that you can quote them.
  - When you are writing for work in a business context or postgraduate academic level, the reader wants to know where you got your ideas, not what those sources said exactly. The reader cares more about what you have done with the ideas. For example, how they have informed or transformed your thinking.
- Paraphrasing is more efficient. Quotations break up normal reading by highlighting that author's work, which can be confusing to a reader or may not be the effect you want, see where the discussion of how a quote changes the tone of the work.

5.4.9.3 How to Incorporate a Quote

Incorporating a quote involves identifying its significance to the reader, building the sentences properly around the quote, using punctuation properly, and understanding proper use of long quotes.

The Three-Step Process to Incorporate a Quote

Now that you know when you should or should not quote, for completeness sake, here are the steps to incorporate the exact wording from another person into your writing. The point with these steps is to explain to the reader the significance of the quote you added, that is what you want the reader to get from the quote. *Remember a quote is never merely a replacement for your words. It was selected for a reason.*

1) Introduce the quotation with a sentence or phrase – Quotes cannot be dropped in somewhere. There needs to be some introduction for the reader to see that someone else's ideas are coming. You can introduce a quote with a full sentence if a longer explanation is required, or maybe just a phrase instead.

2) Insert the quotation – You'll only want to include from the original the words that are pertinent to your point or ideas.

3) Comment on the quotation – The last step is to identify the relevance to the quote in your work. Frequently this comment on the quoted work can come in the form of a phrase as "this shows __."

Other considerations when incorporating a quote or information from a source:

- Depending on the context of the writing and the quote itself, you can dispense with both Step 1 and Step 3, as long as you've provided the significance.
- If you use the words "According to author x" that author ought to be well known to the reader. For example, "According to President Obama." If the author is not well known, then don't mention them in the text. Instead, only cite them at the end of the quote.
- Never start a paragraph with a quote, that is, a topic sentence is never a quote.

Four Common Ways to Incorporate a Quote

There are multiple ways to incorporate a quote into your work. The basic rule of thumb about inserting a quote is that the quote should always make English sense, as if the " " had been removed.

1) Full sentence – in which your sentence provides context for their sentence:

Ian Tuhovsky acknowledges that anger should not be held in, so he points out a way to express it in the workplace safely: "If you want to express your anger in a healthy way and use it to create agreement and build better relationships, stop blaming others for your feelings and direct the beam of consciousness on your emotions and needs" (31).

2) Partial sentence – in which your sentence blends with theirs to create a single, functional sentence:

Ian Tuhovsky urges people that they can reasonably control their anger if they "stop blaming others for your feelings," so that they can focus on their "emotions and needs" (31).

3) Single word quote – your sentence employs only a single key word (or two) from the source:

Some among the communication field propose that anger is not necessarily directed at others, but rather, it is aimed toward the "needs" that remain "unfulfilled" within the angered individual (Tuhovsky 29).

How to Quote and Punctuate Properly, Together

- Ellipsis dots (...) are used to indicate deletions or omissions from a *direct* quote when you delete information from the *middle* of the quote. You will always delete from the front or end of a quote, so no . . . are needed there.
- When an ellipsis is at the end of a sentence, it is followed by a period. (Yes, that means four dots!) However, MLA guidelines call for the ellipsis dots to be placed in square brackets [...].
- Square brackets [ ] are used when inserting clarifying comments into a *direct* quote. Place the clarifying text in square brackets. For example,

  A manager needs to remember to talk to his [or her] employees every week, at least.

In this case, the author wants to ignore that the original author didn't account for women managers and merely fixes the gaffe.

- When quoting text with an obvious error, use [*sic*]. [Notice that *sic* is in italic font, because it is a foreign language. Foreign language words should always be in italic when they are used in an English sentence.] For example,

  A manager needs to remember to talk to his *[sic]* employees every week, at least.

  In this case, the author wants to point out to the reader that the original author doesn't understand that managers can be women too!

- If punctuation is part of the material quoted, it goes inside the " "; if the punctuation is not part of the material quoted, it goes outside the " ."
- Usually periods go inside quotation marks. However, if the sentence includes an in-text citation in (), then the period goes at the end of sentence, after the ().
  - Part of a sentence with "the quoted text" (citation).
  - Part of a sentence, identifies author, with "the quoted text."
- Commas and " " depend on quote location in the sentence:

  Ian Tuhovsky said, "the source of anger always lies in our thinking, beliefs, and attitude."

  "The source of anger always lies in our thinking, beliefs, and attitude," Dr. Julie Miller said.

- Semicolons and colons go outside closing quotation marks.

What to Do When There's Quotes within Quotes

If you have a quote from a document that has a quote in it, then you need to distinguish between them for the reader. The outer quotes use "double quotation marks" and the inner quotes use 'single quote marks.' That way the reader knows which is which.

For example,

> According to Laurie Anderson, "Technical writing offers 'cool' ways to learn how to communicate."

Block Quotes

A block quote is a special kind of quote that does not look like other quotes. It is one that is longer than two typed lines in your document. Follow these rules if you find the need to use a block quote:

- Put the block quote in its own paragraph.
- Indent that paragraph on left and right, to set it off.
- Do not use " " because the indenting shows it's a special kind of quote.
- Put (citation) *outside* the closing period.
- For most academic assignments that have a length requirement, you could not consider the words in a block quote as contributing to your work.

5.4.10 Review Exercises

To refresh your comprehension of this section, see the following questions:

1) When do you need to cite?
2) What don't you need to cite?
3) What are the steps to citing a source?
4) Under what circumstances do you need to cite your sources at the end of a document (e.g., References) if you have no in-text citations?

5) What various heading words are used before the full sources at the end of a document? How do the words indicate different contents?

6) In what order are the references always placed at the end of a document?

7) Why do you need to learn/understand different citation methods?

8) What information do you need to gather from a source to be able to cite it?

9) When should you quote? When shouldn't you quote?

10) How do you incorporate a quote in a document? What are the steps?

11) When/where/how do you cite yourself?

12) What's the difference between a) and b) when seen as an in-text citation?

    a) Sentence [1]. and Sentence (1).

    b) (Quick) and ("Quick")

13) What's the difference between the following when seen as an in-text citation?

    Sentence [1]. and Paragraph of text. [1]

14) If you weren't given a citation system to use, how would you choose one?

EXERCISES ANSWER KEY

5.3.6 Exercises Answer Key

1) Patterns converted into tables

    a) Inductive: Create a table for the Experience section showing rows and columns.

    Uses the time organization for the headings with incorporated reflection:

Heading	**Experience**
In the beginning	
In the middle	
In the end	

This table separates out the reflection into its own column:

Heading	**Experience**	**Evaluation of experience**
In the beginning		
In the middle		
In the end		

b) Persuasive: Create a table for the Arguments and Supports sections showing rows and columns.

This example table has a first column argument, then splits the cells of the corresponding table cells so that there're three supports/arguments along with the support analysis:

Argument	**Supports**	**Analysis**
Argument 1	Support 1	
	Support 2	
	Support 3	
Argument 2	Support 1	
	Support 2	
	Support 3	
Argument 3	Support 1	
	Support 2	
	Support 3	

c) **Process**: Create a table for the Best Practices sections showing rows and columns.

Once it's been converted to a table, and because we read left to right, it makes the most sense to start with the best practice, then add the explanation. If the work is constructed as a table, the reader is already predisposed to follow the best practice, so it can be first. Also, the explanation would be longer than the best practice, making this organization a faster reading structure.

Best practice	Explanation
Command/rule	Why explanation
Command/rule	Why explanation

d) **Problem Solution**: Create a table for the solution sections showing rows and columns.

Solution	Explanation	Alternative solution

If you have multiple, related problems that are being solved using different, related solutions, you could add the specific problem as a column:

Problem	Solution	Explanation	Alternative

6

Show Technical Writing Format for Your Delivery

This chapter covers various best practices, in the form of a table, on how to format your documents so that readers can quickly skim for the information they need. In general, your document page layout and design needs to be varied enough to make it possible to find what your reader is looking for, but not so varied as to distract from, and slow the comprehension of, the delivery of the material.

Remember that your reader is only going to read the part of the document that they need to read to get their job done. Rarely would the reader open the document and read from the first line to the last line, and then act on that information – there's just no time to do that. So your job as the author is to make your document as accessible as possible for the reader.

Writing element	Making a document quickly accessible to the audience
Document title or subject line	The document title or subject line (in the case of an email or memo) tells the reader what they are about to read. All documents need a title/subject line. Don't throw away this tool by leaving it blank or being vague. They need to be sufficiently detailed to help the reader understand when to take the time to read the work. NOTE: This is why an email should never have an empty subject line or say merely hey.
Headings	Headings allow you to break up long content into easily comprehensible chunks of information. They also act like a super topic sentence or transition to orient the reader to the information content in that section. That is, they tell the reader what they are about to read in enough detail so they know whether they can skip it (because they already know it or don't need to read it right now) or whether that's where the information they are looking for lives. Even short one-page documents, letters, and emails can benefit from using headings to break up a long series of paragraphs into smaller chunks to aid in accessibility. Headings need to be clear and precise. It's best if they are more than a word or word phrase, but a longer phrase with a verb. NOTE: The middle part of the work (the "body") should always have headings that describe their content. That is, there should never be a heading called Body – that's just too weird for the audience.
Section orientation	After a major section heading (e.g., heading1), you need to orient the reader as to what information is in that section of the document. This makes it possible for the reader to scan that section, and know whether they need to read further, or continue to another section for what information they need. This can be done with a direct phrase, such as This section covers ___ or In this section, ___. In that phrasing, avoid using will (as in will cover) since it's not in the future tense and the reader is about to read it. Realize that as a section is updated, this orientation ought to be refreshed for accuracy too.

Writing element	Making a document quickly accessible to the audience
Transitions	Transitions are used to tell the reader how ideas are linked together. The idea could signal an addition to the existing idea (e.g., "additionally") or a shift in topic to another idea (e.g., "however") or signal a result (e.g., "therefore"). There are different types of transitions in business and technical writing: • A heading can act as a transition. When well-formed, a heading can transition the reader to the new topic while also helping readers who are skimming looking for a particular topic. • A phrase at the beginning of a paragraph can act as a transition, such as the following sentence from Chapter 7.4 that signals a shift from the discussion of letters to the discussion of memos: *Where a letter is primarily used to send information to someone from one business/individual to another business/individual, a memo is reserved for delivering information inside a business.* • A single word or short word phrase, such as "additionally," "however," "therefore."
Paragraph size	The size of the documents' paragraphs need to match their audiences' attention span. The more likely your audience is to be interrupted (e.g., managers, executives), the trimmer your paragraphs need to be. Highly interrupted readers would keep having to reread large paragraphs to understand their multifaceted content. Correspondingly, highly technical writing with expert audiences would naturally have longer, more complicated paragraphs. In any case, long paragraphs are daunting to the reader.
Clear topic sentence	The role of the topic sentence is to tell the reader what is going to be in that paragraph. Clear topic sentences tell the reader whether they need to read that paragraph.

Writing element	Making a document quickly accessible to the audience
Use of tables/ figures (visual communications)	Tables help the reader get information quickly that would have been formatted in paragraphs of text. Figures help the reader understand information visually that would be difficult to convey in text. These provide rich mechanisms for you to deliver information for the reader. Therefore, just as you've learned to write sentences and paragraphs, you need to learn to create tables/figures, that is, to learn to train your brain to see where text can be condensed into a table or where efforts to explain something could best be shown visually.
Table/figure title (or its heading)	Tables and figures need a title to explain their purpose to the reader. That is, what is the reader supposed to take away from viewing the table/figure? One form is with a separate paragraph line as follows: Table 1: Table title or Figure 1: Figure title The other form is when the only element in a section is the table or figure (no corresponding paragraph discussion is necessary), then you can use a heading as the table/figure title. This form is used in this book (read more in Chapter 5.3 to get more best practices on tables).
Referring to table/ figure	If you have a separate paragraph line for your table/figure title, then you need to refer to in the text before it appears, so that it doesn't spring up on the reader or so that the reader doesn't miss seeing it. The text reference is also a place to locate any discussion about the table/figure that needs to be interpreted for the reader. See Chapter 5.3 for ways to phrase that text reference.

<table>
<tr><th>Writing element</th><th>Making a document quickly accessible to the audience</th></tr>
<tr><td>Use of bullets as lists</td><td>Use of bullets as lists make the reading faster (more accessible) and easier to remember for the reader. Consider as you generate writing, where a list in a paragraph could be more accessible as bullets.

Formatting bullets lists needs to be consistent:
• Use similar white spacing before and after the bullets to ease reading.
• Keep the white spacing evident, especially when the bullets wrap to multiple lines.
• Use similar bullet shapes to deliver content.
• Avoid indenting bullets inside table (like this list) which would be wasted white space.
• Use parallelism in your bullets, as much as possible for quicker comprehension (read more in Chapter 9.1.2).</td></tr>
<tr><td>Use of examples</td><td>Examples help the reader apply the knowledge you're providing.</td></tr>
<tr><td>Including a table of contents (TOC)</td><td>A TOC would be placed at the front of a document after the title page, after an executive summary (if it exists), so that a reader can see the full outline of the document. A TOC works for larger documents.

Whether you include a TOC in a short document would depend on the situation and audience. It's best to format your TOC with leaders (or...) from the headings that lead the reader's eye to the page number that would be flush right.</td></tr>
<tr><td>Including a table of illustrations (TOI)</td><td>A TOI lists all the table titles and figure titles with page numbers. A TOI is placed after the TOC in a document. TOIs are rare, except in scientific writing where there are lots of tables and figures in larger documents.</td></tr>
</table>

Writing element	Making a document quickly accessible to the audience
Inclusion of term definitions Inclusion of glossary	Term definitions may be included as a heading at the end of the introduction to introduce a series of terms for the primary audience. They are usually formatted as a table, for ease of viewing with columns: term, definition. Then the terms do not need to be introduced when first mentioned later in the discussion. Glossary is used for a long list of terms that need explanation for the reader, usually an audience when it's unknown how much background explanation is necessary, that is, if some readers would understand and others not. A glossary is at the end of the document in an appendix (e.g., Appendix A: Glossary of Terms). It can be organized as a table or as separate paragraphs per term, with the term at the beginning of the line using hanging indents, so the list can be easily scanned. Sort the list of terms in alphabetical order.
Headers, footers (see next line for page numbers)	Headers (not to be confused with headings – see above) are fixed information that can be configured for the top of every page in a document. Usually, the header contains the overarching information (e.g., document title). NOTE: You can configure the header not to appear on the first page, usually the desired result, so it's not cluttering up the first page of your delivery. You can also configure the header to have a different look for left/right pages, if you know you're going to format the final work in a book form. Footers are fixed information at the bottom of every page in a document. Usually the footer contains small details regarding the document (e.g., author's name, date last modified, date created). NOTE: You can configure the footer not to appear on the document's first page, usually the desired result, so it's not cluttering up the first page of your delivery.

Writing element	**Making a document quickly accessible to the audience**
Page numbers	Page numbers need to be in any technical document that is longer than two pages. Traditionally in combination with the header, they remind the reader the document they are reading and how far they've read into the document. They have always existed at the bottom of the page; however, now they could be inserted with the header, especially if there is no need for a footer. If your reader needs to know both what page they're currently reading and how many pages still exist in the document, then consider using the Page x of y form to help your reader pace themselves in their reading.
Clear use of proper point of view (POV)	POV tells the reader how to relate to the information they're reading. Clear use of POV keeps the reader engaged in comprehending the content. Improper use of POV (shifting to POVs in unexpected ways) makes comprehension difficult and slower, even impossible (see Chapter 3 for more on POVs, and find which to use in in the pattern summary table for the pattern you're using found in Chapter 4).
Clear establishment of TONE	Tone is the *impression* that you want the reader to be left with after they have read your work. Matching the tone to the delivery is similar to matching the color thread to the fabric. Mismatches are jarring. A consistent, professional tone is acknowledged unconsciously by the reader, while inexplicable changes in tone are slow comprehension. And in some cases, the reader may leave the document to find the information elsewhere. (See Chapter 3 for more on tone.)

Writing element	Making a document quickly accessible to the audience
Clear, precise word choice	Being deliberate in your word choice means your work can be seamlessly comprehended by your audience. Each word is critical to that success. • Using terms that the reader doesn't know slows their comprehension as they try to figure out the terms' meanings and return to your work. • Overuse of passive voice can confuse the reader as who is doing the action in the writing remains unknown. • Use of colloquialisms, abbreviations, clichés, and slang means that many audiences would not understand your meaning (See Chapter 9.3 for more on word usage and use Chapter 2 Stage 2 Revision for more on what to look out for as you revise your work).
White space	It may seem obvious, but you want to use good white spacing in a document. That spacing provides a place for eyes to rest as they read: too tight and the eyes get tired very quickly, yet too much, and the reader is confused because the large white spacing separates the structure so it is no longer visually accessible. White space also needs to be consistent. The amount of white spacing you use before a heading needs to always be the same. Soon as you make that different, the reader will began to get confused about your work.
Vertical alignment	When you use tabs or the → button or other indenting modes to adjust the vertical alignments in your work, you establish an outline correlation between the information. This is useful for the reader. Overused, it can create a document tone that gives the impression that is very rigid. Further, it increases the length of the document because there's less room on each line for content due to the indenting.

6.1 Exercises

1) Look at an older document you created or that you'd been given to read, and evaluate its accessibility based on the best practices explained in this chapter.
2) Rework an old document that is inaccessible to improve its accessibility based on the best practices explained in this chapter. Which change altered the accessibility the most?
3) When you're the reader, which of the writing elements discussed in this chapter do you consider the most important, that is, that help make a reading most accessible to you? Why?
   a) How would your answer vary as you are reading from a different reader's role (refresh your understanding of audience roles in Chapter 3)?
4) In all your revision work, you want to create a document that is low maintenance. Consider creating a "to-do list" of document formatting tasks in an order that minimizes your formatting time, while maximizing the document accessibility for the reader and decreasing the maintenance of the document. See Chapter 5.3 Tables for examples on how to format them for low maintenance as tables grow.

Use Letters Like Email

This chapter discusses letters, memos, and then discusses how emails act more like letters than memos.

7.1 Design of Three Letter Forms

A letter is primarily used to send information to someone from one business/individual to another business/individual.

NOTE: In rare cases, letters can be used inside an organization from one part of the business to an individual; for example, if human resources sent a letter of dismissal to an employee.

To structure a letter, you need to

1) Know the type of information you're going to deliver: good news, bad news, mixed news, or information in the form of a technical writing pattern (read more in Chapter 7.2).

2) Pick the letter form from the three basic forms: full block, semiblock, simplified, based on the type of information you're planning to deliver (read more in Chapter 7.1).

3) Put the information you need to deliver in the correct place in the letter (read more in Chapter 7.3).

   NOTE: *Front matter* refers to standard information that is always the same in the front of a form. Likewise, *end matter* refers to the same information that is always at the end of a form.

How to select which letter form to use, follow these steps:

1) Analyze the content to be delivered, which derives from the purpose. Is it . . . ?
   - Good news
   - Neutral news
   - Bad news
   - Mixed news: a combination of good news or bad news
   - Information to be organized in a technical writing pattern

2) Match the content, what type of news you are bringing to the reader, with the tone. For example, do not use semiblock (medium formal) with bad news, because it leaves the reader with a conflicted message.

3) Match the tone you want to convey with the letter form to use as seen in Table 7.1.

Table 7.1: Matching letter tone with letter form to use

Tone	Letter form	Examples of when to use
Formal	Full block	Bad news, cover letter for resume
Semiformal, familiar to audience, delivers a tone of camaraderie	Semiblock	Thank-you letter, nonprofit organization asking for support or money
Impersonal, SPAM like	Simplified	Warranty renewal, recall notice

7.1.1 Formal Tone Uses Full-Block Form

For the full-block form, one alignment creates a formal tone. See Figure 7.1.

Figure 7.1: Full-block letter form

Your address
City, State, Zip
Month day, year

Recipient's FirstName LastName
Recipient's Title
Recipient's Company
Recipient's Company Address
Recipient's City, State, Zip

Dear FirstName LastName:

First paragraph: One sentence designed to tell the person only the letter's purpose. This way the person knows when and how to deal with the letter. Do not include any bad news words.

NOTE: In this form, all lines are flush left to the edge without any indents, establishing the formal look of the letter. Use white space between paragraphs to help the reader distinguish between them.

Middle paragraphs: More than one paragraphs. Insert pattern here, including headings.

If you're not using a pattern, then explain the details of the letter in a progressive level of disclosure organization. Still use headings for letters longer than one page, but never call a heading "body."

Next steps paragraph: Tell the reader what they can expect to happen next as a result of this letter and/or where to reach you if they have any questions. Include contact information here; don't make the reader hunt for those details.

Sincerely,

SIGNATURE by hand
Author's FirstName LastName
Author's Title

Enclosure [if you've included something else with the letter]

CC: FirstName LastName of person(s) who got a copy of the letter

7.1.2 Medium Formal = Semiblock: Delivers a Tone of Camaraderie

For semiblock, there are three alignments. The last alignment is 2/3 of the way across the page. NOTE: The last alignment is *not* raggedly aligned along the right edge of the page. See Figure 7.2.

Figure 7.2: Semiblock letter form

Your address
City, State, Zip
Month day, year

Recipient's FirstName LastName
Recipient's Title
Recipient's Company
Recipient's Company Address
Recipient's City, State, Zip

Dear FirstName LastName:

First paragraph: One sentence designed to tell the person only the letter's purpose. This way the person knows when and how to deal with the letter.

NOTE: In this letter form, the first line of each paragraph of the letter is indented at the beginning of the paragraph by the same amount. So this letter has three indents: the flush left, indented paragraphs, and 2/3 way across the page for the front and end matter.

Middle paragraphs: Where you insert pattern, including headings. OR If you're not using a pattern, then explain the details of the letter in a progressive level of disclosure organization. Still use headings for letters longer than one page, but never call a heading "body."

Next steps paragraph: Tell the reader what they can expect to happen next as a result of this letter and/or where to reach you if they have any questions. Include contact information here; don't make the reader hunt for those details.

Sincerely,

SIGNATURE by hand
Author's FirstName LastName
Author's Title

Enclosure [if you've included something else with the letter]

CC: FirstName LastName of person(s) who got a copy of the letter

7.1.3 Impersonal = Simplified: Delivers a SPAM-like Tone

For simplified, the letter form uses one alignment, like full block, with other changes to make the tone impersonal. There is no recipient's title or company name, no "Dear" statement, nor is there a salutation, like "Sincerely" since the author isn't sincere. Plus there's no introductory purpose paragraph, which is replaced with a STATEMENT OF PURPOSE fragment in caps. See Figure 7.3.

Figure 7.3: Simplified letter form

Your address
City, State, Zip
Month day, year

Recipient's Name
Recipient's Address
Recipient's City, State, Zip

STATEMENT OF PURPOSE

Middle paragraphs: Insert pattern here, including headings. OR If you're not using a pattern, then explain the details of the letter in a progressive level of disclosure organization. Still use headings for letters longer than one page, but never call a heading "body."

NOTE: In this form, all lines are flush left to the edge without any indents, establishing the stern look of the letter. Use white space between paragraphs to help the reader distinguish between them.

Next steps paragraph: Tell the reader what they can expect to happen next as a result of this letter and/or where to reach you if they have any questions. Include contact information here; don't make the reader hunt for those details.

SIGNATURE by hand

Name
Title

Enclosure [if you've included something else with the letter]

7.2 Letter Content Forms

If you have a prescribed pattern to use to deliver the information, then insert the pattern into the body of the letter.

If you are not using a prescribed pattern, then categorize the information you need to deliver based on one of the following:

- Neutral news
- Good news
- Bad news
- Mixed content (both good and bad news)

7.2.1 Neutral News

Neutral letters merely deliver information: not good, not bad, just news. These letters are devoid of agendas or author feelings. The reader expects the letter to be objective.

Where does information go?

- State purpose in first paragraph
- Put details/pattern in body
- Next steps, add contact information if they have any questions.

7.2.1.1 Neutral News Example

Let's say that you sent a message to Barnes & Noble asking how to read the current balance of your gift card. They responded with a set of solutions – just information, no good news or bad news or mixed news.

In the purpose statement, they acknowledged that they received your message:

We received your message of <date> asking how to read the current balance of your Barnes & Noble gift card.

In the body, the details of the various ways to get the balance are offered, one at a time. Headings for each solution would help the reader follow along.

In the next steps, they offer you a way to reach them, if you have trouble with the solutions.

If you have additional questions or issues with the solutions that I listed, contact me at bnnhelp@bnn.com.

7.2.2 Good News

A good news letter delivers good news. These letters need to be straightforward, telling the reader their good news and following up with details.

NOTE: Do not disguise a sales letter (a letter that is asking for money or trying to make a sale) as a good news letter. The reader is expecting an immediate benefit in a good news letter and would not appreciate a gimmick or reciprocity expectation.

Where does information go?

- State purpose in first paragraph = the good news.
- Put details/pattern about the good news in body.
- Next steps, add contact information if they have any questions.

7.2.2.1 Good News Example

You're being offered a job. What does your letter from the company look like?

Letter purpose = the good news
This letter is to offer you a job as Software Engineer I at company name.

Body of letter would explain the situation further.
You would initially be working on project xyz working for manager's name.

In the body, always use multiple paragraphs for each category of information. It could include paragraphs for salary, salaried benefits (signing bonus, moving reimbursement, etc.), benefits summary (medical, disability, vacation, etc.), and so on.

Next steps, what does the reader expect to happen next? Always written as a separate paragraph.
We ask that you let us know if you are accepting this position by month day, year, after which this offer will expire. To let us know of your decision or if you have any questions or can't meet this deadline, please contact person's name in Human Resources at 123-456-7890 or email them at FirstName@CompanyName.com.

7.2.3 Bad News

When you have bad news, during the prewriting stage, you need to know the larger purpose for the bad news, plus you need to have a way to combat the bad news. Also remember that readers remember what they read last, so what they read last should never be the bad news.

The purpose of the letter is not the bad news because if you started a letter with bad news, the reader may stop reading and never get to the rest of the letter where you offer a way to combat that bad news. For bad news, start with the larger purpose that drove the bad news. After reading the larger purpose, the reader knows they are about to learn something difficult, so don't prolong the bad news until deep into the letter.

Where does information go?

- State purpose in first paragraph = letter purpose = the larger purpose of the situation (no bad news words).
- Put details/pattern in body.
    - State bad news early on as you explain the situation.
    - Always end with a way to combat or overcome the bad news.
- Next steps, add contact information if they have any questions.

NOTE: Even though it's bad news, it doesn't mean the whole letter is bad news. For example, if a person isn't going to get a job they applied for, you can wish them well in their search or thank them for their interest in your company. Or you can even leave the door open with the suggestion to check back as new opportunities may arise later.

7.2.3.1 Bad News Example

You're being laid off. What does your letter from the company look like?

Letter purpose = the larger purpose of the situation.
This letter is to explain how the company has restructured itself to take advantage of the recent changes in the economy.

State bad news early on to explain the situation.
As a result of the restructuring, xxx jobs have been eliminated because of zzz. Your job as yyy is one of these jobs.

In the rest of the body, always end with a way to combat or overcome the bad news.
The company has employed career services consulting to assist you in updating your resume and to help you look for new work in your field.

Then subsequent paragraphs would explain how those services would work. Additional paragraphs would explain how to extend benefits, and so on.

Next steps, what does the reader expect to happen next? Always written as a separate paragraph.

Your last day will be Month Day, Year. We ask that you have your office space be cleared out by Month Day, Year. If you need boxes or assistance transporting any of your belongings to your car, contact Office Maintenance at 123-456-7890. If you have any questions, contact person's name in Human Resources at 123-456-7890.

7.2.4 Mixed: Good News and Bad News

Because mixed news letters have some bad news in them, they mostly resemble a bad news letter. During the prewriting stage, you need to know the larger purpose that is driving the bad news, and you need to have a way to combat the bad news. Again, you need to remember that readers remember what they read last, so what they read last should never be the bad news.

Where information goes?

- State purpose in first paragraph = larger letter purpose of the situation (no bad news words).
- Put details/pattern in body: Organize the mixed news contents according to your situation as follows:
  - State bad news first if you can, so that you can then explain the situation and end with a way to combat or overcome the bad news, and last state the good news. This way, you can end with good news.
  - State the good news first if the reader needs to know the good news before they can understand the bad news. Be sure to always end with a way to combat the bad news, so the reader ends with a solution to the bad news.
- Next steps, add contact information if they have any questions.

7.2.4.1 Mixed News Example

You've borrowed a book from a publisher and it's overdue, but you've also won a raffle that lets you borrow a book. What would this mixed news letter look like?

Letter purpose = the larger purpose of the situation
This letter contains an update on the status of the book Information Should Never Be Random that you've borrowed from our publisher.

For this case, state bad news, then use the good news as a way to combat the bad news.
You borrowed "Information Should Never Be Random" on date. It is currently overdue by 1 week and has accrued a late fee of $amount. If you return the book through the postal mail, then the late fees will be accrued based on the send date of the book. If you return the book by hand at our physical address, then late fees will be accrued based on the date turned in.

Continue with the good news, which is also a way to combat the bad news, in this case.
You have also won the Olympia Timberland Library raffle for the month of August. Winners of the raffle can borrow one book in the month of August or extend an existing book rental by an additional two weeks. As a winner, you can choose use this raffle to hold your borrowed book for another week without any late fees. Or you can pay the late fee and then use this raffle to reserve another book for a total of five weeks.

Next steps, what does the reader expect to happen next? Always written as a separate paragraph.
Please let us know by the end of the week, what you plan to do so we can dispense your raffle reward. If you have any questions, please email at OTLbooks@lib.com.

7.3 Discussion of Each Letter Element

This section explains each of the letter elements in more detail and what information goes there. This section uses the full-block, single-alignment form.

Your street address
Your city, Your state, Your zip

> Front matter contains the address and date information that mimics the outside of an envelope, and can be used by Word to print an envelope. The information is, in this order, with white space in between the bulleted elements and no white space between multiple address lines (use SHIFT + RETURN to establish this effect):
>
> NOTE: A letter begins with your address information. Your name is *not* included at the top because that's how one addresses an envelope.
>
> Use of letterhead: For personal letters (you sending a letter to someone else), never create your own letterhead for yourself. It's pompous. If you own or work for a business and you are writing on behalf of this business to someone outside your organization, then use that business' letterhead. If you're using letterhead, then omit this beginning address information, because it would be incorporated in the letterhead somewhere.

Today's date

> It's best to spell out the date, for example, July 6, 2016, so that all readers know exactly what the date means. Using 7/6/16 can be confusing if the reader is European, since they write their dates 6/7/16. Besides, using the / date form sets an informal tone.
>
> NOTE: There's *no* superscripted *th* or *st* or *rd* after the number day of the week as in *1st, 2nd 3rd, 4th* when you give the date.

FirstName LastName, degrees if relevant
Recipient's title at the company
Company name
Company name full address

Company name street address
Company city, company state, zip code

Recipient's name, title, full recipient's address are each on its own line. For example:

Emma Cowley, M.D.
Practicing Chiropractor
Renton Chiropractic
Sports Office #5006
44437 Seneca Ave NW
Renton, WA 98507

NOTE: Omit any "Mr.," "Miss," "Mrs.," "Ms." For explanation, see "Omit use of titles" later on this page.

Dear FirstName LastName:

Greeting: The use of Dear in this case is not a terms of endearment, but rather a sign of respect. The reader knows it's a sign of respect by the use of a colon at the end of the line. Showing endearment would be, like Dear Mom, with a comma. So use that colon!

If you don't want to use the Dear, then don't, but keep the rest: FirstName LastName: This form still offers enough formality with the colon to show respect to the reader.

If you don't have the FirstName LastName of the recipient, then indicate their role or job title. For example, Dear Search Committee:

Omit use of titles: Along with changes today with respect to the use of Dear, there are similar changes with titles. In business in the United States, use of Mr., Miss, Mrs., Ms. is avoided because it's so easy to get it wrong and you don't want to make the wrong impression on your reader. In these days of gender/transgender hyperawareness, these phrases are not relevant or respectful.

Based on their definition, the use of Miss and Mrs. indicates the marital status of a woman and, unless the topic of the letter has a bearing on the reader's marital status, you should not use them in business. Whereas Ms. is used for women who don't like the labeling of Miss or Mrs. However, you rarely know what your reader prefers. Meanwhile, you might think that using one of these forms shows respect, but it may not. Their use tells the reader you're introducing into the conversation whether the reader is married or a feminist, not who they are as a business person.

Having read all that, you may poll your women friends to ask if they would like being called Miss or Ms. or Mrs. Some may say "oh yes". Others will say, "Never". And for that additional reason, don't use them, because again, when you get it wrong, you'll offend the reader. If you don't use it, the reader won't think "it ought to be there", especially if you've been respectful with Dear and the colon or FirstName LastName followed by a colon.

First paragraph (one sentence).

The first paragraph of a letter is one sentence that explains the purpose of the letter.

This one-sentence paragraph tells the reader what to do with this correspondence. That is, by reading that paragraph, they learn the letter's purpose, and if they need to handle it right away or if it can wait a while.

For these reasons, the paragraph should never be more than one sentence. Additionally, it should never have more information than just the purpose.

For example, a job recruiter would read the first sentence of your cover letter that says, This letter is in response to the job ad for the YYY position your company placed in XXX on DATE. Knowing that much, the recruiter would place your cover letter and your enclosed resume in the pile for YYY position. When the recruiter is ready to read all the resumes for that position, and only at that time, would he or she finish reading the remainder of your letter.

Body paragraphs

<u>Details goes here:</u> If you're using a pattern to deliver the details of the letter, then you would insert the full pattern into the body of the letter – that is, the introduction, body, conclusion form or however the pattern is organized.

NOTE: After the short purpose paragraph, if the pattern calls for an introduction, it might seem redundant – like you're including two introductions – but that's not the case:

- The one-sentence purpose of letter helps the reader determine when to prioritize reading the letter.
- The introduction to a pattern orients the reader to the rest of the pattern – the details to follow.

<u>Headings:</u> If the body is longer than two pages, then it's best to use headings to help the reader follow the letter content. The headings should *not* stand out with a large font. It's best to only change one design element of the heading with respect to the text font to highlight it: either bold, underline, or italic, *not* a combination of these.

<u>Default pattern:</u> If no specific pattern is identified, then use progressive level of disclosure, as is the case when delivering bad news or good news or neutral news.

Next steps paragraph: Always written as a separate paragraph.

Just like there's a small paragraph *before* the introductory paragraph, there's a small paragraph *after* the concluding information in the body of the letter. This next steps paragraph is where you explain what the reader can expect to occur next or what you, as the author, will do next for the reader.

NOTE: After a conclusion paragraph and the next steps paragraph together, they might seem redundant – like you're including two conclusions – but that's not the case:

- The conclusion of the pattern, if it's present, tells the reader what to understand/do based on what they learned in the details of the letter – the "now what."
- The next steps to a letter explains to the reader what they can expect to have happen with respect to only the letter (not the full extent of the information provided). Its scope is immediate, not long term.

  Example phrases you might use:

  Let me know by . . . , what you plan to do about . . .

  If you have any questions, contact me at . . .

  You can reach me at . . .

  I'll call you in . . . to discuss . . .

  We can meet . . . to discuss . . .

Include contact info: Be sure to include any contact information in the next steps if you're offering the point of contacting you, so the reader doesn't have to go looking for it. If you say "email me," then include your email address. If you say "call me," then include the phone number with area code.

Closing salutation. For example, "Sincerely" (omit for the SIMPLIFIED letter form)

Leave white space after the salutation so you can sign the letter above your typed name.

Sign your full name by hand in pen, after the letter is printed.

Author's FirstName LastName
Author's title or role (what role do you play in relation to the letter)

Enclosures

The word Enclosures is added at the end of a letter if you have included additional pages of information with the letter. This word signals to the reader that there are additional documents, if they got separated from the letter.

Typically, you merely use the word Enclosures where the reader figures out what is included with the letter based on the context/details of the letter. However, if you are including multiple enclosures, you may choose to include a bulleted list after the word, so the recipient can inventory the packet to verify everything was included.

CC FirstName LastName:

The letters CC would be added at the end of a letter to show that the author copied this same letter and sent it to someone else. Everyone who got a copy of the letter would be named after the CC: delineated with commas.

7.4 Memos

Where a letter is primarily used to send information to someone from one business/individual to another business/individual, a memo is reserved for delivering information inside a business.

Any information can be delivered in a memo. Their use, frequency, and type of information are determined by the workplace. Some workplaces may use them heavily, rarely, or not at all, especially with the use of email and other forums.

7.4.1 Memo Form

The front matter form of a memo is shown in Figure 7.4, and an explanation of each element follows afterward. Then see Figure 7.5 for an example.

Figure 7.4: Front matter of a memo

MEMO	
To:	Primary audience
CC:	Secondary audiences
From:	Your name followed by your initials written *by cursive hand*, after printing
Date:	Date
Subject:	Precise indicator of content

MEMO: The word Memo or Memorandum needs to be at the top of a memo as a signal to the reader.

To: The primary audience can be a list of comma-delimited individual names, or it could be the name of an internal group.

CC: The carbon copy (CC) list is for those readers/audiences who also need the information, but who do not need the information directly for their job.

NOTE: Be careful about who is placed in the CC list. Someone in the CC list is not expected to act on the information you provided. Many readers who see themselves as a CC will wait to read it, or maybe even store the information away and not read it until they need to.

Carbon copy comes from the days of typewriters. To create carbons, the author would position multiple pieces of paper together in the typewriter with carbon pages in between each page. Those who got the carbons knew it because of the type print quality. However, the only way the original receiver of a letter/memo knew if someone else got a copy was with the CC line.

From: Your first name and last name, followed by just your *initials, written by cursive hand* after you've printed the memo.

For a letter, there's a salutation, your signature followed by your typed name in the end matter to signal your authorship. However, for a memo, that end matter doesn't exist. So you need to signal your authorship by cursively writing your *initials* right after your typed name in the front matter of the memo after you've printed the memo.

Date: The date is usually of the form month date, year. If you use mm/dd/yy, then be sure that your audiences are all Americans, because that form is not the same in other countries. Also consider the tone you want to deliver.

Date form and Tone:
month date, year is a formal form of the date.
mm/dd/yy is an informal form of the date.

Subject: Make the subject line a clear indication of the document's purpose.

Colon: The colon after the words To, CC, From, Date, and Subject occurs immediately after the word.

TABS: Each element (To, CC, From, Date, Subject) has a tab *after* the colon. This creates an alignment so that the reader need only read down the column of unique information.

NOTE: These lines (To, CC, From, Date, Subject) must always be in the same *order*. This is because readers skim this top front matter, looking down the column created by the tabs, to find unique information. Readers to not read the front matter across like paragraphs of text. Therefore, if the front matter information is in a different order, then the reader would become confused as they scanned for what is important to them.

LINE and white spacing:
A line after the memo front matter followed by white spacing is required before the beginning of the information in the memo.

Figure 7.5: Example front matter of a memo

MEMO

To: Julia Min

CC: Sirius Camus

From: Erin Yu

Date: December 12, 2018

Subject: How to Cite in MLA

7.4.2 Memos as a Delivery Mechanism

The information that follows the front matter of the memo would be organized into patterns or use progressive level of disclosure.

7.4.3 Memo Uses

- As a written record of a meeting (also known as *meeting minutes*):
  Written after a meeting concludes, usually organized along the lines of Progress, Decisions, Outstanding Items, and Next Steps. The minutes would be stored in a global/cloud directory for everyone that needs that information and those that attended the meeting to read again to refresh their memory.
- As acknowledgment of work completed:
  Sometimes it's customary to acknowledge when someone did something so that their participation can be recognized. A memo is a common form for this type of acknowledgment.
- A semiformal announcement:
  If a company is making an announcement, which it wants to be delivered in a more formal tone than email, it might write it as a memo. (Memos can deliver a more formal tone than an email because they usually have a corporate logo attached and other signposts not available in email app.) The memo might be delivered on paper, posted on bulletin boards throughout the company, or emailed as an attachment in an email message.

- Memos are designed as a one-way conversation to tell the reader the included information.
- There are many more uses of memos depending on a business' policies.

7.5 Comparison: Letters, Memos, and Email

Letters and memos compare to email in the following ways:

Comparison	Letters	Memos	Emails
Used for	Communicating TO a single person about a topic Might COPY other recipients	Communicating TO a single person or group of people Might COPY other recipients	Communicating TO a single person or group of people Might COPY other recipients
Tone delivered	Formal (full block) Semiformal (semiblock) Informal (simplified)	Formal, but can vary formality by varying fonts, use of headings, etc.	Semiformal to informal depending on whether any formatting is used in the email
Used when	To communicate to someone in another organization Could be used for inside an organization when a one-to-one formal tone is required	Used to communicate only inside an organization	Used to communicate inside an organization OR outside an organization OR a combination based on the email addresses
Distinctive features	Possible letter head	Memo front matter. Memo or Memorandum must be on top	Email subject, CCs

7.6 Relationship of Letters and Memos to Email

This table shows how the email form evolved from both memos and letters. And since emails are designed primarily as a conversation, you can use your understanding of letters and memos to create better email communications.

Parts of	Letters	Memos	Emails
Front matter	Your street address Your city, Your state, zip Date First Name Last Name Recipient's title Company name Company full address Company street address City, state, zip	MEMO To: recipient CC: copied From: Your name *INITIALS* by hand Date: month day, year Subject: subject line	To: CC: From: Date: Subject:
Salutation or purpose statement	Dear First Name Last Name: *Purpose paragraph*	NONE	First Name: *Purpose paragraph*
Body or pattern	Pattern OR order of information based on neutral news, good news, mixed news, bad news	Pattern	Pattern OR order of information based on neutral news, good news, mixed news, bad news
Next steps	What the reader can expect with this letter	NONE	What the reader can expect with this letter
End matter	Sincerely (or equivalent) *SIGNATURE BY HAND* Author name Author title	NONE	Sincerely, (or equivalent) Author name Author title Optional postal address Your street address Your city, Your state, zip

7.7 Review Exercises

1) When do you use each of the three business letter forms?
2) When do you use a memo?
3) When do you an email?
4) What is the difference between mixed news and neutral news?
5) What goes into the middle/body of a letter?
6) How do you discern who is your primary audience and who is your secondary audience?
7) How would using a company letterhead change the look of a business letter form?
8) How are headings formatted in a letter? What headings should be used? Why should you never use the word "body" as a heading?
9) What can you do to make it easier for the reader to get information they need without violating the integrity look of a letter?
10) What is the minimum number of paragraphs in an email if you form it as a letter?

7.8 Exercises

1) Search for news articles to see where they mention the use of a memos. What can you learn about how organizations use memos?
2) Find a job ad that you might consider applying for. Write the cover letter that would go with your resume.
3) Write an email to your local library asking for a guide to their services. Analyze their response and if necessary, reformat it to match a format mentioned in this chapter.
4) Write a memo after your next meeting that records the "meeting minutes."

7.9 Practice Letters

This practice gives you the opportunity to write three letters. In all cases, the scenario begins the same, then the scenario alters so that there's bad news, mixed news, or good news. For this practice, you cannot change the scenario by adding or deleting information. In this way, you can see where to put information based on the three forms. Maximum length of each letter would be one typed page.

SCENARIO: Hans Meyer is a sales representative for a start-up called GenT Tech, 9250 Lichen Street, Orlando, FL 93004, main phone 033-226-4899. Yesterday, Hans had a call from Judy Brook owner Brook's Books, 334th Street, Seattle WA, 98024 to settle payments for GenT completing Brook's Books new app. In total, Hans charged Judy $43,000 for the project.

In this scenario, you write the draft letter to the customer on behalf of your manager who is too busy to create that initial version. (This practice was created this way to have you practice your tone of voice [it's your manager's, not yours], and because it's not uncommon in a business setting for individual contributors to be asked to compose messages another person uses.)

<u>Option 1. Addition to scenario: bad news</u>

. . . But Hans <u>did not bill</u> Brook's Books for the maintenance hardware because it was his understanding that the equipment <u>was under warranty</u>. However, when Hans met with his manager, Shane Dougal, he learned that the hardware <u>was no longer under warranty</u> and Brook's Books would need to be <u>billed</u> an additional $1,800.84 for the hardware. Brook's Books has been an excellent client and previously claimed that they would consider recommending GenT's services to other companies, so Shane to be respectful and careful in his letter requesting the additional money.

Based on this scenario, outline Shane's bad news letter.

<u>Option 2. Addition to scenario: mixed news</u>

. . . But Hans <u>did not bill</u> Brook's Books for the maintenance hardware because it was his understanding that the equipment <u>was under warranty</u>. However, when

Hans met with his manager, Shane Dougal, Hans learned that the hardware was no longer under warranty and Brook's Books would need to be billed an additional $1,800.84 for the hardware. At the same time, Hans learned that Brook's Books is GenT's "customer of the month" and will get a 10% discount on the total project cost.

Based on this scenario, outline Shane's mixed news letter.

Option 3. Addition to scenario: good news

. . . Hans billed Brook's Books for the maintenance hardware since he understood that it was not under warranty. However, when Hans met with his manager, Shane Dougal, Hans learned that the equipment was still under warranty. Brook's Books would be credited $1,800.84 for the hardware. The credit could be returned to them by check, or it could be applied toward an extension of their equipment warranty that expires in two months. That warranty notice will be sent by their Accounting department within four weeks.

Based on this scenario, outline Shane's good news letter.

Critique Other's Writing with Care

There are some best practices,* which when followed, ensure a successful critique encounter that can strengthen each other's writing: your work by seeing another's work and the author's work by receiving constructive input to improve their work.

8.1 Why Critique

You might have wondered why you should engage in critiquing someone else's work.

* The ideas about critiquing derived from this video: *Student Writing Groups: Demonstrating the Process*. Directed by James J. Hupf. written and produced by Connie J. Hale and Tim Mallon. Wordshop Productions, Inc. © 1998.

8.1.1 As the Reviewer

You need to build the skill of reviewing other people's work, because on the job, you'll need to work on large documents with others, or need to review other's work when in a review process.

In addition, you can extend the skills you learn here with respect to critiquing a document to critiquing someone's design or code – activities that will certainly be expected of you on the job.

8.1.2 As the Author

Having your work critiqued is an efficient way to find out how it is received and understood. You can't follow up face-to-face with the recipient of every document or email each time you send out your work to see whether it's understood or whether they have any questions. That's unrealistic. However, if your work was not understandable to the reader, then your additional explanation would be needed. And that's not sustainable. Therefore, you need to know that your work is well received on the job, and learn how to fix it to become understandable before it's sent out.

You can extend the skills you learn from accepting critiques of your writing, to accepting critiques of your design or code, which would likely occur on the job.

8.2 How to Critique

The type of critique you provide is critical to its successful outcome.

8.2.1 As the Reviewer

This section explains your role as the reviewer.

8.2.1.1 Don't Use "You" or "Your" (2nd POV) in the Critique

When you hear "you" in a sentence, you automatically put yourself inside the sentence – see how you did that? The brain does this unconsciously. You really can't stop it. Once you've put yourself inside the upcoming sentence, you live out that sentence as though you are doing/thinking the action. This is the power of how the 2nd POV inserts the listener into the language.

However, when you're in a situation where someone is going to critique your work, when the reviewer uses "you" and your brain inserts yourself into the sentence, then your brain realizes that you're about to hear something that is critical, and with no interest to experience pain, the brain's next automatic action is to turn off your ears, so you don't hear it. "Whannn, Whannn, Whannnn." The sound bounces around your head and nothing registers.

So it's the job of the reviewer, knowing what the brain does, to discuss the work in terms of the 3rd POV instead. See Table 8.1 for a sampling of words to avoid and use instead. You can extrapolate from this table to other language you need to use.

Table 8.1: Examples of words to use instead during a critique

Do not use these phrases in a critique	Use these phrases instead
Your work	The document
Your table, your graphic	The table, the graphic
Your writing	The paragraph, the sentence, and so on

8.2.1.2 Say What Doesn't Work, and What Does Work to Give Balanced View

By our nature, we're trained to hear the bad about what we've done. Correspondingly, we're equally trained to only provide the bad news when providing a critique. However, a one-sided critique, that is, hearing only the bad when someone provides a critique gives the author a balanced view of their work.

Instead, it's helpful to hear what is good or working about their work too. That way the author will know when not to try to fix something that is already working. That is reassuring and can save them time.

You can start with what works, and continue with what needs fixing. Or you could go through the document section by section saying what works and doesn't work – whatever method is appropriate for the situation. As the reviewer, it's important to log both categories of critiques as you read the work, so you can provide a complete feedback.

8.2.1.3 Don't Fix Their Work and Become Their Editor

When you provide feedback on what doesn't work in a document, don't explain your critique in terms of how to fix it. For example, rather than say, fix these commas here, here, and here. Instead say, you need to follow the proper comma rules in these sentences.

The difference is that when you fix their work, the author doesn't know what is wrong with their writing, only how to fix it. That means that you've turned into the author's editor, a role you probably don't want to play for the duration of your encounters. For example, you could find yourself the resource for this author who keeps coming back to you every time they've edited their sentences to ask for verification they've used commas correctly.

Once you've explained what to fix, then you can offer to teach the person how to fix their own work. In that way, you're helping them learn, rather than editing their work.

8.2.2 As the Author

As the author, the first task is to keep track of everything that you hear. If you're nervous about what you'll hear, then just write it all down. This way, you have logged the information and can review it in comfort later.

When someone states that some part of your work does not work, do not say anything. Even though, common nature may be to speak up and defend yourself; resist that urge. That action stops the process: the reviewer doesn't want to argue with you and will stop giving you the information you need.

Furthermore, if you defend yourself, you'll never learn how to make your work stand on its own. You need to know what others thought of your work.

Once the critique process is concluded, if there's still time, you can always ask for suggestions on how to fix your work. Remember, of course, that with the knowledge of what's not working, it's your job to learn how to fix it, so that you can grow as a writer.

When there's time in the process, you can ask your reviewers for another review of your revised work before you declare the work final.

8.3 How to Use This Critique Method

This section suggests a way this critique method could be used in a classroom setting and on the job.

8.3.1 In a Class

For a class, this critique process assumes that students are in writing groups or are assigned another person's work to critique.

1) If you're in groups, students first read each other's work.
2) As you read a work, comment on a separate page or rubric what is excellent and what needs improvement.
3) Once everyone has completed reading everyone else's work, then pick one person in the group and begin to offer overall verbal comments on their work summarizing your thoughts.
4) Each person provides their critique of that one person.
5) After everyone has completed their comments, you move to the next person in the group and provide summarized critiques of their work by each member.
6) Continue in this way till all verbal critiques are completed.

Assuming all this activity is done in class, this process

- Maximizes quiet time, since everyone is reading quietly and recording comments at the beginning. That way, there's a quiet time that helps concentration. Eventually one group will finish first and begin talking, but that's okay.
- Maximizes group time, that is, if you don't finish all verbal critiques by the time class ends, as least each person has the written comments from each member.

8.3.2 On the Job

If where you work doesn't have a critique process, here are some ways you might use this process on the job:

1) Have everyone read the document before arriving at the meeting where it will be discussed.

2) Go page by page or section by section asking everyone for substantive comments in that area. That way, if there are debates about content, it can be resolved while everyone is available.

3) Collect comments about typos, grammar, punctuation at meeting's end. These errors don't need airing in the meeting.

9

Revitalize Your Grammar for Business and Technical Writing

This chapter is not a full English grammar guide. Instead it covers the most common difficulties encountered in business and technical writing: sentence structure, verb choice, word usage, and punctuation.

9.1 Sentence Structure

This section examines transitions – helping the reader see your connections in your writing – and subordination – connecting ideas together in a sentence – where you decide on the level of importance of information in a sentence by the words that glue them together.

9.1.1 Reviewing Transitions – or How to Relate Ideas for the Reader

As someone reads, they want to build on existing information, this is the role of the transition – to signal how ideas are connected. Just like the turn signal in a car tells you the vehicle ahead of you is changing lanes or exiting the roadway, a transition in your document prepares the reader for the type of information that follows, so that information doesn't spring up and confuse the reader.

If you do not help the reader understand your flow of content, then they must guess. Guessing is never a good practice for readers when reading technical writing. Remember technical writing is not fiction; so techniques you were taught in English composition about creating suspense in your writing no longer apply. It's important for the reader to know where your ideas are going before they get there so that they know how to understand what they are reading.

This section covers the various ways that you can create transitions for the reader, beyond using a simple word, such as "also" that lets the reader know you're adding content.

9.1.1.1 Signaling Connections with Headings

One way that you can signal a transition is with a heading or subheading. Well-formed, clearly articulated headings can work to inform your reader of where you're taking them.

Examples of not-well-formed and well-formed headings and subheadings

Not Well-Formed Example	**Well-Formed Example**
Instrument Learning	Mastering a New Instrument
Practice	Establishing a Practice Regiment
Experts	Talking to Experts
Performance	Performing to Audiences

9.1.1.2 Signaling Connections with Section Introductions

The phrase "this section covers" can be found after a *heading1* (a heading at the highest level in a table of contents) to orient the reader as to the contents of that major section of a document.

This phrase is best used as a transition for your reader when the following conditions apply:

- When a heading follows another heading in the document. Two headings that follow one another puts all the pressure on the headings to explain to the reader what the sections contain.

  For example:

Don't do this:	**Do this instead:**
Heading	Heading
Subheading	This section covers . . .
Some content	Subheading
Subheading	Some content
Some content	Subheading
	Some content

- When you don't know how else to orient the reader to what is covered in this section.

Do not use "this section covers" phrase when the following conditions apply:

- When you have other introductory material to discuss after the *heading1* that would orient the reader regarding that section.
- When it is not a *heading1* section.

9.1.1.3 Signaling Connections between Paragraphs

Once your reader is oriented to a section of the document, then you want to make sure they follow the series of paragraphs within that section. From one paragraph to the next, orientation can follow by a simple single-word transition (e.g., "Additionally" or "Furthermore") or you can use a more descriptive phrase at the beginning of the first sentence of the paragraph.

> Example:
>
> (Paragraph about Project Delta's "vast array of features")
>
> Project Delta's vast array of features come at the cost of high power consumption, so the team plans to add additional hardware support. (Paragraph continues to talk about the specific "hardware support")

9.1.1.4 Signaling Connections between/within Sentences

When you change the direction of ideas in a paragraph, but you're still building on the idea of the topic sentence, then you need a transition between sentences. This is probably the most common transition you're familiar with.

- One method of sentence transition is to repeat key words (but do not do this excessively):

  ORIGINAL: The time it takes to master a new skill is dependent on the dedication of the person. The dedication of the person needs to be high enough for the person to maintain long and frequent practice of the new skill.

  REVISED: The time it takes to master a new skill is dependent on the dedication of the person, and it needs to be high enough for the person to maintain long and frequent practice of the new skill.

- One problem area with transitions is overuse of or vague "this" subjects. Avoid overusing them, and make sure when you use them that what "this" refers to is clear to the reader.

ORIGINAL: New hobbies are fun to do by oneself, but other hobbies such as gaming require other people. This often leads to huge gatherings where people can get a feeling of camaraderie from others with similar interests.

REVISED: New hobbies are fun to do by oneself, but other hobbies such as gaming require other people. This need for company often leads to huge gatherings where people can get a feeling of camaraderie from others with similar interests.

- One transition to watch for is when restating not just the previous sentence, but the sentences that came before. This may be used in a concluding sentence.

  EXAMPLE: Long-time durations, frequency, and mental engagement are each individually crucial to acquiring a new skill, but together, they can exponentially cut down the amount of time it takes to achieve full mastery of a skill.

- When you're looking for a signal, you ought to know what direction you're planning with the next paragraph or sentence so you can find the right word/phrase to use. You can signal a transition, given your goal, using these sample words/phrase.
  - To add to a previous point – and, or, nor, furthermore, indeed, also, moreover, in fact, first, second, in addition
  - To illustrate or expand on a point – for instance, for example, similarly, likewise
  - To summarize or emphasize a point – therefore, thus, hence, consequently, on the whole, all in all, in other words, in short, in conclusion
  - To qualify or illustrate a point – frequently, occasionally, in general, specifically, in particular, usually
  - To shift to a different point of view or signal a contradiction – but, however, yet, conversely

- To make a concession – although, though, whereas
- To connect an explanation to a statement – because, as, since, for
- To qualify and restrict a more general idea – if, provided, in case, unless, lest, when

9.1.2 Signaling Subordination or Connections within Sentences

Sometimes as you build a sentence, you change or add to ideas within the sentence and you need to signal to the reader what that change means. In this case, subordinating ideas tell the reader how one idea ranks in order with the other ideas in the sentence.

- Conjunctions signal how ideas are related. You can signal sentence conjunctions, given your goal, using these sample words.
    - Coordinating – and, but, for, nor, or, so, yet
    - Correlative – both/and, either/or, neither/nor, not only/but also
    - Relative – that, which
    - Subordinating – after, although, as a result of, as far as, as if, as soon as, as well as, because, before, even though, once, only, since, so far as, though, unless, when, wherever, where, whereas . . .
- Prepositions offer transitions.
    - Spatial – about, above, against, around, at, behind, below, beneath, beside, between, beyond, by, down, from, in, inside, into, on, off, out, outside, over, through, to, toward, up, upon, with, . . .
    - Time/sequence – after, before, during, since, till, until, . . .
    - Compound (use sparingly as they add extra words the reader needs to read) – according to, along with, due to, except for, in addition, in front of, in order to, in spite of, on account of, instead of, with regard to, with respect to, . . .

9.1.3 Reviewing Sentence Structure: Parallelism and Faulty Modifiers

This section discusses

- parallelism – creating structure in lists. Sentence parts are underlined to show their parallelism.
- faulty or misplaced modifiers – creating clarity with the location of idea phrases within a sentence.

9.1.3.1 Reviewing Parallelism

Parallel structure is the use of the same grammatical form or structure for equal ideas. The balance of equal elements in a sequence helps show the relationship between ideas.

> The baseball coach reviewed how their team threw the ball and how they swung the bat.
>
> Crafting the school banner allowed the photographer to start planning the yearbook picture.

Nonparallel structure occurs when items are not in the same grammatical form or structure.

> [Faulty] Potential employees need to consider not only their pay, but also be thinking about their employee benefits, such as stock options.
>
> [Corrected] Potential employees need to consider not only their pay, but also think about their employee benefits, such as stock options.

9.1.3.2 Understanding where to use Parallelism

Parallelism should be present in all the following places:

- In each of the list elements in a list within a sentence
- In each of the bullet elements in bullets at the same level

- In each of the headings at the same level in an outline or table of contents
- In each of the list elements in a numbered list
- When possible, in each of the table cells in the same row or column. This is more difficult to create, but a little effort at parallelism, even with some inconsistencies, can create a more readable table.

9.1.3.3 Reviewing Dangling/Misplaced Modifiers

A *dangling* modifier is a word or phrase that refers to (or modifies) a word or phrase that has not been clearly stated in a sentence. *Misplaced* modifiers are words whose placement alters the understanding of the sentence.

Common characteristics of these faulty modifiers include the following:

- Cause ambiguity and even humor
- Are located at the front or at the very end of a sentence
- Often have an –ing verb or a to + verb phrase near the start of the phrase

Examples are as follows:

> Aiming too quickly to close the deal, the stakeholders gradually adopted annoyed expressions on their faces.
> (Were the stakeholders the ones making the deal?)

> Unable to bear the stress of work, the ID machine read the engineer's card for the last time.
> (The ID machine is a machine that's unable to feel stress.)

Dangling Modifiers

A dangling modifier is a modifier that is about a noun, which is not part of the sentence.

A few examples of dangling modifiers in action:

> Bored out of his mind, the book's end was nowhere in sight.
> (the book doesn't have a mind)
>
> Forgetting to bring sunglasses, the frisbee was sure to miss.
> (the frisbee doesn't have eyes)
>
> Pressing the power button, the movie screen looked crisp.
> (the screen can't push buttons)

To fix dangling modifiers, you need to find out what piece of information is missing and rewrite the sentence.

> Original: Bored out of his mind, the book's end was nowhere in sight.
>
> Fixed: Tim was bored out of his mind because the book's end was nowhere in sight.
>
> Fixed: The book's end was nowhere in sight as Tim became bored out of his mind.
>
> ---
>
> Original: Forgetting to bring sunglasses, the frisbee was sure to miss.
>
> Fixed: Since Jerry forgot to bring sunglasses, the frisbee he threw was sure to miss.
>
> Fixed: The frisbee Jerry threw was sure to miss because he forgot to bring his sunglasses.
>
> ---
>
> Original: Pressing the power button, the movie screen looked crisp.

Fixed: Pressing the power button, Nathanael saw that the movie screen looked crisp.

Fixed: Nathanael was pleased that the movie screen was crisp after he pressed the power button.

Misplaced Modifiers

A *misplaced* modifier alters the wrong word or phrase because it is so far away from what it refers to (or modifies).

The assembly line workers were told that they had been fired by the personnel director.
(Note: Were the workers told by the personnel director that they had been fired, or were they told by someone else that the personnel director had fired them?)

Single-word modifiers should be co-located with the words they modify. Understand how one-word placement difference completely alters the concept of the following two sentences:

I easily learned how to draw a person.
(Note: The person's learning process was easier for them)

I learned how to easily draw a person.
(Note: The person learned a simple way to draw a person)

9.1.4 Sentence Structure Exercises

1) Rework the following paragraph using *transitions* to build bridges between the sentences and part of sentences. Use underlines to show where you've added transitions.

Notice first how difficult it is to follow the paragraph's ideas and to retain them. A role of transitions is to help you build a tree of knowledge as you read by knowing where to place the next piece of information before you get to it.

Project Delta is the name of a Bluetooth laptop computer accessory that we are developing. It can be used as a computer microphone. It can be used as a webcam. The accessory can share live camera feed to the computer. The computer's interface with the accessory enables it to filter and edit the camera feed with advanced machine-learning software. The accessory can create a hotspot to connect the laptop to the Internet wherever it is. The accessory can be ready for marketing in 6 months.

2) To practice *subordination* within a sentence, choose connectives to make a single sentence of the following short, choppy, disconnected sentences. You must retain *all* the main ideas of *all* the sentences. Do *not* just throw a conjunctive between each sentence to make an unyielding run-on sentence. A maximum of two "and"s are allowed. How many words are in your sentence?

The day was Saturday. Freddy was driving.
The car was a blue Ford Galaxy. It was going fast.
The road curved sharply. The car skidded.
It missed a cat. It hit a tree.
Freddy wasn't hurt. He had no insurance.
The car was totalled.

3) Match the *conjunctions* from the table to the correct or most appropriate sentences. Conjunctions can be used only once.

In addition	If	Because
Therefore	For example	But

i. Pianos are large and expensive. ________, they require investment to acquire and then learn to play.

ii. The art of fishing may seem at first to be a matter of doing nothing _______, everything changes when you catch your first fish.

iii. Mathematics is a staple school subject. _________, it is a pastime for many aspiring engineers.

iv. There are many martial arts with different applications. ________, Karate emphasizes unarmed combat and Aikido focuses on redirecting the force of the opponent.

v. Hobbies that can be done by oneself are often easier to practice _________ it can be difficult depending on the environment to find other people to practice with.

vi. Guitars are large instruments with six strings. _________ you want an easier instrument, you might consider the ukulele because it has two less strings to focus on.

4) Take some recent reading. Identify where the transitions and subordination occurred and how they helped to build knowledge as you read.

The sentences in the following paragraph make an attempt at the use of *parallel* sentence structure. Fix those that don't. Your revised sentences need to still be the same number of sentences with all the original content.

5) Your revised sentences need to still be the same number of sentences with *all* the original content.

During the Korean War, Jerry traveled to South Korea to teach mathematics and to serve in the Signal Corps. During his time in Korea, he learned that it was easier for him to speak to the Korean soldiers in Japanese than translating their speech to English. The need for interpreters as well as their search for specialists to pass their skills to the Koreans made Jerry an ideal teacher. Although his Japanese heritage was useful for establishing friendly relations with Koreans, it made it difficult bonding within the American military because of anti-Japanese sentiments from World War II. The art of avoidance was a familiar concept to Jerry from his time dodging around his older brother. Adding to this skill, Jerry gained the virtue of patience, the knowledge of army politics, and the tactic of negotiation. During his breaks from service, Jerry would study physics, go exploring Korea, and try to visit other military bases. In later years, Jerry chose to only tell his grandchildren about how he traveled around the military bases in Asia, and when they were older, his experiences with relational conflicts within the military. His grandchildren didn't know what to think, but the familiar warmth within Jerry's eyes taught them this: their grandfather nonetheless experienced a joyful life of adventure.

6) Only technical workers share relevant business information to their managers. Understand how the meaning of these sentences changes as the word single-word modifier, "only," moves throughout these sentence.

Technical workers only share relevant business information to their managers.

Technical workers share only relevant business information to their managers.

Technical workers share relevant business information only to their managers.

7) Revise the following sentences to correct the *dangling* modifier. Your revised sentences need to still be the same number of sentences with all the original content.

Turning off the alarm, the sun began to shine through the uncovered window.

Preoccupied with the stirring the oatmeal, the omelet began to smoke dangerously.

After planning out the next run, the dog joined Germaine on the streets.

Depleted of energy, Germaine turned off his phone and took a nap.

By setting lunch on the desk, there was motivation to begin the work quickly.

To complete the entire report, the clock was hidden from view.

Answers at end of the chapter.

9.2 Understanding Passive Voice

There are different ways to identify issues with passive voice: weak verbs, missing subjects, expletives, and nominalizations.

9.2.1 Weak Verbs

Passive voice in English can be identified by weak verbs, such as such as to be (is, are, was, were, have/has/had, been), to have, or to do. Although weak verbs serve essential language roles as auxiliary or "helping" verbs, when they are overused, they steal understanding/clarity from your writing. Very often a verb with more context/content is located in another word in the sentence along with the to be verb.

> Lawsuits had been overwhelming the company. (Weak)
> Lawsuits overwhelmed the company. (Strong)
> Lawsuits overwhelmed the company from top of the organization to the bottom. (Stronger with clarity)

Overall in technical writing, there will be a fair amount of weak verb use. It's only a problem when its overuse makes it difficult for the reader to get the information they need from the reading, or the structure makes the reading so dull (especially for large documents) that the reader is uninterested in finishing the reading, even though they need to read it.

9.2.2 Missing Subject

Passive voice is also identified as when the subject is unidentified or unclear in the sentence. Consider the following sentence:

> Mistakes were made. (Weak verb and unknown subject. Who made the mistake?)

Depending on the type of writing, it may be advantageous to keep the subject as a mystery. For example, in the case of the mistakes, if your company didn't want to identify who within the organization made the mistake, just that it occurred, then the focus isn't on who, but what to do about rectifying the mistake.

In other cases, obscuring the subject is just confusing.

> The performance was declared to be unimpressive. (Passive voice: Who made this declaration?)
> The manager declared the performance unimpressive. (Subject identified)

When your writing obscures the subject, the reader is left with an unclear understanding of the content.

9.2.3 Expletives

Expletives are variations of there is and it is (i.e., there is, there are, there were, ...it is, is was). These passive voice constructions blunt your sentences by hogging both the subject and the verb in a sentence, pushing all the content in the sentence into a dependent clause. These constructions throw away not only your verb potential but your subject too.

> There were dancers filling the stage.
> There is a musical about world hunger.

When expletives are overused in a document, it becomes stilted and remote slowing reading speed and increasing comprehension difficulty.

The best solution, after recognizing their overuse, is to selectively identify expletives and rewrite to convey your ideas better. When you rewrite them be careful not to substitute another passive voice construction. That is, sometimes you have to identify a subject.

> There is a musical about world hunger. (Expletive)
> You should attend this musical about world hunger. (Subject identified: clearer)

9.2.4 Nominalizations

Nominalizations are nouns that end with a –ion, just as nominalization does. These are sometimes referred to as "shun" words because of the sound –ion makes when these words are spoken aloud and are discussed here because they frequently are accompanied by weak verbs.

Nominalizations are another example of wording, like expletives, that when overused, cause problems with the way your document comes across to your audience. In the case of too many nominalizations, your document sounds as though your intent was to appear more knowledgeable than your audience or to sound like you want the audience to be impressed with your knowledge. Because of this perceived intent, very often the opposite occurs: your audience thinks you're not very knowledgeable nor are they impressed.

You can fix a nominalized verb by converting the –ion noun into the verb that lives within the –ion word. In some cases, you may need to make up a subject if it was absent due to the nominalizations occurring in a passive voice sentence.

The active voice is easier to understand than the passive because the active voice explains who is doing the action.

> The event organizat**ion** that was done by the media team was for the manager's birthday. (Not as clear)
>
> The media team **organized** the event for the manager's birthday. (Clearer with active verb)

9.2.5 Passive Voice Exercises

Revise the following sentences to correct the passive voice constructions. Your revised sentence needs to still be *one* sentence with *all* the original content.

1) Fix these sentences with weak verbs.

- **i.** The time had been wearing away at the customer's patience.
- **ii.** The business pitch needed to have been significantly shortened by the rookie presenter in order to retain interest.

   iii. Instead, he thought he needed to have to stretch out the content to cover every single detail.
   iv. Fortunately, the senior presenter, who was partnered with the rookie presenter, anticipated that he needed to have been trained more by her.
   v. The senior presenter's coworker had been pretending to be the customer the entire time.

2) Fix these no subject sentences. Insert a subject (if needed) that fits with the sentence's context.
   i. The songs were sung beautifully well.
   ii. Despite major obstacles, the character was very accurately portrayed.
   iii. Although fights were started over who should be the lead dancer, the matter was eventually handled.
   iv. Major improvements need to be made before the cast is ready to perform.

3) Fix these sentences by removing the expletives.
   i. Consider that there are good and bad consequences to each business decision so it is to be expected that not everyone can be appeased.
   ii. There was an important absence at the meeting because the organizer forgot to CC the missing person.
   iii. The manager carefully noted that there was a surplus of employee candidates because it was the time when the college students graduated and sought work.

4) Fix these sentences by removing the nominalizations.
   i. Workers should always be prepared for an evaluation of their efforts.
   ii. One workplace skill that should not be the subject of underappreciation is conflict resolution.
   iii. Each job position is a chance for people to create an evolution of their skillsets.
   iv. It has been said that you must always include extra time considerations for unforeseen circumstances when planning projects.
   v. New workers should be punctual in order to show they have commitment to the company.

Answers at end of the chapter.

9.3 Word Choice

Each word chosen in your writing conveys meaning. To expedite the reader's ability to absorb that meaning quickly, it's important to pick each word with care and avoid wordy constructions.

The topics covered in this section are included based on what is most often misunderstood while commonly used in business and technical writing. They are the proper use of acronyms, abbreviations, jargon, noun stacks, clichés, colloquialisms, and quoted words. Also covered are reminders of homonyms and gender bias (pronoun problem) issues.

9.3.1 Using Slang, Colloquialisms, Clichés, Affectation, Jargon, Abbreviations, Acronyms Noun Stacks, Quoted Words

If it's not clear, then it's not a good technical writing. This table explains various word constructs that may or may not be useful or used in technical writing.

Constructs	Definitions and examples	Used in technical writing?
Slang	Language that is primarily shared and understood depending on their group, such as age and physical setting. They can add new meanings to other words by using them outside of their usual context to create unique figures of speech. They are often misunderstood by people outside of the group For example, that is sick, low-key, woke	DO NOT USE – These constructions imply rather than tell; therefore, the reader must figure out what you really mean. Also slang is not good for English Language Learners (ELL) who may not understand the cultural context.
Colloquialisms	A conversational, informal speech For example, y'all, Hey	

Constructs	**Definitions and examples**	**Used in technical writing?**
Clichés	Trite and overused metaphor expressions that evoke an image For example, we are what we eat, shooting fish in a barrel, dry as dust, dumb as a post, what goes around comes around, meet your maker, easy as pie, break a leg, until pigs fly	DO NOT USE – Clichés are great when they work, but they rarely work, especially in technical writing, because their exact meaning is unclear. Also they are not good for readers who may not understand them.
Affectation	Language that is written with pretense or used to display one's ability to communicate For example, disseminate rather than share. Or utilize versus use	IT DEPENDS DO NOT USE – When the intent is to sound superlative or to impress, which obscures your meaning. OK to use – If that word is really the right word for the job.
Jargon	The specialized language of a specific trade or profession. All professions have significant jargon that is common for their profession. For example, transmission control protocol (TCP)	OK to use – Jargon is appropriate given an audience who understands it. If you're writing to an audience unfamiliar with the words, then define the terms first before you use them. If you're introducing a lot of jargon in a document, then consider including a glossary.

Constructs	Definitions and examples	Used in technical writing?
Acronyms and initials	A word that consists of the first letters or parts of a multiple word term/name/concept.	OK to use – Acronyms are appropriate given an audience who understands them. In most cases, it is best to spell them out with the first occurrence. If there are a lot of them that the audience is learning as they read, you may need to consider a glossary.
Abbreviations	An abbreviation is when letters followed by periods are used to refer to a phrase. This is different than acronyms or initials, because the resulting letters are not necessarily the first letter of each word. For example, Washington D.C. for District of Columbia Other abbreviations are used to abbreviate words, such as ft for feet.	IT DEPENDS DO NOT USE – When the abbreviation eliminates words for brevity that are not standard conventions For example, comm for communications, abbrev for abbreviation, or msg for message OK to use – When it's an accepted abbreviation For example, POTUS for President of the United States or FBI for Federal Bureau of Investigation, ft for feet

Constructs	**Definitions and examples**	**Used in technical writing?**
Noun stacks	A jammed/stacked modifier, also known as a noun stack, is when there are a string of modifiers stacked before the noun acting as adjectives. These can be very difficult to parse and make the reading difficult. However, they are extremely effective when the audience knows what you mean, and in that context, they may be referred to as an acronym or jargon depending on its form.	OK to use – Noun stacks are appropriate given an audience who understands them. In most cases, it is best to spell them out with the first occurrence. If there are a lot of them that the audience is learning as they read, you may need to consider a glossary. For example, internet control message protocol, hypertext transfer protocol
"Quotes" around words	You quote a word, because (1) You are quoting the exact words that someone said, such as quoting from an outside source. (2) You are identifying a word you're about to define. (3) you don't want the reader to apply the conventional definition to the word, but rather some other view. For example, The students didn't come to class because they were "sick." (What were they if they weren't sick?)	IT DEPENDS OK to use (1) Are you quoting someone? Then okay to use, and cite the source. (2) Does a follow-on sentence explain what the quoted word means? Then okay. DO NOT USE: (3) If you quote a word to tell the reader you don't really mean this word, but don't explain what you really mean, it's ambiguous and thus poor technical writing.

9.3.1.1 Convention: Introducing an Acronym

When you use abbreviations and acronyms, you want to write it out first, then use the letters in parentheses, for example, English Language Learners (ELL) readers. After spelling it first, all later instances would only need to use ELL in a sentence.

This is the convention because from a punctuation perspective, information in parentheses is extraneous (see Chapter 9.4), that is, not required to read and explained as follows:

- Do not say ELL readers, the first time, because that means that the reader would encounter ELL and be confused if they are not familiar with the acronym. If the full spelling of the acronym follows in parenthesis, they may not read it and so their confusion is never resolved.
- Someone who can't figure out what an abbreviation or acronym means knows to search for the acronym in parentheses earlier in the document to find out its full meaning spelled out. For that reason, use the convention.
- If you didn't follow the convention, then if the reader skipped into a document and later saw ELL and searched for (ELL), they wouldn't find it.

9.3.2 The Pronoun Problem and Gender-biased Problem Words

The phrase "the pronoun problem" refers to the use of "he" to refer to more than the male gender – to refer to essentially any human being. Although hundreds of years ago, this phrasing was common place and understood to mean men and women, today it's not possible to use he to refer to all genders and be accepted as a forward-thinking individual. In fact, many would believe you to be biased against, or not accepting of, all genders if you used he with the belief it refers to all genders.

That's because the long-ago universal belief that the use of he being gender inclusive no longer holds true. Women want to be identified for themselves with their own pronoun. Nonbinary individuals want their self-view recognized. Likewise, transgender people want a pronoun of their choice used for them.

9.3.2.1 Importance of Learning How to Solve the Pronoun Problem

There are many ways to solve this problem, and you need to be able to recognize these forms as you read other work, so you can understand what is meant in their work.

Furthermore, it's important for you to know these various forms, so you can vary which you use at any time in your own work depending on the circumstances. That is, the same method may not always be the one that works.

9.3.2.2 Common Methods to Fix the Pronoun Problem

This table shows the most common methods to fix the pronoun problem. NOTE: Some methods, although common, are not recommended in technical writing, because they can cause confusion, but are explained, so you can recognize them.

Method	**Description and technical writing use**	**Example**
Use most frequently in technical writing.		
Remove pronoun No possession pronoun available	Use one of the approved methods when referring to the noun in the sentence, and remove the possessive pronoun. NOTE: This is a great option to use in conjunction with the upcoming fixes.	The guitarist needs to buy guitar strings.

▶

Method	Description and technical writing use	Example
They as singular Possession pronoun their	Using they to refer to the individual person. While even ten years ago, this was considered bad grammar; today, this form is recognized as acceptable. Frequently used for those who prefer not to be associated with the male/female connotations of our society.	They need to buy guitar strings. They need to buy their guitar strings.
He/she Possession pronoun his/her	Using he/she when referring to the person.	He/she needs to buy guitar strings. He/she needs to buy his/her guitar strings.
He or she Possession pronoun his or hers	Conceptually the same as he/she. However whichever you choose (he/she **OR** he or she), you must be consistent through the whole document. NOTE: Likewise, if you use he or she, do not reverse the order (she or he) for variety. Consistency is key. In this case, the repetition works.	He or she needs to buy guitar strings. He or she needs to buy his or her guitar strings.
They in the plural Possession pronoun their	If you make the nouns plural in the sentence, then the pronoun you'd use is they, which refers to everyone, regardless of gender. NOTE: Using they for singular or plural means that that the audience doesn't know whether there are more than one subject or not, but that can usually be derived by the other information provided.	They need to buy guitar strings. They need to buy their guitar strings.
One Possession pronoun ones	Use one to refer to the person. This form changes the language to an formal tone, so use one only in those situations; otherwise, your work will sound stilted and awkward.	One needs to guitar strings. One needs to buy one's guitar strings.

Method	**Description and technical writing use**	**Example**
You Possession pronoun your	Use you to refer to the person. This form changes the point of view (POV) to be 2nd person. This form can be used only if this shift works for your document. NOTE: If you shift POV, then the whole document needs to be shifted to 2nd POV, not just this sentence with the pronoun problem.	You need to buy guitar strings. You need to buy your guitar strings.
Use sparingly in technical writing.		
Repeat the noun Repeat the noun with possession punctuation to show possession	Use the noun rather than a pronoun to refer to the subject. Then repeat the noun when needed for the possessive. NOTE: While overuse of the same noun is repetitive and that can be okay, repeating the noun too much will become annoying to the reader, so use this option sparingly.	Guitarists need to buy guitar strings. Guitarists need to buy guitar strings.
Remove the pronoun (subject) No possession pronoun available	Removing the subject from the sentence turns the sentence into passive voice. NOTE: Shifting to passive voice may cause a new problem as it removes the subject. Thus, use this option sparingly.	Guitar strings need to be bought.
Do not use in (formal) technical writing. They cause ambiguity.		
s/he	This is using the knowledge that the / means OR, so this alternative is an abbreviation for she/he. As with many abbreviations, it's unclear and therefore should not be used in technical writing. NOTE: This form really only works when you don't need to use the possessive pronoun. There's no shorthand for her/his.	S/he needs to buy guitar strings. S/he needs to buy _??___ guitar strings.

Method	Description and technical writing use	Example
Alternate he and she	Some authors decide to avoid these inclusive phrasings (he/she OR he or she) because they are cumbersome or wordy, and decide to alternate use within a document/book, so they put a notice in the front of the document saying "This document [/book] alternates between use of he and she in each section [/chapter]." However, alternating is a bad idea. Usually no one sees this notice. So the reader sees and believes the author when they say that only men do what's discussed in one of the sections/chapters, and only women do what is discussed in the other sections/chapters. In confusion, they might find the notice. So, always avoid potential confusion in technical writing.	He needs to buy guitar strings. He needs to buy his guitar strings. NEXT TIME guitar strings are mentioned . . . She needs to buy guitar strings. She needs to buy her guitar strings.
New English pronouns	The English language is always evolving and adding new words. Many are at work to find out how to create a new, inclusive, gender-neutral singular pronoun for the English language. The many varied new pronouns' use goes beyond the scope of this book. Check with your employer Human Resources department to see how gender identity pronouns are used in your company.	<u>Examples using Xe and Zie</u> Xe needs to buy guitar strings. Xe needs to buy xyrs guitar strings. Zie needs to buy guitar strings. Zie needs to buy zir guitar strings.

9.3.2.3 Gender-biased Words and their Alternatives

Just as the last section was about how "he" needed to be changed as English as evolved, using words with "man" in them to refer to all people are also no longer suitable. So you need to learn the replacement words. This table covers some of the more common gender-biased words that are used in technical writing and offers alternatives.

Gender-biased word	Alternative word
Mankind	Humankind
Man hours	Staffing
Unmanned	Pilotless
Fireman	Firefighter
Chairman	Chair
Congressman	Congressperson
NOTE: Not every word with "man" in it needs to be changed. For example, neither *manager* or *managing* is derived from the root word "man" as in, only a "man" is doing the managing.	

This section isn't designed to be all inclusive, but rather to make you aware of the problem. When you realize that your draft work uses a word that needs to be changed to avoid gender bias and if you don't know what alternative word to use, then google "alternative word for *word*" and you ought to find an option that will work instead.

9.3.3 Understanding Homonyms and Commonly Misused Words

Due to the number of homonyms in the English language, it's very easy to accidentally or unknowingly use an incorrect word if you're not careful. Homonyms mean that you can use the wrong word by not knowing there's another word with the same sound, different spellings, and different meanings. Some common examples are their and there; than and then; *principle* and principal; complement and compliment; insure, ensure, and assure; queue or que.

Another problem exists where commonly used words are misunderstood and used inaccurately in writing. For example, ability and capacity.

To solve this problem, you need to brush up on your spelling vocabulary and dictionary definitions. It's the only way because, in these cases, your spell checker probably won't help.

9.3.4 Word Choice Exercises

1) Affectation, jargon, and clichés: Revise the following sentences to remove the affectation, jargon, and clichés.

- **i.** Exemplary manners at the table may not give indication of relation to work, but austere behavior can implicate the company as vulgarian.
- **ii.** I would like to request your personage to our sick gathering of like-minded associates.
- **iii.** We need you to go through the SMART goals process before we can give the thumbs up.
- **iv.** The current employee registry is janky, so for now, current employees can only connect Mac systems with OS systems complying with the old 2018 regulations.

2) Noun stacks: Revise the following sentences to improve readability of the noun stacks. There are more than one way to rewrite the sentences.

- **i.** The standardized international business ethics of economic negotiation can vary in complexity depending on the countries' cultures that are involved.
- **ii.** The lower level executive management team controls the operations of the workers, but the higher level executive management team controls the goals and directives of the company.
- **iii.** Often, a company may send its employees to foreign company-owned branches to gain more experience with the company's values in different settings.

3) Pronoun problem: Eliminate the pronoun problem in the following sentence, using the first <u>nine</u> methods defined in the table in Chapter 9.3.2.2.

The piano player with small hands knows he needs to stretches his hands before practicing.

4) Sexist language: Reword the following sentences to eliminate the sexist language. You may need to search for a replacement word.

- **i.** Experience in the workplace can often cause you to vote for particular statesmen.
- **ii.** Before engaging in a project, consider how much manpower is needed to complete it.
- **iii.** This product could shape the course of mankind.
- **iv.** Overseas business trips are compensated with hotel rooms and maid service.

5) Homonyms and commonly misused words: Use your favorite dictionary for best results.

Circle the appropriate words to create a correct sentence.

- **i.** The company provides (complimentary, complementary) products – that is, you get the operating system free with the purchase of the personal computer. In addition, you have the option of purchasing (complimentary, complementary) products, such as a word processor, spreadsheet, or database program.
- **ii.** Let me (ensure, insure, assure) you that you must (ensure, insure, assure) every asset to (ensure, insure, assure) you receive compensation if they are stolen.
- **iii.** The start-up currently has the (ability, capacity) to take on only two consumer requests at a time.
- **iv.** The long-winded (antidote, anecdote) in what was supposed to be a brief proposal only drove the speaker (farther, further) away from the main point.
- **v.** Managers need to be (effective, efficient) problem-solvers to make vague proposals into real success, but they must also be (effective, efficient) workers to make the most of their time and capitalize on their successes.
- **vi.** A good proposal for a project (ensures, insures, assures) stakeholders why the project should have a high chance of success.
- **vii.** In group project summaries, you should (cite, site) each worker and their tasks so that each person can be properly credited.
- **viii.** Be sure to ask where the (cite, site) of the project will be, if your company has multiple buildings.
- **ix.** I know that this product line seems like a useless (dessert, desert), but our idea can help stir up the field and solve new problems.

x. Make sure to finish your (dessert, desert) before you leave the company dinner.

xi. When my team decides between (alternate, alternative) ideas we keep a list of the ideas so that even after we have decided, we have a line of (alternate, alternative) ideas.

xii. My boss was (anxious, eager) to see the fruits of our efforts, especially after they dealt with being extremely (anxious, eager) as the deadline approached.

xiii. (Great, big, large) inventions often come from how people dealt with (great, big, large) and pressing problems, although the physical size of these inventions nowadays tends to not seem as (great, big, large) as something like the computers of the 20th century.

xiv. Although managers may seem like they are the (middle, center) of the project because of their constant communication efforts, other workers should also reach out to the team for help and information.

xv. Remember to take care of yourself. Many businesses encourage you to efficiently use your time to work, but don't forget during your downtime to not (lose, loose, louse) your sense of fun.

xvi. Consider researching how to negotiate your salary so that you don't end up with a salary that is (less, fewer) than what you wanted at the beginning of a job.

Answers at end of the chapter.

9.4 Punctuation Review

This section reviews all the various punctuation marks.

9.4.1 Commas

Effective comma usage requires and depends on an understanding of the sentence construction. For example:

> When the meal is cooking the chef should take the time to clean up their workspace.

The subject seems to be about the meal is cooking the chef. So the correct sentence construction clarifies this confusion with proper comma usage.

When the meal is cooking, the chef should take the time to clean up their workspace.

This section does not cover *all* possible comma rules, just the most common ones.

1) **Linking independent clauses**

What's an independent clause? It's a clause with a subject and verb of its own that could stand as an complete or independent sentence. Use a comma before a coordinating conjunction that links independent clauses (e.g., for, and, nor, but, *or*, and sometimes yet, and so). NOTE: The first letter of these conjunctions spells FANBOYS so that's an easy way to remember them.

The host had prepared a large meal for her guests, for she knew that these particular people had a limitless appetite.

2) **Enclosing elements**

If you're including a phrase that is parenthetical in nature, use a comma to set it off, both at the beginning and the end.

The kitchen knives, which were recently sharpened, cut through the meat and the cutting board entirely.

3) **Introductory phrases**

If your sentence starts with a dependent clause like this sentence you're reading now, set it off with a comma. By doing that, you give an indication of where the independent clause begins. Always place a comma after a long introductory clause or phrase. Get in a habit of placing commas after introductory clauses, even with short ones.

After adding the lime juice to accelerate the process, the meat finished cooking.

4) **Separating items in a series**

In technical writing, serial commas are most commonly used to avoid ambiguity that can result in omitting the comma before the last item in a series.

Sandwiches, curry, berries, rice, fish and chips are all good food for lunch.

Does fish and chips refer to the meal, "fish and chips" or a fish meal and potato chips? So put in that serial comma.

Sandwiches, curry, berries, rice, fish, and chips are all good food for lunch.

5) **Clarifying and contrasting**

Use a comma to separate two contrasting thoughts or ideas.

The project was finished on time, but not within the budget.

The sandwich was delicious, but the spaghetti was terrible.

Use a comma after an independent clause that is only loosely related to the dependent clause that follows it.

I got all the groceries for my breakfast, even though strawberries are not quite in season.

6) **When present with other punctuation: periods, question marks, exclamation marks, or dashes**

Conjunctive adverbs (however, nevertheless, consequently, for example, on the other hand) that join independent clauses are preceded by a semicolon and followed by a comma.

The presentation of the dish was well executed; however, the taste was terribly bland.

Commas always go inside quotation marks.

"That's right," he said.

The exception to that rule is with *abbreviations*; a comma should not be used with a period, question mark, exclamation mark, or dash.

Exceptions to that rule is in the commonly used notions i.e., that translate to "that is" and e.g., that means "for example" – then a period and comma go together. The periods are used to show the abbreviation, the comma to set off the abbreviation from the list elements that follow.

(i.e., "an explanation")

7) Commas with adjectives

Use commas to separate two or more adjectives that describe the same noun equally.

Fresh, warm bread

Sweet, juicy blueberries

However, not all adjectives in front of a noun describe the noun equally. When they are not equal (or coordinate) adjectives, do not use commas to separate them.

Stainless steel refrigerator (the refrigerator is made from stainless steel)

Three small onions

8) Unnecessary commas

This section covers commas that ought to be eliminated but are frequently inserted erroneously. Commas are omitted when the word or phrase does not interrupt the continuity of thought. Also, never place a comma between a subject and verb or between a verb and its object.

The manager of the new restaurant gave(,)the struggling chef a job.

No comma is placed between the subject The manager of the new restaurant and its verb gave, nor the verb gave and its object the struggling chef a job.

Do not place commas between the elements of a compound subject consisting only of <u>two</u> elements.

The director of the engineering department(,)and the supervisor of the quality control section were opposed to the new schedules.

The table(,)and the dishes were set for a nice(,)and simple dinner for two.

Do not place a comma before the first item in a series.

Don't forget to always have(,)knives, cutting boards, pots, pans, and stirring spoons in an industrial kitchen.

Here's a final word about commas. Many were told to use commas where they paused in their reading their work aloud in their head. Although this rule can be useful depending on when you breathe when you're reading in your head, it can also lead to confusion about where commas go. It also leads to the impression that there are no exact rules on using commas – and that's not true; there are. The truth is that once commas have been placed properly in a document and you're reading it aloud in your head, you can pause wherever you see a comma. However, pausing isn't indicative of where to place a comma.

9.4.2 Semicolons

There are *two* main uses for semicolons: the strong connective and the series of items containing commas.

1) In the strong connective capacity, semicolons are placed between two complete sentences, in which you are calling special attention to the relationship between the sentences.

> The presentation of the dish was well executed; however, the taste was terribly bland.

2) If you have a list within a list, then you need to distinguish between the inner list and the outer list. Therefore, in a series of items containing commas, the semicolon functions something like a *super-comma*. That is, since the items themselves contain commas, the semicolon distinguishes them.

> Opening a restaurant is like starting a business. You need to have the following requirements to be met: a product, a unique menu in this case; a target audience, people who want to consume your food; and a basic team, such as yourself, a partner, and investors.

9.4.3 Colons

Colons are used to introduce something. They do so with a more direct emphasis than do commas. The clause that precedes the colon must be a complete sentence.

> The best entrepreneurs often share a particular trait: self-motivation.
>
> Turning an idea into a product for a new business can be considered in the following dimensions: time, cost, and complexity.

You cannot put a colon between a verb and its object, or between a preposition and its object. Notice the *incorrect* colon use in the following two sentences:

> The secret to a successful business is often found in: quick decision-making.
>
> Although swiftness is important for a growing business, you should also mix: speed with thoroughness in order to make sure that as many problems and questions are answered at once.

9.4.4 Dashes and Hyphens

The meaning of a dash is directly *opposite* to that of a hyphen – a dash indicates a complete break between two words, while a hyphen joins them. A dash is typed using two hyphens; see previous sentence.

Hyphens are used to connect words together, for example:

> decision-making, wi-fi, yo-yo
>
> Williams-Suzuki (combined last name)
>
> In order to pay for my meal, I presented two-, five-, and fifty-pence coins. Unfortunately, I forgot I was in America.
>
> The fast food chain, Lucky's Shack, decided to close down the Brooklyn-, Georgetown-, and Bellevue-Shacks.

Dashes create an informal tone and therefore should be used sparingly in technical writing, unless an informal tone is okay for that work. They are used to add emphasis to what follows the dash, for example:

> The next time you serve a dish – assuming we even get another chance – you need to make sure the diners are not allergic to the ingredients.
>
> The restaurant managed to cover the entire town with advertisement flyers – but without the restaurant's address.

9.4.5 Possession and Contractions

If you're wondering whether you need to use an apostrophe, then ask yourself the following questions:

- Does something in this sentence constitute an aspect or possession of something or someone?
- Is it singular or plural?
- Am I forming a contraction?

Remember that where possessive pronouns do *not* take apostrophes (e.g., yours, his, hers, theirs, ours, its, my), pronouns *do* take apostrophes when they're linked in contractions, such as it + is, you + are, and they + are.

> Although the meal was delicious in taste, its presentation was lackluster.
>
> Although the meal was delicious in taste, it's a shame that the restaurant ran out of ingredients for seconds.

9.4.6 Punctuation Review Questions

Test your comprehension of the punctuation marks.

1) There are seven common comma rules. Distinguish their use.

   i. Linking independent clauses with the FANBOYS
   ii. Enclosing elements rather than with ( )
   iii. Introductory phrases
   iv. Separating items in a series/list
   v. Clarifying and contrasting
   vi. Commas with adjectives
   vii. With other punctuation (e.g., quote marks or with periods [e.g., or etc.])

2) Why is the comma rule in a series not optional in technical writing?

3) How do you ensure clarity for the reader using punctuation when you have a list or commas in a list of elements? Give an example.

4) What does a hyphen do?

5) What does a dash do?

6) When typing, how do you differentiate a hyphen from a dash?

9.4.7 Punctuation Exercises

These questions ask you to apply your knowledge of the punctuation marks.

1) What are **two comma rules that are optional** in English composition, but become important for clarity in scientific/technical/business writing?

2) What is a **comma splice**? What are four easy ways to fix it, without rewriting the sentences?

3) Under what two conditions are **semicolons** (;) used in writing?

4) When is a **colon** used in scientific/technical/business writing?

5) What do **parentheses** ( ) do?

6) How is the **slash** (/) used?

7) What's the rule for using **apostrophes**? When each person owns something? When a group owns something?

8) How is US **money** written out using the $ punctuation mark?

9) Which punctuation marks evoke **emotions**, and thus should be used sparingly in scientific/technical writing (business) setting?

10) Insert **commas** as needed in the following sentences:

i. We wanted to start a business but we did not know what we would specialize in.

ii. The vegan industry an unreached local community in our area seemed to be an audience with a need that our new business could answer.

iii. Even before we started our business we began meeting stakeholders building trust and convincing others that our innovative profitable product worth investing in.

iv. We decided to pitch the idea of the "Wonder Salad" that contained all the nutritional value that vegans typically struggle to gain; however we had to consider how to keep it interesting such as by adding different fruit blends to the salad.

v. Our company was new to the vegan market so we decided to observe other vegan companies and adapt some of their marketing strategies to support our business.

vi. When our vegan food business grew steadily we decided we needed to partner with other vegan businesses who shared our company values in order to increase our growth gain more experienced members and build our network in the vegan community.

vii. In our first attempt to strike a deal with a local vegan business we failed for we accidentally fed the representatives milk products through the ranch dressing.

viii. It took time to redeem the company's image but we eventually received help from other vegan businesses to make cheap easy-to-make Wonder Salads.

ix. Wonder Salads are now the famous tasty vegan meal at the big markets such as QFC and Costco.

11) Fix the punctuation in the following sentences using only **semicolons**, **colons**, and **dashes**, as necessary, in the following sentences:

i. Some examples of common vegetables include: broccoli, lettuce, kale, carrots, and peas.

ii. I thought I prepared all the ingredients, that my grandfather very specifically requested, for breakfast – but – it turns out I forgot them back at the grocery store.

iii. Although the workers handled most of the physical cooking tasks, the head chef cut the fish for the customers herself: the shape of the fillets are always flawless in her restaurant.

iv. The kitchen is a place where chefs aim to: create new dishes, experience new flavors, and hone their culinary skills.

   v. Landon's friend Brandon asked him to cook a new dish for him; Landon decided to take many precautions before making his first attempt: clean the kitchen area, prepare extra ingredients, and watch multiple video examples.

   vi. Sierra was invited out to a potluck, she brought some tikka masala to the gathering.

   vii. We will need some people to bring food for the picnic. Currently, we need a few things a side dish, such as chips and guacamole, a fruit dish, such as strawberries, a vegetable dish, such as green beans, and a drink, such as soda.

12) Correct the use of apostrophes in the following sentences: if necessary, add in or take away apostrophes where appropriate, or add in the correct possessive form.

   i. I forgot to bring Michelles pots and pans for the cooking session.

   ii. Its time to make some cupcakes!

   iii. Did you sanitize your cutting board?

   iv. When you use a blender, make sure to read its instruction manual first.

   v. I believe this warm dinner is yours.

   vi. Michael borrowed his parents ornate plates to more nicely present his dish. (there are two valid options with different meanings)

   vii. The kitchens windows were open in case smoke appeared during the cooking. (there are two valid options with different meanings)

   viii. The recipes all seemed to appeal to the tastes of Mindy's guests.

   ix. The waters purpose in the dinner was to prepare Mitchell for the morning run.

   x. That bread recipe is not yours. Its actually theirs according to this website.

   xi. Mira brought extra ingredients, but its only necessary if we mess up the baking recipe.

   xii. Although the habanero pepper was spicy enough on the first bite, its seeds burned my mouth upon my second bite.

xiii. Mickey asked his friends at lunchtime what their favorite restaurant was.

xiv. Mimis and Milsons ideas on how to cook the perfect egg were very different from each other.

xv. Mika and Miguels friend made a five-course meal in under an hour.

13) When do you place the period indicating the end of the sentence *inside* the closing parenthesis? Seen as ".)" When do you place the period indicating the end of the sentence *outside* the closing parenthesis? Seen as ")."

Seen as ".)" ______________________________

Seen as ")." ______________________________

14) Punctuate, or fix the punctuation in, the sentences in the following paragraph, using *only commas, semicolons, colons*, as necessary. Since this is a paragraph, it's easier to check your work with the answer key, if you circle ◯ each mark you fix.

It does not take a lot of skill to become a casual cook, it only takes a bit of curiosity and a willingness to try. Materially speaking you will need a fair number of basic cooking tools knives, cutting boards, plates, stirring spoons, pots, mixing bowls and pans. It is worth keeping a list of quick simple meals that you want to cook in the future, you can then store ingredients that are needed for multiple recipes on your list. While it is nice to enjoy meals in isolation you should have other people try out your dishes on occasion. The first basic meal at least for breakfast that you should consider learning to make is scrambled eggs. The only absolutely necessary ingredient should be clear from the name, eggs are the only necessity but other helpful ingredients include milk, assuming you are not lactose intolerant, butter, assuming you are not lactose intolerant, salt, such as kosher salt, and pepper. The Internet has plenty of online tutorials that, can guide people toward the basics. Cooking as a hobby can start out as a struggle and sometimes some people's environments are not as conducive but it can open up many opportunities such as control over your diet, and opportunities to host.

Answers at end of the chapter.

EXERCISES ANSWER KEY

9.1 Sentence Structure Exercises Answer Key

1) Transitions

Project Delta is the name of a Bluetooth laptop computer accessory that we are developing. It can be used as a computer microphone <u>and</u> a webcam. <u>In addition</u>, the accessory can share live camera feed to the computer. <u>Furthermore</u>, it enables it to filter and edit the camera feed with advanced machine-learning software. <u>On top of its other features</u>, the accessory can create a hotspot to connect the laptop to the Internet wherever it is. The accessory can be ready for marketing in six months.

2) Subordination

There are lots of ways to create one sentence from that series of sentences. The samples show how the importance of the information changes based on where it is located in the sentence and what subordinate constructs are used.

Freddy wasn't hurt, but his uninsured blue Ford Galaxy was totaled on Saturday, when he sped around a sharp curve in the road and skidded, missing a cat, but hitting a tree.

(32 words)

On Saturday, although he wasn't hurt, Freddy totaled his blue Ford Galaxy when he was driving too fast, with no insurance, down a sharp curve, skidded, hit a tree, while missing a cat.

(33 words)

Saturday, Freddy wasn't hurt when driving his uninsured blue Ford Galaxy, which was totaled after just missing a cat and skidded into a tree because he was going too fast on a sharp curve in the road.

(37 words)

On Saturday, Freddy was speeding in his uninsured blue Ford Galaxy when the road curved sharply, causing the car to skid; although Freddy managed to avoid hitting a nearby cat and escaped injury himself, he totaled his car by hitting a tree.

(42 words)

3) Matching

i. Pianos are large and expensive. <u>Therefore,</u> they require investment to acquire and then learn to play.

ii. The art of fishing may seem at first to be a matter of doing nothing, <u>but</u> everything changes when you catch your first fish.

iii. Mathematics is a staple school subject. <u>In addition,</u> it is a pastime for many aspiring engineers.

iv. There are many martial arts with different applications. <u>For example,</u> Karate emphasizes unarmed combat and Aikido focuses on redirecting the force of the opponent.

v. Hobbies that can be done by oneself are often easier to practice <u>because</u> it can be difficult depending on the environment to find other people to practice with.

vi. Guitars are large instruments with six strings. <u>If</u> you want an easier instrument, you might consider the ukulele because it has two less strings to focus on.

5) Parallelism

ok	During the Korean War, Jerry traveled to South Korea **to teach mathematics** ***and*** **to serve in the Signal Corps.**
fix	During his time in Korea, he learned that it was easier for him **to speak to the Korean soldiers in Japanese than to translate their speech to English.**
fix	**The need for interpreters** *as well as* **the need for specialists** to pass their skills to the Koreans made Jerry an ideal teacher.
fix	Although his Japanese heritage **was useful for establishing friendly relations with Koreans, it was also difficult bonding within the American military** because of anti-Japanese sentiments from World War II.

ok	**The art of avoidance** was a familiar concept to Jerry from his time dodging around his older brother. Adding to this skill, Jerry gained ***the virtue of patience, the knowledge of army politics,*** and **the tactic of negotiation.**
fix	During his breaks from service, Jerry would **study physics, explore Korea,** *and* **visit other military bases.**
fix	In later years, Jerry chose to only tell his grandchildren about **how he traveled around the military bases in Asia,** and when they were older, he told them about **how he experienced relational conflicts within the military.**
fix	His grandchildren didn't know what to think, but the familiar warmth within Jerry's eyes told them **what to learn from this;** their grandfather nonetheless experienced a joyful life of adventure.

6) Faulty modifiers

i. Only technical workers share relevant business information to their managers.
(It's just the technical workers that share info, not other workers.)

ii. Technical workers only share relevant business information to their managers.
(The workers only share. They don't do other actions.)

iii. Technical workers share only relevant business information to their managers.
(The workers sharing consists of only relevant business info.)

iv. Technical workers share relevant business information only to their managers.
(This information is shared to just the managers.)

7) Dangling modifiers. NOTE: In some cases, multiple sentences are provided to show how various interpretations of the missing context would lead to different results.

i. Original: Turning off the alarm, the sun began to shine through the uncovered window.

Fixed: [insert name] turned off the alarm as the sun began to shine through the uncovered window.

ii. **Original:** Preoccupied with the stirring the oatmeal, the omelet began to smoke dangerously.

Fixed: The omelet began to smoke dangerously as [insert name] was preoccupied with stirring the oatmeal.

iii. **Original:** After planning out the next run, the dog joined Germaine on the streets.

Fixed: After Germaine planned out the next run, the dog joined Germaine on the streets.

iv. **Original:** Depleted of energy, Germaine turned off his phone and took a nap.

Fixed: Germaine was depleted of energy, so Germaine turned off his phone and took a nap.

v. **Original:** By setting lunch on the desk, there was motivation to begin the work quickly.

Fixed: By setting lunch on the desk, [insert name] motivated themself to begin the work quickly.

vi. **Original:** To complete the entire report, the clock was hidden from view.

Fixed: To complete the entire report, [insert name] hid their clock from view.

9.2 Verb Choice Exercises Answer Key

These answers offer one way to resolve these passive voice sentences.

1) Weak verbs

i. **Original:** The time had been wearing away at the customer's patience.

Fixed: The time wore away at the customer's patience.

ii. **Original:** The business pitch needed to have been significantly shortened by the rookie presenter in order to retain interest.

Fixed: **The rookie presenter needed to significantly shorten the business presentation** in order to retain interest.

iii. Original: Instead, he thought he needed to have to stretch out the content to cover every single detail.

Fixed: Instead, the rookie presenter thought he **needed to stretch** out the content to cover every single detail.

iv. Original: Fortunately, the senior presenter, who was partnered with the rookie presenter, anticipated that he needed to have been trained more by her.

Fixed: Fortunately, the senior presenter, who was partnered with the rookie presenter, anticipated that she **needed to train him more**.

v. Original: The senior presenter's coworker had been pretending to be the customer the entire time.

Fixed: The senior presenter's coworker **pretended** to be the customer the entire time.

2) No subject sentences

i. Original: The songs were sung beautifully well.

Fixed: The vocalist sang the songs beautifully well.

ii. Original: Despite major obstacles, the character was very accurately portrayed.

Fixed: Despite major obstacles, the actor very accurately portrayed the character.

iii. Original: Although fights were started over who should be the lead dancer, the matter was eventually handled.

Fixed: Although the cast started fights over who should be the lead dancer, they eventually handled the matter.

iv. Original: Major improvements need to be made before the cast is ready to perform.

Fixed: The cast needs to make major improvements before they are ready to perform.

3) Nominalizations

i. Original: Workers should always be prepared for an evaluation of their efforts by others.

Fixed: Workers should always be prepared for others to evaluate their efforts.

ii. Original: One workplace skill that should not be the subject of underappreciation is conflict resolution.

Fixed: One workplace skill that should not be underappreciated is conflict resolution.
(Resolution is also a nominalization, but the resulting sentence would be longer to fix resolution into resolve. Turning underappreciation into a verb form results in less words overall.)

iii. Original: Each job position is a chance for people to create an evolution of their skillsets.

Fixed: Each job position is a chance for people to evolve their skillsets.

iv. Original: It has been said that you must always include extra time considerations for unforeseen circumstances when planning projects.

Fixed: It has been said that you must always include extra time considerations for unforeseen circumstances when planning projects.

NOTE: This answer is also a passive sentence without a subject. It could also be changed to include a subject ("Who said what") to improve clarity.

v. Original: New workers should be punctual in order to show they have commitment to the company.

Fixed: New workers should be punctual in order to show they can commit to the company.

4) Expletives

i. Original: Consider that there are good and bad consequences to each business decision so it is to be expected that not everyone can be appeased.

Fixed: Consider each business decision has good and bad consequences, so expect that not everyone can be appeased.

ii. Original: There was an important absence at the meeting because the organizer forgot to CC the missing person.

Fixed: Someone important was absent from the meeting because the organizer forgot to CC the missing person.

iii. Original: The manager carefully noted that there was a surplus of employee candidates because it was the time when the college students graduated and sought work.

Fixed: The manager carefully noted the surplus of employee candidates the college students recently graduated and are seeking work.

9.3 Word Usage Exercises Answer Key

1) Affectation, jargon, and clichés

i. Original *affectation*: Exemplary manners at the table may not give indication of relation to work, but austere behavior can implicate the company as vulgarian.

Fixed: Good manners at the table may not relate directly to work, but improper behavior can ruin the company's image.

ii. Original *affectation/slang*: I would like to request your personage to our sick gathering of like-minded associates.

Fixed: Are you able to come to our meeting with friends?

iii. Original *jargon/ cliché*: We need you to go through the SMART goals process before we can give the thumbs up.

Fixed: We need you to evaluate your goals before we can move forward.

iv. Original *jargon/slang*: The current employee registry is janky, so for now, current employees can only connect Mac systems with OS systems complying with the old 2018 regulations.

Fixed: The current employee registry is not working, so for now, current employees can only connect Mac systems that were released before 2019.

2) Noun stacks

i. Original: The standardized international business ethics of economic negotiation can vary in complexity depending on the countries' cultures that are involved.

Fixed: Business ethics in the international domain of economic negotiation can vary in complexity depending on the cultures of the involved parties.

ii. Original: The lower level executive management team controls the operations of the workers, but the higher level executive management team controls the goals and directives of the company.

Fixed: The managers on the lower level of the company control the operations of the workers, but the managers on the higher level of the company control the goals and directives of the company.

iii. Original: Often, a company may send its employees to foreign company-owned branches to gain more experience with the company's values in different settings.

Fixed: Often a company may send its employees to other company locations to gain more experience with the company's values in different settings.

3) Pronoun problem

The piano player with small hands knows he needs to stretches his hands before practicing.

i. Eliminate: The piano player with small hands knows hands need to be stretched before practicing.

ii. They (singular): The piano player with small hands knows they needs to stretches their hands before practicing.

iii. He/She: The piano player with small hands knows he/she needs to stretches his/her hands before practicing.

iv. He or she: The piano player with small hands knows he or she needs to stretches his or her hands before practicing.

v. They (plural): Piano players with small hands know they need to stretches their hands before practicing.

vi. One: One with small hands knows one needs to stretches one's hands before practicing.

vii. You: You with small hands know you need to stretch your hands before practicing.

viii. Repeat noun: The piano player with small hands knows the piano player needs to stretch the piano player's hands before practicing.

ix. Eliminate subject: Hand stretches need to be done before practicing.

4) Sexist language

i. Original: Experience in the workplace can often cause you to vote for particular statesmen.

Fixed: Experience in the workplace can often cause you to vote for particular state representatives.

ii. Original: Before engaging in a project, consider how much manpower is needed to complete it.

Fixed: Before engaging in a project, consider how much effort is needed to complete it.

iii. Original: This product could shape the course of mankind.

Fixed: This product could shape the course of humanity.

iv. Original: Overseas business trips are compensated with hotel rooms and maid service.

Fixed: Overseas business trips are compensated with hotel rooms and housekeeping.

5) Homonyms and commonly misused words

i. The company provides **complimentary** products – that is, you get the operating system free with the purchase of the personal computer. In addition, you have the option of purchasing **complementary** products, such as a word processor, spreadsheet, or database program.

ii. Let me **assure** you that you must insure every asset to **ensure** you receive compensation if they are stolen.

To "ensure" is to check and verify something. To "insure" is to apply your insurance policy. To "assure" is to build up the confidence of someone else.

iii. The start-up currently has the **capacity** to take on only two consumer requests at a time.

An "ability" refers to the current state of being able to do a certain action. A "capacity" refers to the potential to store or receive something. For example, a server has the capacity to handle (receive) multiple user requests at the same time, but it has the ability to connect multiple computer users together at the same time.

iv. The long-winded **anecdote** in what was supposed to be a brief proposal only drove the speaker **further** away from the main point.

"Farther" is used to describe an increasing physical gap like in meters. "Further" is used to describe a nonphysical gap, such as (in this case) focus on the topic.

v. Managers need to be **effective** problem-solvers to make vague proposals into real success, but they must also be **efficient** workers to make the most of their time and capitalize on their successes.

"Effective" is used to describe something/someone that works at a high level or consistently solves a problem. "Efficient" is used to describe something/someone that takes up a low cost. A race car is an effective vehicle for speed, but it is not as efficient as a modern hybrid car in terms of mileage.

vi. A good proposal for a project **assures** stakeholders why the project should have a high chance of success.

To "ensure" is to check and verify something. To "insure" is to apply your insurance policy. To "assure" is to build up the confidence of someone else.

vii. In group project summaries, you should **cite** each worker and their tasks so that each person can be properly credited.

viii. Be sure to ask where the **site** of the project will be, if your company has multiple buildings.

ix. I know that this product line seems like a useless **desert** of fruitless efforts, but our idea can help stir up the field and solve new problems.

x. Make sure to finish your **dessert** before you leave the company dinner.

xi. When my team decides between **alternative** ideas we keep a list of the ideas so that even after we have decided, we have a line of **alternate** ideas.

"Alternate" can be used as a noun or as an adjective to describe a substitute to a certain implied subject. "Alternative" can be used as a noun or as an adjective to describe an idea that someone is choosing between.

xii. My boss was eager to see the fruits of our efforts, especially after they dealt with being extremely **anxious** as the deadline approached.

Although "anxious" has some positive uses, in technical language it is best to use "eager" instead when referring to excitement.

xiii. **Great** inventions often come from how people dealt with **large** and pressing problems, although the physical size of these inventions nowadays tends to not seem as **big** as something like the computers of the twentieth century.

"Great" is used to describe something that is important or has a significant impact. "Big" is used to describe physical size. "Large" is used to describe substance or an uncountable quantity.

xiv. Although managers may seem like they are the **center** of the project because of their constant communication efforts, other workers should also reach out to the team for help and information.

"Middle" is often used to imply a situation where things are on all sides of the described place. It is less precise than center. "Center" is often used to imply something that other things not only surround, but also revolve around.

xv. Remember to take care of yourself. Many businesses encourage you to efficiently use your time to work, but don't forget during your downtime to not **lose** your sense of fun.

xvi. Consider researching how to negotiate your salary so that you don't end up with a salary that is **less** than what you wanted at the beginning of a job.

9.4 Punctuation Exercises Answer Key

1) What are **two comma rules that are optional** in English composition, but become important for clarity in scientific/technical/business writing?

  i. Comma after introductory phrases

  ii. Comma before the and/or in a series/list

2) What is a **comma splice**? What are four easy ways to fix it, without rewriting the sentences?

When two sentences are connected using a comma, which is incorrect punctuation, but commonly done when the author hasn't finished their idea, but a sentence is concluded, then finished in the next sentence.

Four ways to fix a comma splice:

  1) Add one of the **FANBOYS** words, and leave in the comma.

  2) Replace the comma with a **semicolon**. Easy solution, but not to overuse as the reading gets overly complicated to follow, and can only be used once in a sentence.

  3) Use a **colon** instead, if the second sentence is a sample/example of what is explained in the first sentence. For example:

    My friend has a fat cat: he weighs 25 pounds.

  4) Replace with a **period**. This may require the first sentence to be rewritten so its idea is ended, thus using a period. Oddly enough, if an idea is not ended, but there's a period; the reader will conclude that they didn't understand and look backwards in the document to understand, and rarely go forward to the next sentence.

3) Under what two conditions are **semicolons** (;) used in writing?

When fixing a comma splice, that is connecting two complete sentences.

When you have a list within a list and need to distinguish between the outer list and inner list elements.

Any other semicolons are incorrect!

4) When is a **colon** used in scientific/technical/business writing?

   There are many uses and probably why they get misused. Here's the most common.

   i. Between two sentences when the second sentence is a sample/ example of the first sentence

   ii. At the end of the complete sentence that introduces a list

   I have a number of favorite things I like to do on the weekends: read a book, binge watch a newly discovered TV series, and practice new recipes.

   iii. When showing time in USA English

   iv. In a ratios

   v. Between a title and subtitle

   vi. After names on a legal record

   vii. Dear _____:

5) What do **parentheses** ( ) do?

   Parentheses offer additional information that is not needed to understand the content of the sentence. This is relevant because many people will skip reading when they see *a* (*till they see the ending*). NOTE: If there is too much information that you want/need to put in parentheses, then put it in a footnote at the bottom of the page.

6) How is the **slash** (/) used?

   Shorthand for OR, for example, his/her.

   The only time that use of a slash is ambiguous is with and/or. Recommendation:

   Not: X and/or Y

   Use: X or Y or both

7) What's the rule for using **apostrophes**? When more than one person owns something? When each person owns something?

   a) When more than one person own something:

   Frank and Jo's lakeside cottage makes a great weekend getaway.

b) When each person owns the something:

Frank's and Jo's passports were renewed for their overseas vacation.

8) How is US **money** written out using the $ punctuation mark?

The $ goes <u>in front</u> of the numerals, not after, even though, when speaking, it's said after the numeral.

Written: $20

Spoken: twenty dollars

9) Which punctuation marks evoke **emotions**, and thus should be used sparingly in scientific/technical writing (business) setting?

!

– (dash)

10) Insert commas as needed in the following sentences. Also included is the rule that was used to punctuate the sentence correctly.

i. __5__ We wanted to start a business, but we did not know what we would specialize in.

ii. __2 7__ The vegan industry, an unreached, local community in our area, seemed to be an audience with a need that our new business could answer.

iii. __3 4 7__ Even before we started our business, we began meeting stakeholders, building trust, and convincing others that our innovative, profitable product worth investing in.

iv. __6 6 5__ We decided to pitch the idea of the "Wonder Salad," that contained all the nutritional value that vegans typically struggle to gain; however, we had to consider how to keep it interesting, such as by adding different fruit blends to the salad.

v. __1__ Our company was new to the vegan market, so we decided to observe other vegan companies and adapt some of their marketing strategies to support our business.

vi. __3 2 4__ When our vegan food business grew steadily, we decided we needed to partner with other vegan businesses, who shared our company values, in order to increase our growth, gain more experienced members, and build our network in the vegan community.

vii. __3 1___ In our first attempt to strike a deal with a local vegan business, we failed, for we accidentally fed the representatives milk products through the ranch dressing.

viii. __1 7___ It took time to redeem the company's image, but we eventually received help from other vegan businesses to make cheap, easy-to-make Wonder Salads.

ix. __5___ Wonder Salads are now the famous tasty vegan meal at the big markets, such as QFC and Costco.

11) Fix the following punctuation using *semicolons*, *colons*, and *dashes*, as necessary.

i. Some examples of common vegetables include: broccoli, lettuce, kale, carrots, and peas.

REWRITE the colon is at the end of an incomplete sentence. The colon must end a complete sentence and not be between the verb and its corresponding object.

There are a few common vegetables to remember: broccoli, lettuce, kale, carrots, and peas.

OR fix the punctuation, keeping the sentence structure and removing the incorrect punctuation.

Some examples of common vegetables include broccoli, lettuce, kale, carrots, and peas.

ii. I thought I prepared all the ingredients, that my grandfather very specifically requested, for breakfast – but – it turns out I forgot them back at the grocery store.

FIX. Demonstrates improper use of dashes. The dashes are supposed to accompany a parenthetical. Can also add in the dashes for the parenthetical that is actually present:

I thought I prepared all the ingredients – that my grandfather very specifically requested – for breakfast, but it turns out I forgot them back at the grocery store.

iii. Although the workers handled most of the physical cooking tasks, the head chef cut the fish for the customers herself: the shape of the fillets are always flawless in her restaurant.

FIX. The relationship between the two sentences is not introductory or emphasis (which calls for the use of a colon), but rather strongly connected (semicolon); therefore use a semicolon not a colon.

Although the workers handled most of the physical cooking tasks, the head chef cut the fish for the customers herself; the shape of the fillets are always flawless in her restaurant.

iv. The kitchen is a place where chefs aim to: create new dishes, experience new flavors, and hone their culinary skills.

REWRITE. You cannot put a colon between a preposition and its object. Colons require a complete sentence. If you really wanted to use the colon, then the sentence would need to be rewritten.

Chefs aim to do many things in the kitchen: create new dishes, experience new flavors, and hone their culinary skills.

OR FIX keep the sentence structure and remove the punctuation.

The kitchen is a place where chefs aim to create new dishes, experience new flavors, and hone their culinary skills.

v. Landon's friend Brandon asked him to cook a new dish for him; Landon decided to take many precautions before making his first attempt: clean the kitchen area, prepare extra ingredients, and watch multiple video examples.

Perfect as is: no fix is necessary. The semicolon connects two complete, related sentences. The colon emphasizes what follows.

vi. Sierra was invited out to a potluck, she brought some tikka masala to the gathering.

FIX. Demonstrates comma splice (improper comma use).

Sierra was invited out to a potluck; she brought some tikka masala to the gathering.

vii. We will need some people to bring food for the picnic. Currently, we need a few things a side dish, such as chips and guacamole, a fruit dish, such as strawberries, a vegetable dish, such as green beans, and a drink, such as soda.

FIX. Need colon to present the list. Then need to separate the list elements using semicolons. Need to separate each list element from its parenthetical information that's been included.

We will need some people to bring food for the picnic. Currently, we need a few things: a side dish, such as chips and guacamole; a fruit dish, such as strawberries; a vegetable dish, such as green beans; and a drink, such as soda.

12) Decide whether and where to place an apostrophe in the following sentences.

i. I forgot to bring Michelle's pots and pans for the cooking session.

ii. It's time to make some cupcakes!

iii. Did you sanitize your cutting board?

iv. When you use a blender, make sure to read its instruction manual first.

v. I believe this warm dinner is yours.

vi. Michael borrowed his parents' ornate plates to more nicely present his dish.

Michael has two living parents who share the ornate plates.

vii. Michael borrowed his parent's ornate plates to more nicely present his dish.

Michael borrowed the plates from one parent.

viii. The kitchen's windows were open in case smoke appeared during the cooking.

There is only one kitchen. This is likely talking about a house.

ix. The kitchens' windows were open in case smoke appeared during the cooking.

There are multiple kitchens whose windows were open. This could be a building with multiple kitchens.

x. The recipes all seemed to appeal to the tastes of Mindy's guests.

xi. The water's purpose in the dinner was to prepare Mitchell for the morning run.

xii. That bread recipe is not yours. It's actually theirs according to this website.

xiii. Mira brought extra ingredients, but it's only necessary if we mess up the baking recipe.

xiv. Although the habanero pepper was spicy enough on the first bite, its seeds burned my mouth upon my second bite.

xv. Mickey asked his friends at lunchtime what their favorite restaurant was.

xvi. Mimi's and Milson's ideas on how to cook the perfect egg were very different from each other.

xvii. Mika and Miguel's friend made a five-course meal in under an hour.

13) When do you place the period indicating the end of the sentence <u>inside</u> the closing parenthesis? Seen as ".)" When do you place the period indicating the end of the sentence <u>outside</u> the closing parenthesis? Seen as ")."

Inside:

You place a period INSIDE the parenthesis when a complete sentence is written within ( ).

(See Figure 1.)

(See Appendix A.)

(Refer to Chapter 10.)

Outside:

When what is written within the ( ) is parenthetical and part of a larger sentence, the period goes OUTSIDE the closing) to complete the sentence. This rule is true even if the information inside the ( ) is a complete sentence, for example (see Figure 1).

You often find parentheses at the end of a sentence (for list, examples, or ideas not germane to the rest of the sentence).

14) Using *only commas, semicolons, colons*, as necessary.

It does not take a lot of skill to become a casual cook; it only takes a bit of curiosity and a willingness to try. Materially speaking, you will need a fair number of basic cooking tools: knives, cutting boards, plates, stirring spoons, pots, mixing bowls, and pans. It is worth keeping a list of quick, simple meals that you want to cook in the future; you can then store ingredients that are needed for multiple recipes on your list. While it is nice to enjoy meals in isolation, you should have other people try out your dishes on occasion. The first basic meal, at least for breakfast, that you should consider learning to make is scrambled eggs. The only absolutely necessary ingredient should be clear from the name; eggs are the only necessity, but other helpful ingredients include milk, assuming you are not lactose intolerant; butter, assuming you are not lactose intolerant; salt, such as kosher salt; and pepper. The Internet has plenty of online tutorials that can guide people toward the basics. Cooking as a hobby can start out as a struggle, and sometimes some people's environments are not as conducive, but it can open up many opportunities such as control over your diet and opportunities to host.

Index

C

D

E

F

G

H

I

J

L

M

N

O

P

Q

R

S

T

U

V

W